If I Were
PRIME MINISTER

If I Were
PRIME MINISTER

Introduction by
MEL HURTIG

Hurtig Publishers
Edmonton

Hurtig Publishers Ltd.
10560 – 105 Street
Edmonton, Alberta
Canada T5H 2W7

Canadian Cataloguing in Publication Data

Main entry under title:

If I were Prime Minister

Bibliography: p.

ISBN 0-88830-315-7

1. Canada — Politics and government —
1984–   — Miscellanea.*
FC630.I33 1987   320.971   C87-091326-3
F1034.2.I33 1987

Printed and bound in Canada

CONTENTS

INTRODUCTION

What would *you* do if you were prime minister?

Most of us are very adept at criticizing our governments in Ottawa, and virtually everyone would agree that in recent years we've had lots of good reasons to do so. Today, few Canadians don't have strong opinions about what's wrong with our federal government.

At the same time, most of us think *we* know what could and should be done in many areas of public policy. If only the dolts in Ottawa would listen! A Chamber of Commerce luncheon, or a dinner party or public meeting, or a session at the nineteenth hole or local pub rarely goes by without plenty of vigorous suggestions about how we could easily run the country a helluva lot better than it's being run now.

However, some interesting things happen when you are asked to spell out succinctly and write down, for public scrutiny and for examination by your friends and foes (not to mention book reviewers), exactly what you would do if you had the opportunity to lead the nation. When faced with the challenge, could you confidently articulate your policies and beliefs? Or would you become more cautious and conservative? Or perhaps the opposite, even bolder? On the following pages you will find some surprising examples of both processes.

I had two reasons for wanting to put this book together. First, and most obviously, there's the dismal performance of our federal governments during the past few years, going back to the last years of the Trudeau administration, right through the first three years of Brian Mulroney's disappointing leadership after he had received an unparalleled mandate for change and new policies. The day I am writing this introduction, a new public opinion poll has just been published, indicating that only 17 per cent (surely a record low) of Canadians surveyed feel the current prime minister would be their choice today. At the same time, I think it's true that most Canadians were clearly unhappy with the last few confused and often arrogant Liberal years, and with the ineptitude that led to such ill-considered programs as the Scientific Research Tax Credit boondoggle (as but one example), which so quickly and neatly ripped off the people of Canada for billions of dollars.

The second reason for the book is more positive. Everywhere I travel across Canada I keep meeting really bright, energetic people who have really bright, imaginative ideas about how to make Canada a better country. Some are Conservatives, some Liberals, and some are from the NDP. Most, like most Canadians, are not formally active in any political party.

When we first began planning this book, we thought of a much smaller volume. But it kept growing. The response from those we approached was most enthusiastic. Everyone thought it was a great idea, and that was part of our problem. Almost everyone we selected agreed to contribute, and it soon became apparent that we had some less than adequate balances. We needed more women, more western- ers, more from the right, more francophones, more native Canadians. From our planned thirty contributors and some sixty thousand words, we expanded to fifty pieces and one hundred thousand words. Still our editors felt we needed broader representation, hence this final product of sixty authors and some one hundred and thirty thousand words.

Certainly we can't claim a perfect balance, but we did try hard to present a good variety of opinions. Any book containing Peter Wor- thington and Mel Watkins, John Crispo and Dave Barrett, or Donald Macdonald and Bob White can't be completely one-sided.

But the book *is* big. My advice is to try not to read it too quickly— ideally, no more than three or four essays at a time. You'll be delighted with many of the authors, and furious with others. Some pieces need to be read more than once, not because the writing is unclear but because the ideas may seem impractical or unrealistic at first yet somehow stick in the back of the mind so that you want to go back for a second look.

Obviously, you'll find totally different and quite conflicting visions of Canada. But you *will* find more than a few visions. And you will find common, commonsense themes and pleas for reform. Clearly, these Canadians are completely fed up with the patronage, pork- barrelling, and corruption in Ottawa. And there are numerous other common themes on the pages that follow, in economic policy, social policy, foreign and defence policy, and other areas.

I was surprised that some contributors decided to limit themselves to a single topic. Two of the finest essays in the book, in my opinion, are in this category. Elsewhere, one arch-conservative has presented some remarkably progressive suggestions, while one author from the left sounds surprisingly conservative.

I would like to have had others in the book. Among those who declined (for various reasons) were Bob Blair, John Bulloch, Dalton Camp (who accepted but then some sort of government appointment apparently intervened), Bill Davis, Remi De Roo, Wendy Dobson, Eugene Forsey, Northrop Frye, George Grant, Eric Kierans, Michele

Landsberg, Roger Lemelin, Maureen McTeer, Judith Maxwell, Roy Romanow, Maurice Strong, and David Suzuki.

The next few months may well be the most important period in Canadian history. Economist Richard Lipsey, one of the contributors to this book, has said elsewhere: "The debate about free trade is probably the most important thing that's ever happened in our country in our history. And it's certainly the most important thing that's ever happened in our country since the end of the Second World War." Aside from the need for a common market in Canada, I suspect that this is one of the few things I will ever agree with Professor Lipsey about. But I certainly do agree that our nation is at a vital crossroads in our history. The prime minister and many of our most integrationist economists and some of our business community's Canada-lasters say that free trade (by which they really mean a comprehensive bilateral economic union and harmonization with the U.S.) is *the only answer* to our problems. Others suggest it would be a massive—and, likely, fatal—surrender of our sovereignty. Perhaps, after reading the pages that follow, you will be able to decide for yourself whether or not there is indeed only one solution to our problems.

Other questions keep reappearing in these essays or returning to mind as you read them. Is it really a lack of ideas that is our problem, or is it the political system itself? Why do we seem to have such lack of vision in Canada, such a lack of direction? Is it the people or the politicians who are to blame? Or both? Should we really have a national dream, national industrial policies and blueprints for the future? Or should we simply leave it all to "the market"? Private industry wouldn't dream of not planning ahead and budgeting carefully for the future, but should government do the same and intervene accordingly? Should governments assume the role of elected representatives of the people and provide leadership and direction, or should they govern by public opinion polls as they have so often in recent years? It's true that these are age-old questions, but it seems to me, after reading this book, that they are at the very basis of our national schizophrenia.

The decision-making process is clearly under attack in these pages. Parliamentary reform, the Senate, Commons committees, and public appointments are the focus of much attention. Perhaps, before we can go on to loftier goals, it may well be that we must first pay much more and very careful attention to the reform of our democratic institutions.

I think it's fair to say that most of us feel Canada has not lived up to its potential for quite some time. We seem to have somehow become bogged down, to have accepted a society where between one and a quarter and one and a half million Canadians are unemployed and over four million Canadians, including a million children, live well below commonly accepted definitions of the poverty line. We have treated our native people very poorly. Our once widely accepted international role as a middle-power, peacekeeping, conciliatory country has now been largely replaced by our image as an economic and military satellite of the United States. We are increasingly involved in testing various delivery systems for nuclear weapons. For over a generation our tax system has clearly benefited the wealthy at the expense of the middle class and the poor. In relative terms of income, the bottom fifth of our population is about where it was forty years ago. Our internal and external (current account) deficits are heavy burdens. We are close to the top in the list of the world's largest per capita foreign debtors. Almost half of all our non-financial industry profits go to non-Canadians, a shocking figure by any comparison. Still, we are back at it again, "open for business" again, selling off the ownership and control of our country just as quickly as we can. At the same time, we friendly, generous Canadians give or lend or provide tax breaks for the world's biggest and wealthiest foreign corporations at the rate of hundreds of millions of dollars in taxpayers' money every year.

The twentieth century was supposed to belong to Canada. At the present rate we will be fortunate if Canada belongs to Canada.

Despite the negative picture I have painted above I remain totally convinced that most Canadians, the overwhelming majority, consider themselves very fortunate to live in Canada. We continue to have one of the highest standards of living in the world (in terms of real purchasing-power parity, we are still number two). We have developed a relatively peaceful, relatively compassionate, relatively tolerant, multicultural and comparatively well-educated nation, which still has a relative abundance of natural resources, fertile lands, and fresh water. Visitors from abroad are inevitably astonished by the beauty of our land, our mountains, our forests and lakes, and our immense, magnificent coastlines. In so many ways we have so much going for us. In so many ways we have splendid opportunities for the future.

Perhaps, looking at the pluses and minuses, it would be tempting to say we should be content with our lot. Altogether, we're not in bad shape. Personally, I don't buy this at all. It seems to me the quality of our political leadership in recent years has been poor. While so many other nations are improving their lot in leaps and bounds, are planning ahead for a rapidly changing economic environment, are joining business and labour and government in well-planned national policies and strategies, Canada seems prepared to stagger blindfold into the twenty-first century, putting the welfare of millions of our citizens in jeopardy.

The following pages do not represent a blueprint or a panacea or even a simple basic outline for our future. But they do represent some

4

interesting, well-thought-out opinions about how we might change. After reading the words of these sixty Canadians I am even more optimistic about the potential of our country. As I have said in a thousand speeches across the country, the greatest asset we Canadians have is our ability, as Canadians, to determine our own future. If we can stop the current government from giving this away, I'm confident that we can go on to build a truly great country, which in turn can go on to play a greater role among the world community of nations. I suspect that quite a few people who write on the following pages will be deeply involved in that process.

Mel Hurtig
Edmonton
April 1987

DORIS ANDERSON

One of the biggest concerns that I, as prime minister, would have is the manner by which I attained my high office. The House of Commons is not representative of the people—if it ever was—and the way we decide who will govern us is certainly not very democratic. As well, the public is beginning to lose faith in our present system's ability to respond to our needs. In an age where technology is changing at breath-taking speed, our parliamentary system is as slow to react as a brace of Maritime oxen in a mud hole, and its lack of flexibility is bred in the system.

If it can't be changed to represent us better, people will participate in the democratic process even less than they do now—perhaps even as little as they do in the United States, where only just over half the people even bother to vote.

Canada is presently run mainly by an oligarchy of male WASPS, who try to keep in touch with the needs of the voter by polls and, lately, by trekking expensive parliamentary committees around the country— with the purpose of educating our elected members of parliament by making them listen to the people they are supposed to be representing. In fact, the situation in Canada today is somewhat similar to the situation in England when large numbers of ordinary people were represented only by landowners.

To begin with, the cost of maintaining the House of Commons is not cheap—about $321,000 per member of parliament, and for the whole government administration $332 million a year. That figure is not out of line for running a country of this size, but we're not getting our money's worth.

Members of parliament, especially if they are backbenchers of the party in power, have little influence on legislation except to vote robot-style for the government's bills. Even in their constituencies they do more of a public relations job for the government, rather than bringing back to Ottawa the concerns of their constituents. Question period, which is all that most Canadians ever see of how the country is governed, is a zoo where the name of the game is to bait the government and get on television. Speeches—no matter how well informed— are generally irrelevant as far as influencing any votes, although they often perform the useful function of informing the press and the public of the issues at hand. The Senate is a joke and should either be reformed and made an elective body or abolished as an expensive pay-off for faithful party workers.

Consequently, more and more people who feel they are not adequately represented work outside the system—since they have so little input in it. They work mostly on a volunteer basis, as lobbyists, trying to persuade the government to make the reforms it would be making if it were truly representative. Such lobbies are relatively new, though we have always had strong, well-financed business lobbies.

But it's an awkward, cumbersome, inefficient way to run a country, and it gradually leads to frustration and distrust by the public and lack of respect for our national institutions. In other countries and in other times, such situations have led to rebellions. Democracies, hopefully, have built-in self-renewing qualities that avoid such draconian changes.

In a country where everyone over eighteen is privileged to vote and where anyone, supposedly, can work his or her way up through the political party system to run for parliament, why is the House of Commons so monotonously white, three-piece-suited, lawyer-laden, and male?

It isn't as though it takes exceptional ability and merit to sit in parliament. In a democracy, anyone should be capable of being elected—and almost anyone has. We've had used car salesmen, hockey players, eminent lawyers, scholars, successful businessmen, as well as bankrupts, wife beaters, income tax evaders, forgers, influence peddlers, and fraud artists. One member of parliament took counsel on important matters by communing with his dog and his dead mother. He became prime minister.

Lofty personal qualities are clearly not essential. Some members who look like potential prime ministers fail miserably. Others, with no obvious distinction, succeed brilliantly. But what clearly has been a decided asset in the past has been to be male and a WASP—and, of late, French Canadian.

Let me digress for a minute. If we were honest about a fair system, we should decree that for the next twenty years at least, all members of the House of Commons, with the exception of 10 per cent, must be women, Italians, Germans, Dutch, Inuit, blacks, etc; that all judges for the next thirty years, with the exception of 2 per cent, must be women and minorities; and that five out of every seven appointments made to any board, from Air Canada to the National Advisory Council on Aging, must be the same mix.

Preposterous? Why? Women, for example, have had the vote for over sixty years. On the average, they have been at least as well educated as males, and most of them have been working for most of the last twenty years, both in the home and in outside jobs. Yet they have been overwhelmingly represented in all our institutions by the other sex. Why not even things up? Considering our not-so-remarkable record, could we lose?

"Balderdash!" I can hear the reader saying. "If women or anyone else want to get into parliament, they simply have to work for it—as men have done."

But getting elected to parliament is carefully controlled—by the nomination process, and ultimately by the party itself. If you are lucky enough to be the party's choice for a prized safe seat, you may never make a speech, rarely even attend sessions, in fact distinguish yourself in no way at all—and still be returned to the House of Commons election after election. Liberals in Quebec, Tories in the West—it's like being endowed with a fairly easy, prestigious job with generous holidays, plentiful perks such as travel, and a handsome indexed pension forever, as long as you do what you're told.

The problem, of course, is getting the nomination. For example, in 1968 when Trudeaumania swept the land, only one woman ran for the Liberal party in the whole of the country—Margaret Rideout—and she couldn't easily be ousted because she already held her New Brunswick seat. In the last federal election, when it was clear the Conservatives were going to win, the party ran only three women west of the Lakehead (where they were bound to make a sweep), and one of them, Pat Carney, was already a sitting member. In Quebec, where the Conservatives expected to gain only a few seats, the party ran close to half women. But they did much better than they had expected—and thus, by a fluke, we got more women into the House of Commons than ever before in our history: 10 per cent.

Once in office, a lot of other power-wielding decisions are made by the government, from picking who will sit in the cabinet to who become judges and who sit on over 3500 government boards and commissions.

To change the system so that we are represented by more women, and a better racial and ethnic mix, several reforms must take place. Spending on nomination meetings must be limited—as it now is on election campaigns by the Canadian Federal Election Act. Trucking busloads of people in from other ridings to pack the meeting has to be stopped. Anyone eligible to vote at a nomination meeting must have been a member of that riding organization for at least a month and must not belong to any other riding organization. All-in-good-fun dirty tricks (such as the riding executive switching the date of the nomination meeting without telling all of the candidates) must be outlawed. The NDP has such a system in place, and the Liberals are moving in that direction. If all of these reforms were instituted by all

9

parties, it wouldn't change the system entirely, but it would result in a better mix of people in the House of Commons.

Yet it's still difficult for people who don't feel comfortable in any of our three major parties to be represented in our parliament. We would be better off and would involve more people in the democratic process if we had more choice, as many European countries have. I believe that a party like the Green Party in Germany, which is supported by feminists, environmentalists, and peace activists, might be a welcome addition to the political spectrum in Canada today, if only to remind the other major parties that there is a substantial number of votes to be lost if these objectives aren't being pursued more vigorously. But we abhor minority governments in Canada even though, during minority governments, we have generally managed to get a lot of legislation through the House with a lot less posturing and speechmaking and much more compromise.

As you can see, I am not likely to become prime minister. But since this is the theme of the book, let's imagine for the next few minutes what I would do if I did. One of my first priorities would be to provide jobs for people, particularly young people. There is no lack of jobs that need to be done, though the jobs are no longer extracting minerals out of the earth and harvesting our forests or working on assembly lines. Those jobs are now being done by machines for the most part.

We need a highly educated and skilled labour force, and we need to concentrate on those things we do especially well so that we can compete on world markets. To do this we have to move, and make up time, on research; and we have to develop—after twenty years of talking about it—a viable industrial strategy. Somehow, workers have to be more involved, and unions and business must learn to co-operate better.

We should be moving ahead to develop our tar sands and offshore oil resources so as to make ourselves, as a northern nation sitting on the edge of the Arctic Circle, more secure in time for the next erratic move by OPEC.

The way we care for our old people and our children—particularly children of working parents—is shocking. We have thousands of homeless people wandering the streets of our cities and millions more with inadequate housing. Clearly, if we did all the jobs that needed to be done, there would be more than enough work for everyone.

We are not a major power, but as a middle power Canada can exert much more influence than at present to support—along with New Zealand, Australia, and the Netherlands—de-escalation of the arms race, as well as continuing peacekeeping operations and exerting, as we now are doing, a strong voice at the United Nations.

Since we don't need masses of unskilled workers any longer, we need to cherish and look after our young a lot better than we have done in the past. Every Canadian baby has the right to be wanted, loved, raised outside the spectre of poverty, and given as equal an opportunity as possible. Yet more and more Canadian children are being raised below the poverty level. This must be stopped—and this means, as well, that women must have access (as the law stipulates) to safe therapeutic abortion.

For people who are unable to work, we must provide a guaranteed annual income and get rid of the gim-rickety system of welfare we now have in place.

Finally, since the dawn of history, in the occasional lull when the world has not been struggling to survive (mostly from the aggression of one nation towards another), we have attempted to plan Utopias where we would all live in peace and harmony. Today, the world's problems, stated in the simplest terms are:

- to avoid getting blown up in a nuclear holocaust,

- to look after the environment better,

- to learn to look after each other better.

I think a large body of Canadians would agree with these broad aims. Where we differ, of course, is in how to achieve them. For we Canadians at least—a law-abiding, modest, urban, overly talkative and cautious middle power—the last two objectives could easily be within our collective national grasp, within the lifetime of our youngest citizens. Then why don't we do it?

THOMAS S. AXWORTHY

Most of us are deluded about the power of the prime ministership. Believing that simply holding high office is sufficient to achieve societal change, as prime ministers fail to deliver we question their integrity instead of assessing their influence.

The truth of the matter is that political leaders spend most of their time explaining, cajoling, and pleading rather than strategizing, deciding, and commanding. Arriving in office full of hope, politicians quickly discover that resources are limited, demands are enormous, and events are overwhelming. "I agree with you," President Kennedy once told an anxious supplicant, "but the government may not."

Leadership involves a perpetual battle to preserve some element of choice from the pressure of onrushing events. To maintain any sort of an agenda, the primary resource of the prime minister is the power to persuade. A prime minister can focus attention on society's ills, chart a new course, or return to old verities. Political office is "a bully pulpit," to quote Theodore Roosevelt. Transforming society's values is a more enduring accomplishment than rearranging budget figures.

Amidst all of today's problems, is there one paramount crisis that puts all others in the shade? Is there one dominant issue that should command the sustained attention of the prime minister's bully pulpit? I believe there is. The single most important problem of mankind is how to avoid nuclear war.

On 16 July 1945, in the desert of New Mexico at a test site named Trinity, mankind invented the means to destroy our species. With that first explosion of the atomic bomb we became the first generation since Genesis, in the words of the American Catholic bishops, "with the capacity to destroy God's creation."

There is no precedent for the enormity of this fact. Wars have always been with us, but the ability to end all life is the terrible secret of our generation alone. Peace, therefore, is the moral priority of our time. All other objectives, however worthy, recede when compared to our obligation to future generations to leave them a planet capable of sustaining life.

In the vast sweep of time measured by biologists, the forty-two years since Trinity is but the blink of an eye. Forty-two years without war between the major powers, however, is a significant time indeed.

We have already exceeded by twenty-one years the period of peace enjoyed after World War I.

This is the awful dilemma posed by nuclear weapons. So awesome is their power that adversaries shun the ultimate confrontation. By most normal historical standards, the Soviet Union and the United States should have gone to war sometime after 1945. Because of nuclear weapons, we have avoided the fifty million casualties of World War II.

But if this restraint ever falters, all is lost. We are playing Russian roulette with a nuclear revolver containing a hundred chambers instead of six, but it is still Russian roulette. Sometime, somewhere, that trigger will go off. We must use the present uneasy coexistence won by nuclear deterrence to implement a program to replace nuclear deterrence. Man invented nuclear weapons. We can also abolish them.

What, then, is to be done? Is the dream of a nuclear-free world simply airy-fairy idealism, or are there solid grounds for hope? My sense of urgency, even of desperation, arises from the belief that the world now faces a critical divide. For the first time since 1945, we have a real chance to undo the folly of Trinity. History, technology, and geopolitics are creating real conditions for peace. An historic compact between the superpowers is possible. Creative leadership alone is absent. Canada cannot decide the issue. But we can do everything in our power to ensure that our alliance is on the right side of history.

A program aimed at the long, medium, and short term is essential:

- We must reconcile the interests of East and West. In the long term, true security will only come from internal changes within the Soviet Union. But we can aid the process.

- We must reduce reliance on nuclear weapons over time. In the medium term, we should set a goal of a nuclear-free world by the year 2000.

- We must reduce the immediate risks of nuclear war. In the near term, as we move towards abolishing nuclear weapons, we must ensure a stable balance of power.

Building Peace

Canadians cannot blind themselves to the reality that the historic rivalry between East and West will endure. The Soviet Union, like czarist Russia before it, is an expansionist state. Having won an empire in Eastern Europe, the Soviet Union is desperate to retain the prize. Leninist ideology is also hostile to the West, so a competition over values is added to the conflict over geography. In seeking some accommodation with the Soviet Union we must never forget that the conflict originates in fundamentally opposed world views. Security must be based on a balance of interests, not on good intentions.

But it is this very desire of the Communist regime to endure that may now be forcing the pace of change. The Soviet Union is a failing society—economically depressed, repressive, and rigid. It can produce rocket boosters but it cannot deliver the good life. The crucial point is that the Soviet leadership knows this. Military might has made the Soviets into a superpower, but economic failure is reducing them to Third World status.

Not surprisingly, Mr. Gorbachev is seeking a solution. First, he wants to avoid worsening the situation through a new burst of military competition with the United States. Next, as his recent actions on Soviet dissidents reveal, he sees political and economic reform as one way to stop the rot. It is in our interest to help him succeed. A bear is never so dangerous as when cornered. Through trade, tourism, and scientific exchange, we must aid Mr. Gorbachev's policy of openness by exposing the Soviet Union to Western values. Ours must be a policy of sustained engagement. Andrei Sakharov knows the abuses of the Soviet system firsthand. Yet he is willing to give Mr. Gorbachev the benefit of the doubt. So should we.

Towards the Year 2000
Until Ronald Reagan met Mikhail Gorbachev at the Reykjavik Summit in October 1986, nuclear disarmament seemed to be the preserve only of a crackpot fringe. No longer. In one of the great ironies of history, Ronald Reagan has made nuclear disarmament respectable again. Such a breakthrough must not be allowed to fade. Nuclear disarmament in the year 2000 can be a meaningful, achievable goal.

There are 50,000 nuclear weapons in the world today. They should be reduced to zero. Nuclear deterrence has brought us an uneasy coexistence; it has not brought us true security. True, a non-nuclear world would still endure the strains of Soviet-American rivalry; it might even be more expensive to maintain a conventional balance of power. But it would be a world free of the psychic pain brought on by nuclear terror. It would be a world where children no longer have to ask, "What do you want to be *if* you grow up?" Most of all, it would be a world that we can pass on to our descendants.

The elements for a grand compromise are plain. In exchange for American forbearance from testing and deployment of a space-based defensive missile system, the Soviets would agree to a mutual deep cut of 50 per cent in strategic rocket forces. After reducing strategic weapons to 5000 for each side, phase two would be the elimination of the 20,000 intermediate and tactical nuclear weapons. Finally, after a ten-year period of digestion, phase three would require the elimination of all remaining strategic nuclear forces. Of course, there would have to be adequate verification and enforcement safeguards. France, China, and Great Britain would have to be persuaded to give up their nuclear armaments, and protection would have to be assured against one of the superpowers or a rogue state squirrelling away a few nuclear warheads. But even if such complete safeguards could not be attained, reducing the arsenals to only a fraction of their present strength—say, 500 weapons each as the U.S. Navy proposed in the late 1950s—would make the world a vastly safer place. Let us begin.

Reducing Risk

While putting in place a long-term strategy of sustained engagement with the Soviet Union and a medium-term goal of reducing reliance on nuclear weapons, we can also take several immediate concrete steps to lessen the likelihood of nuclear war. Bad as our situation is today, it would be infinitely worse if a larger number of states already had the bomb. Strengthening the non-proliferation treaty is vital. The nuclear cancer must not be allowed to spread. And while prohibiting the horizontal spread of weapons, a test-ban treaty banning underground experiments will prevent new weapons of destruction from emerging.

Within NATO, Canada has agreed to a western defence posture that calls for the early use of tactical nuclear weapons. This madness should cease. For a relatively small investment in defence expenditure—$20 billion over five years—NATO could achieve conventional military parity with the Soviet Union. It is a price worth paying. Canada should contribute a fair share.

These are all steps forward. But most urgent of all, we must do what we can to stop the United States from taking a giant leap backwards. The Reagan administration has already exceeded the arms limits set by the SALT II treaty and it plans to reinterpret the ABM treaty to allow the testing of Star Wars. If the Reagan administration chooses to destroy the ABM treaty—the most significant arms control achievement since 1945—it will be turning its back on the possibility of a nuclear-free world. Canada must protest this monstrous step with our every breath.

Albert Einstein said that "the splitting of the atom has changed everything except our way of thinking." Now is the time for politics to catch up with physics. The anti-nuclear momentum of Reykjavik must gather force. This should be Canada's primary purpose. We have a planet to save.

LEONE BAGNALL

To be given the opportunity to serve as prime minister of Canada is, I believe, a great privilege and one that entails tremendous responsibilities and requires wisdom, courage, and a sincere love for Canada and all Canadians. As prime minister, I would seek the guidance and assistance of my Heavenly Father and of capable Canadians who are ready and willing to put the best interests of their country before personal gain or recognition. Relying on such assistance, my program would be as follows.

First, I would challenge and encourage all Canadians to concentrate upon the positive things in our society that unite and strengthen us as a nation, and I would minimize and strive to eliminate the things that divide and weaken our country. I would try to increase trust among all potential divisions in our nation (e.g., east/west, labour/management, large/small).

After consultation with the provincial governments to seek their co-operation, I would enter into serious land claims negotiations with the native peoples of our country, with the view to achieving a just settlement which would restore to them an acceptable portion of their heritage in land and resources. In so doing, I would return to the native peoples their right and responsibility for self-reliance and self-determination.

As a keynote to my economic policy, I would challenge Canadians to meet the absolute need to control our national deficit, bringing about a balanced budget in a reasonable period of time before the carrying charges of our national debt are so great that a balanced budget is impossible to achieve. I would pass legislation that would require sinking funds to be set up to provide for the payment of all future borrowings of the federal government. And I would endeavour to create a climate in which our society would not deem it necessary to squander our inheritance and mortgage all future generations.

Overall, I would strive to create an economic regime in which our renewable resources of land and sea—namely our forests, our soil, and our marine life—would not be exploited beyond a perpetually sustainable yield level and in which non-renewable resources would be conserved rather than squandered. I would work with all governments on this continent to reduce pollution to ensure a safe environment for all forms of life. In particular, I would commit ongoing effort in every way possible to bring peace to our world and to prevent the eclipse of human life by nuclear war.

I would build on the strengths of each region of Canada to remove once and for all the regional disparity that has plagued our country for over one hundred years. Regional economic development, I believe, must be achieved by working with the communities involved and thus allowing the communities within the region to select, create, and support economic development projects that are specifically suited to their communities, to build on their strengths and opportunities, and always to strive for excellence.

My energy policy would encourage the development of hydroelectric power, both for the benefit of the Canadian economy overall and for the benefit of individual electrical consumers. Canada is lacking a truly national policy for the development and marketing of electric power. We have many of the world's greatest sites for hydroelectric development, but they remain undeveloped. Moreover, hydroelectric power is environmentally benign (safe, acceptable) and is renewable, efficient, and generally inflation-free. As prime minister, I would take decisive action to develop its potential, first, by installing generation capability and, secondly, by erecting transmission capability to deliver electricity to markets within Canada and for export. A national power grid would be a first step towards a national pricing policy for electricity, similar to steps already taken for gas and oil. This would result in new markets for electricity at an equitable price for all Canadians, regardless of the province in which they live. This policy would have a second major benefit—contributing to the elusive goal of regional economic development in Canada. Hydroelectric projects would produce industrial development, employment, and related economic activity in several regions of the country where it is badly needed.

Recognizing that efficient, modern transportation systems via road, rail, air, and water are essential for present and future economic development in all parts of Canada, I would make an ongoing effort, in co-operation with provincial and territorial governments, to ensure that such systems are in place and are maintained so as to assure that every province and region has access to transportation systems at a cost to producers, industries, and business that is competitive with the rest of Canada.

I would recognize the importance of the primary producers of Canada and would work with them to guarantee a just return for the quality food they produce, as well as ensuring that interested young producers have an opportunity to enter the industry.

I would endeavour to remove the detrimental effects of unemployment—which causes severe social damage by the ever-increasing personal sense of failure, depression, and lack of hope for the future—and to end the unforgivable loss of productive human contribution to our country. Along with continuing every effort to strengthen our national economy, and thus to provide long-term meaningful employment, I would immediately select an advisory committee of knowledgeable, concerned Canadians to formulate a new definition of employment—one that recognizes that although there is and may well continue to be a shortage of jobs, there definitely is not a shortage of worthwhile, productive work. This new definition of employment would be such that it would encourage all Canadians to contribute, to their fullest capability, to their community and country. The advisory committee would also be required to recommend the necessary steps for the immediate implementation of a new income security system to support Canadians as they in turn contribute, in order to ensure that Canada becomes a stronger, more compassionate, and more progressive nation.

An educated society is fundamental to the achievement of a stable, tolerant, empathetic society, as well as to successful economic development and employment creation and flexibility. I would therefore cooperate with the provincial and territorial governments to ensure that all Canadians receive the best education possible.

I would immediately convene a national conference on the family to seek ways to strengthen and support Canadian families. And I would require that all legislation be such that the family, as an institution, would be strengthened rather than eroded, since I believe that the survival of our civilization depends on the family flourishing as a peaceful, stable, supportive, productive unit within our society. Included in this effort would be the establishment of a realistic value on the work and service to society provided by a parent, perhaps applying the concept of "equal pay for work of equal value." Then, and only then, will a parent be given a real choice to remain at home while the children are growing up, or to continue education or training, or to work outside the home. If continuing education or entering the work force were chosen, then I would ensure that the financial support given would be more than adequate to pay for quality child-care services.

Among the many other measures I would take as prime minister, I would:

– ensure that all Canadians are provided with adequate, affordable shelter, as it is unacceptable that our country should ignore the individuals and families who are forced to live in totally inadequate housing, as well as ignoring the homeless within our midst (second-stage housing for victims of domestic violence, ex-prisoners, etc., is also of critical concern and this need would be met);

– strive to maintain, in co-operation with the provinces, our excellent health-care system, while remaining sensitive to changing needs and aiming to provide equality of service in all parts of Canada; meanwhile, there would be increased emphasis on illness prevention and healthful living;

– explore and support programs and policies, in co-operation with provincial and territorial governments, that would bring the youth and the senior citizens of our country together for educational, cultural, recreational, social, and spiritual purposes;

– strive to provide for greater regional control of and input into the major cultural agencies of our country; and continually endeavour to identify, share, celebrate, and treasure the cultural traditions and identities that are authentically part of our provincial, territorial, and national heritage;

– restructure the Senate to make it consist of an equal number of elected members from each province (and future provinces) who would serve for a specific length of time;

– enact legislation that would require all new employees of the federal civil service to have had five years of employment in the private sector or to have been successfully self-employed for five years (or a five-year combination of both);

– seek the co-operation of public-sector unions and the private sector to formulate and implement a system whereby there would be ongoing regular interchange of personnel between the public and private sectors of our country;

– reserve the time to return often to my beloved island province and stroll along the peaceful white-sand beaches and the country roads to renew my mind and spirit, and thereby maintain my roots and my sense of being.

Finally, and perhaps of greatest importance by word and action, I would encourage my fellow MPs to rise above partisan rhetoric and concentrate on the problems, issues, and challenges (e.g., unemployment, poverty, economic development, deficits, provincial equality) which must be solved if our country is to survive. If politicians are to regain public trust and respect, and re-establish the integrity of parliament and government as a worthwhile institution, members of parliament must put the needs of others before personal gain and prestige. Indeed, if the problems that face the world today are to be solved, there will have to be a universal desire to put the well-being of others before oneself and to live together in an atmosphere of love and respect. Many would say this is an impossible dream. I don't agree, and I believe that it is a goal that we must continually, prayerfully try to achieve.

Having striven to accomplish all this, I would gladly retire.

George Bain

What I would do if I suddenly found myself prime minister would be to sit down and read up some more on Lord Melbourne. Melbourne, who was Queen Victoria's first prime minister, is the patron saint of prime ministers of the if-it-ain't-broke-don't-fix-it school. It was his ingrained belief that it was at least even money that whatever any government did, it was likely to make things worse. This philosophy was summed up succinctly in his comment, when he was home secretary and faced with widespread civil disorder after the Lords defeated the Reform Bill of 1831: "When in doubt what should be done, do nothing."

I would model myself on him. Whenever a minister brought a proposal to the cabinet table, my immediate response would be to say, "Let's don't." If I detected signs of mutiny, I would appoint a cabinet committee to study the proposal so that we wouldn't have to do anything right then. Meanwhile, I would have the staff hunt around for as innocuous a something as could be laid hands on, to be substituted in case it became unavoidable that we give the appearance of having done something. But that would never happen before I had played my last card—namely, had tried to get an argument going and then given them the old clincher. "Look," I would say, "obviously we have not achieved a complete meeting of minds on this. Therefore, I suggest we remember the wise words of that great British statesman, William Lamb, the second Viscount Melbourne, who said...." Et cetera.

There is a lot to be said for a prime minister concentrating on just keeping his head above water, without actually doing things. Politics, remember, is the art of the possible, and in Canadian politics not very much is ever possible. This has been recognized by all our most successful prime ministers, success in Canadian politics being measured by years in office, not by what was done with them. So long as you don't make the mistake of committing yourself to anything (an almost certain recipe for getting people upset), the other side can be relied on to make enough mistakes to keep you in office. William Lyon Mackenzie King knew that, and he was prime minister forever—or, as it seemed in his case, longer.

At the end of World War I he wrote a book called *Industry and Humanity*, which analysed the ills of industrialized society and laid down an intellectual foundation upon which might be built an economically, sociologically, and spiritually better world—and, not at all incidentally, upon which W. L. M. King might become Liberal leader and prime minister. Principles were defined there that King remained true to for the rest of his life. Two or three he even did something about. When King stepped down after twenty-two years, he had been in office longer than any prime minister in all of British Commonwealth history. He also had, as social reforms he could lay claim to (the list may not be comprehensive, but it's close enough), a modest old-age pension, family allowances, and the outline of unemployment insurance—which worked out to significant reform at the dizzying rate of one every seven years and four months. However, he was canny enough to reserve most of this feverish activity until after his last election, in case a vengeful public might descend on him crying, "Change! Change! Change!—Is that all you ever think about?"

King was a manager. What he managed best was to keep himself in office. This he did by cultivating a personality with the iridescent charm of wallpaper paste, by not scaring people with precipitate action, ever, and by always playing great dee-fence. His successor, Louis S. St. Laurent, was also a manager. He reigned in a time of rare political and economic euphoria. This was the 1950s when cars put out fins, cities put out endless suburbs of ranch bungalows, and the Young Marrieds (as the homemaker magazines liked to call them) put out the future dropouts and flower children, generically known as the Now Generation, later transformed into Yuppies and Dinks (double income/no kids). No prime minister in his right mind would have been tempted to disturb the calm by setting out to change anything drastically, and Uncle Louis was in his right mind and not tempted to change anything.

Do you begin to get my drift? Consider John Diefenbaker. Renegade in power or not, it was never John Diefenbaker's mistake that he did a lot that was alarmingly different. He didn't. A northern vision here, a bill of rights there; your ordinary workaday prime ministerial sort of thing. With the Dief, it was that visionary's lightning blue gaze of his and the billowing voice, like an overripe Shakespearean's, that did him in. He made people uneasy thinking that he *might* do something radical. A sense of insecurity developed on a national scale akin to what anyone might feel as an individual, leaving home for work every day wondering if a favourite chair would be in its familiar corner when one came home again in the evening. Consequently, Diefenbaker was in, quickly in again with the largest majority in history, and then out, all in six years.

Or look at Lester B. Pearson. His short career illustrates exactly the reverse of the coin from King's, namely the perils of doing. It was instantly evident that his promise of sixty days of decision was a mistake. Having managed to be elected in spite of it, what he needed was a show of indolence to demonstrate insincerity. Unfortunately, the Pearsonians had a lust for legislation—Canada Pension Plan, medicare, new flag, Canada Development Corporation, and so on— and if various entertaining scandals had not intervened to divert public attention from the pace of change, their first parliament might have been their last. But scandals can do only so much to cleanse a government of the stigma of reformism, and in a second election in 1965 the electorate expressed itself in an unseemly show of vigour by again denying Pearson a majority.

We now come to Pierre Trudeau's fifteen-year custodianship. Trudeau got off on the right foot by bringing with him an admirably short list of things he wanted to get done—make the French language accessible to Canadians in all national public institutions and embed a charter of rights in a patriated constitution. However, two mistakes nearly cut his reign short at four years.

One was to create an air of electricity around the Prime Minister's Office. Regional desks were set up through which, in theory, anyone in the realm might reach Numero Uno, or come close. Then it was let out that in the name of participatory democracy the mind of the public would be plumbed and the collective wisdom brought to bear on issues of the day as never before. Professional managers were retained to plot on flow charts the progress of every item of public business. Nothing much came of this, but it smacked of doing things and created public unease, which was compounded when Trudeau unwisely opted, at one go, to throw half his essential program into the hopper in his very first term. Even if we disregard the Canadian weddedness to the status quo, this must be seen to have been a mistake. Very many French-speaking Canadians found it no big deal that they would now be able to buy stamps in French if they found themselves in Orangeville, Ont., whereas at least as many English-speaking Canadians found it a very big deal indeed that posters advertising the post office's next commemorative issue (on Canadian covered wagons) would be thrusting The Other Language at them. In 1972 the Liberals were reduced to 109 seats, fewer even than Lester B. Pearson had in either of his elections.

A chastened Pierre Trudeau was careful not to do anything between 1972 and 1974, except to say that Robert Stanfield should not be allowed to make a reckless experiment in zapping inflation—a bold stroke against change which restored him sufficiently in public esteem to give him a majority again. We are now left with the conundrum of 1979. Again, it is activity, and even the public perception of the possibility of it, that causes governments to be defeated, not inactivity. As the Trudeau government was faultless in this regard between 1974 and 1979, political scientists have been left to speculate that the defeat resulted from public apprehension in case, if re-elected, Trudeau would be unable to go on resisting the impulse to *do* something. That apprehension defeated him. When Joe Clark found himself in office and unwisely made an undisguised attempt to introduce change, and fiscal change at that (short-term pain for long-term gain, remember?), the voters unceremoniously threw him out too. And, of course, they proved to have been right in questioning Trudeau's ability to resist the siren call of legislation if re-elected. Between 1980 and 1984—now, however, like King, contemplating retirement and safe from the threat of electoral retribution—he completed the second half of his fundamental program. The voters promptly hanged his successor.

It should not be thought that Canadians knowingly oppose change. Assume a study by, let us say, Canadian Research Analysis and Polling, to find the terms by which Canadians themselves think they are best described. What would their answers be? "Confident." "Outgoing." "Forward-looking." "Progressive." "Adaptable." "Buoyant." "Optimistic." "Zestful." And there would be the one respondent who would sum it all up: "For my part—and I think the same is true for most Canadians I know—it is not that I am opposed to change. Far from it. But I don't think it should make things different."

It is this typically Canadian viewpoint that we see reflected in the response to the two main economic thrusts of the Mulroney government: debt reduction and the restructuring of trade with the United States. True, the new government was foolish to set out to create a record for itself, overlooking the prime rule of Canadian politics: as with a prisoner in the dock, the best record is the one with the least on it. True, too, that with rare exceptions the pundits in 1984 said that Canadians had voted for change. But what they failed to recognize, and the government as well, is that no one actually expected to get change. Undoubtedly, very many people accepted in the abstract that at some point, preferably somewhere short of the Government of Canada not being able to raise enough revenue to pay the interest on the national debt, expenditures would have to be cut. What they did not accept was that anything should be changed by this, and consequently exceptions would have to be made for all social programs, the Canadian Broadcasting Corporation, cultural organizations in general, environmental programs, foreign aid, subsidies to create jobs in areas of high unemployment, assistance to western farmers suffering from depressed grain markets, relief for oil producers, the armed services (at least as related to sustaining Arctic sovereignty), scientific research, payments to the provinces relating particularly to health care and higher education, multicultural programs, postal services, VIA Rail, and jobs of all sorts in the public service. Beyond these sacrosanct areas and a few more, the government would have a free hand to get on with deficit reduction.

Similarly, the government misread early polls, which purported to show 70 per cent of Canadians favourably disposed to free trade, as indicating that many Canadians were favourably disposed to free trade even at the risk of its costing anything. As the realization settled in that the Americans probably would be hard to persuade to sign an agreement under which only they gave and only we got, the list daily grew longer of things to be kept off the table in case the U.S. negotiator saw them and, in his greed, forgot the biblical injunction against coveting his neighbour's ass.

On second thoughts, if I suddenly found myself prime minister, what I would do is I wouldn't.

DAVE BARRETT

As a political veteran, I know that advance assembling of an agenda for a prime minister can be like compiling a grocery shopping list. That's the easy part. The hard part is bringing home the bacon. The difficulties occur when you actually get to the store and discover that some items are unavailable because they're out of season, some have wilted, and others have price tags too high. So you adjust your list in order to come out with a balanced purchase to meet your overall needs. My shopping list for improving Canadians' lives is just such an idealized agenda, by no means complete, which would be subject to changes in priority and to additions or even delays as circumstances and opportunities presented themselves in the real world beyond these pages. But it forms a basic package which I believe our political system can deliver to our citizens if government energies are harnessed to that goal.

Sadly, the list has to begin with any and all measures that can restore the sense of fundamental public trust in the parliamentary system which existed when I grew up, proud of the basic integrity and noble traditions of public service in Canada. This is not nostalgia—it is sheer necessity. In a democracy in which government depends on the consent of the governed, trustworthiness is absolutely vital. Otherwise, no political agenda will be achievable.

This does not involve simply scrubbing clean the malodorous corners of patronage and political scandals. It must also revive the spirit of pioneering, the sense of excitement and the fulfilling challenge in pursuing the dream which Tommy Douglas called the New Jerusalem. We must regain the awareness that we still are a young, vigorous, and bountiful nation. We should seek greatness, not through the self-defeating resort to arms or through exploitation of others but through the creation and cultivation of a civilization within our own borders that puts people first and liberates all the aspirations, energies, and dynamism of the growing human family that lives in the home we call Canada.

Some gestures towards reassuring voters of the integrity of the system have indeed been taken, but they have been used to project the image of reform rather than providing the substance. No major overhaul of some of these measures is needed, just the political will to realize their potential value. Among them would be a conflict-of-interest prohibition with teeth. A more detailed and comprehensive disclosure of the financial affairs of every member of parliament and senior government administrator, and their families, should be required. And to it should be added a direct prohibition against financial holdings that conflict with public responsibilities.

The committee system in the House of Commons should be strengthened to ensure that all members of the House, on both sides, have a more direct and positive impact on the form in which legislation is introduced, not just on the final votes for adoption or rejection. Our parliament has sunk into a mire in recent years, with its unremitting partisan warfare. A glimpse of what can be done by using the energies of elected representatives to work for the people, and not just for the parties, was revealed by what happened in Ontario when the aftermath of the last election boded virtual deadlock and political chaos. This was averted by an *ad hoc* agreement on a public agenda which spanned the aisle dividing the government and opposition. Similarly, a greater role for parliamentary committees and a greater willingness to use "free" votes could make our national political forum into a productive instrument for consensus and action.

Another long step towards reviving respect for the system would be the abolition of the Senate, which has largely been used by both of the old-line parties as a political pay-off. What a signal of changing attitude it would be if this symbol of institutionalized patronage were to be abolished and the $28 million annually going to sustain a few score sycophants in the Red Chamber were spent instead on enabling thousands of young Canadians to serve their communities in locally initiated worthwhile service projects.

Our nation's problem is much more than the difficulty of a business cycle. The rapid transformation of the world's economy has brought our own to an historic crossroads. It is now belatedly clear that the direction we have pursued as a resource-based, export-oriented, branch-plant economy has not fulfilled Sir Wilfrid Laurier's declaration that the twentieth century belongs to Canada. We do face an emergency, but we don't have to panic and we don't have to hide behind a royal commission. A change of direction will be possible if we fashion a renewed national consensus such as Sir John A. Macdonald forged. That one grew out of the consultation of community leaders at soirées, meetings, and tête-à-têtes. To achieve the same result in a much more populous and complex society, we need to assemble a larger and more formal prime minister's conference, representing the full spectrum of our widespread society—business, labour, consumers, civic leaders, academics—in an effort to shape a co-operative commonwealth in which all Canadians would share both the burdens and the benefits of an agreed itinerary towards the future. Since this would be a consultative effort, I would be repudiating its very nature if I prescribed in advance what it should propose for economic and social improvement. But I am sure that most of the following would be discussed thoroughly.

The increased productivity and rapid rise of our Gross National Product brought about by the enormous technological changes of the past generation have been accompanied by a steady ratcheting upward of the unemployment rate, by an erosion of our middle-income earners, and by the return of food banks and soup lines. Clearly, providing work is the top economic priority. Technological change has brought us much greater wealth, but instead of using it to spread jobs around so that everyone shares in the prosperity, we have allowed the gains to be monopolized for profit margins. Much of the profit is siphoned off by the foreign-controlled multinational giants, some of it even escaping our tax laws. It's past time to consider a whole host of job-spreading measures such as shorter work weeks, voluntary early or phased retirement, longer vacations (five weeks has been standard in Europe for years), and sabbaticals for all workers who wish to retrain, travel, spend time with their families, or simply take a rest break to prevent loss of health or burnout. All of this could be achieved progressively and without prejudice to the steady growth of GNP by an agreed schedule of improvements to our labour standards legislation. We must also make real strides towards the goal of equal pay for work of equal value.

Technological innovations that produce new products (unlike those that increase productivity by reducing labour) automatically create completely new jobs. Yet our research and development investment is barely half that of the leading industrial nations, and we give inadequate assistance to home-grown companies and training programs. Just one example of what could be done: there could be R & D assistance to produce a cheap, advanced mini-computer in Canada and a policy to purchase enough to put it into all our classrooms. This would foster a massive increase in a modern, domestically owned industry and would prepare all our youth for the kind of world in which they will have to compete.

We should revolutionize our approach to national development, which in one sense has been a continuation of the pre-Confederation view of Canada as a treasure house of resources to be shipped out. You can't build a nation by selling it. Britain, the United States, Japan, and many others have demonstrated that developing the domestic market is the foundation for steady industrial growth. Import substitution and value-added exports should be encouraged by domestic economic policies that use our own pools of capital in a concerted fashion. The principles of a conserver society, consciously building on our strengths at a methodical pace, would harmonize our economic, environmental, and social stability while nourishing the diversity of our people and regions.

Government does not have to do it all. Our mixed economy—using both the private market mechanism and public intervention—is ideally suited for evolving even more decentralization of power while pursuing the national interest.

Along with a more balanced development strategy, we must also structure a more balanced income distribution. Tax reform is desperately needed. Where once corporation and individual income tax revenues were in rough equilibrium, today's firms carry only about one-fifth of the load. (The justification that all taxes eventually are paid by individuals anyway doesn't wash in a branch-plant economy like ours, since every tax dollar dodged by the multinationals, or by our own mailbox head offices registered in tax havens abroad, enriches foreign profits at the expense of our economy.) The overwhelming bulk of the tax load falls on individual households, and particularly heavily on our working poor. Statistics also show that the top 20 per cent of income earners grow richer, both relatively and absolutely, while our middle-income earners—the backbone of our economic structure—actually decline, and our poor stagnate.

It's past time for a thorough reform, providing a suitable level of guaranteed annual income through a negative income tax and evening up the total tax load. Besides introducing greater justice, this would be a good business move for the long run. In order to ease the strains of technological and industrial change so that a Luddite backlash doesn't break out, workers must be given greater security for themselves and their dependants. The guaranteed annual income could provide such basic security for the entire labour force, including the unemployed. This is an essential precondition for the peaceful and productive transformation of our economy. And it would revive the principle that the purpose of an economy and of national development is to improve the life of people, not just to improve profits.

Education, more than ever before, is at the centre of any economic and social improvement—in fact, is at the heart of survival. It was free university benefits for returning veterans that provided the professional and intellectual steam to help drive our enormous postwar boom of the fifties and sixties. Today, too, we need to develop our brains. It's an investment for survival in the post-industrial struggle. We must also reduce the tragically high unemployment rate among those in their teens and early twenties. They learn nothing of value, only bitterness, lining up for the dole. The country's most precious asset, its youth, is being wasted; and any country that wastes a generation today will go down tomorrow. We must fight back by offering all our youth hope and opportunity while serving their country.

This could be accomplished through a program of public service like President Roosevelt's Civilian Conservation Corps. The cost of paying young people during their service would not be much greater than the present cost of the dole and its administration. The added investment of such a program would be free college education for any youth wishing it. One spin-off of this would be to break the recent trend towards a closed system of elitism. It has been becoming more difficult, not less, for ordinary Canadians to send their kids through college, and this sets up a self-perpetuating circle in which more and more of the fruits of our economy are reserved for fewer and fewer. At its extreme, it is underscored by the recent revelations that the Canadian economy—or at least what's left of it in domestic hands—is effectively controlled by four hundred families through interlocking directorships. We are returning to the evils of the Family Compact.

One of the contributing reasons for this incipient revival of oligarchy has been the disappearance of the succession duties and estate taxes which provinces used to levy. A couple of decades ago, we used to collect about $150 million across the land in succession duties. Such a sum would pay a substantial amount towards the annual tuition of almost a hundred thousand university students, and it would go a long way to ensuring that no Canadian was excluded from university by a financial barrier.

The concentration of power and wealth in a few centres must also be tackled. Rather than shelling out billions to bail out blundering banks and big corporations, we should invest about $14 billion on urban infrastructure over the next decade, as proposed by the Federation of Canadian Municipalities. Investment in repairing and expanding roads, sewers, and other civic facilities would be a sensible mortgage payment for better communities to live in, and it would provide a significant number of permanent jobs immediately. More than $20 billion is owed the treasury in deferred corporate income taxes, and we could gradually draw down that credit by collecting $1 billion each year for rebuilding our communities and improving our economic base.

Developing the Canadian community would hardly be worth the effort if it is to be destroyed or eliminated as a result of international events. For this reason, we should put some real muscle behind our so far limp efforts to help foster a worldwide control of the arms race. As an immediate step, Canada should declare itself a nuclear-free zone and, like New Zealand, should prohibit any nation, not just the United States, from visiting or transiting our territory with nuclear-armed ships or aircraft. We should also refuse to be the testing ground for cruise missiles. And until nuclear reactors are assuredly accident-proof (and especially until a means of safely storing nuclear wastes throughout their lengthy half-life cycle has been found), we should place a moratorium on them. Nor is it just physical destruction we must guard against. Loss of our national independence can occur through economic domination. Any comprehensive trade treaty with the United States should be subject to ratification by a vote of the Canadian people, who can best judge whether it would improve their lot or make them vassals of a foreign power.

Expenditures alone do not shape the ethos of a society. Our nation is one of three grand experiments in the New World. Of these, only Canada—without jingoism and without the sham of a forced patriotism—seeks to let its citizens flower as themselves, roots and all. We are building a multicultural society within a single nation, a co-operative commonwealth spread across half a continent. In our unified diversity, we are the prototype of the global village, the vanguard for all humankind seeking to live and work together in peace.

For this reason, there is an urgency to right the wrongs of the past. We have begun to acknowledge the harm done to our native people, and to Canadians of Japanese descent, and others. We must complete this task. Nor should we delude ourselves with self-praise. Our tradition of sanctuary for refugees, begun with the "underground railroad" for escaping slaves, has been breached in the past and will be again if we forget how many Jews, fleeing to our gates from the Nazi terror in the prewar years, were locked out. Today, there are refugees from murderous regimes in Latin America, Asia, and Africa who seek our haven. As a multicultural society, we risk our soul if we lose compassion for the oppressed in any corner of the earth.

Because we are the hope of a better world.

CARL E. BEIGIE

Many years ago, I read a definition of "class" that has stuck in my mind ever since. It was suggested that class was revealed in the time perspective of a person's current actions. The greater the number of generations into the future one planned for in actions taken today, the higher was one's true class. I believe that this definition applies for countries just as it does for individuals. If I were to find myself prime minister of Canada one day, I would try to make this a "higher class" nation by encouraging more informed reflection about the impact of my generation's policies and attitudes on the generations of Canadians that are to follow us.

In an age of increasingly sophisticated interest-group lobbying techniques, the focus I am advocating is unlikely to make the contemplation of being prime minister more than an idle diversion. People alive today are becoming so adamant about having their wants satisfied now that it takes a rare—and almost certainly a relatively unsuccessful—politician to reflect, for more than a brief moment, on the needs of the yet unborn.

But this is enough cynicism. Let me carry on, starting from the assumption that the problem lies not so much in a failure of will to move outside our narrower, inward-looking instincts but in the absence of a clearly articulated alternative to the established course. Formulating such an alternative is a key role for modern senior political leadership to undertake.

The needs (as opposed to mere wants) of people alive today merit immediate attention and concern. I would advocate supplying these needs in a manner that in no way diminishes the capacity of the nation to provide at least as much to people in the future. If we set this as a minimal goal, then three policy imperatives spring out as necessitating new thinking about what we are doing today and how we measure its impact on the future.

First, environmental degradation must be halted and reversed. To this end, there is a need to devise better ways of measuring the long-term costs of pollution, even if they are imperfect at the outset, to serve as a highly publicized counterweight to reported domestic output performance. What we are allowing to happen to our air, land, and water in the pursuit of growth should be a source of shame. We leave the mess for the yet unborn to live with, oblivious to what that legacy will ultimately entail.

Second, some form of social price must be placed on our non-renewable natural resources which are used up in the process of producing material output. Such resources on or in the ground should, in my opinion, be developed for sale in domestic and foreign markets; I am not an advocate of "warehousing" them. At the same time, however, I regard these resources as a form of capital. Once they are consumed, the nation's capital base has been diminished. Accordingly, I would urge that we strive to replace the diminished capital base below the ground with a parallel expansion in the capital base above the ground. This would mean greater attention to reinvesting (as opposed to consuming) a high proportion of the returns received from sales of the nation's non-renewable raw materials.

This point, by the way, is a major problem in Canada's external economic relations. We have traditionally run large trade surpluses in the area of natural resources. Yet our net imports of other goods and of services have usually exceeded these surpluses, thereby causing Canada to experience deficits on its international current account in most years. We balance these deficits by obtaining net savings from other countries, in effect, but these foreign funds bear interest and dividend costs which add to the magnitude of our now perpetual services trade deficits. In short, we have been consuming so much more than we have been producing in our international merchandise goods trade that we have had to sell off large amounts of our below-the-ground capital to try to make up part of the imbalance. But we are nevertheless falling behind and have had to borrow to settle accounts. Yet this borrowing adds to our payments outflows, and we have not been investing enough of the borrowings to keep the net debt burden from rising.

Third, Canada must get its budgetary accounts in far better balance. The issue here is often badly misunderstood. An imbalance that is solely the result of temporary (what economists call cyclical) short-falls in economic performance presents no major problem, so long as the situation is turned around without too long a delay. The far more serious problem is what can be called structural deficits—those imbalances that cannot be eliminated by economic growth alone. It is very difficult to obtain a precise estimate of the cyclical versus the structural elements of Canada's budget deficits in recent years, but I am convinced that both have been very substantial. The cyclical component is virtually impossible to wipe out in Canada so long as there is a large U.S. budgetary deficit (of either variety). But we can, and I believe we must, work to eliminate our structural deficit through our own initiatives.

Although I have rather orthodox business views about the negative longer-term consequences of structural budget deficits, I am less predictable about the role of government in our modern society. Government deficits create liabilities on the right-hand side of the national balance sheet. If there were no compensatory rise on the left-hand side in terms of effective national assets—in short, if we merely consumed the proceeds of deficit financing—we would be leaving a bitter legacy indeed to the future. As prime minister, I would be more tolerant of what are called government budgetary deficits—even if, technically, structural in character—if they arose from a logically framed capital-building exercise. In other words, borrowing by government for investment purposes is not really objectionable per se; borrowing on a long-term basis to pay for an excessive level of consumption, however, is very objectionable to me.

Too many of my business colleagues fail to realize that in modern society a politician who wishes to remain in office can no longer regard the profit motive merely as an end in itself. Profits are an honourable means, in my scheme of things, but the end they help achieve must also be regarded as improving the long-term performance of the economy. There are other means than the private profit motive alone for this purpose, and government can play an important role in many of them.

I share the conventional businessman's bias towards encouraging society to devote a reasonably substantial share of its current output to investment purposes. My understanding of the forces that will be pressuring our economy as we move into the next century has led me to become stronger in this preference with each year that passes. There has been relatively little problem in terms of Canadians' saving habits. Although in some Asian nations saving rates are 25 per cent of disposable income or higher, our rate of around 10 per cent is more than twice that in the United States and not grossly out of line with any of the other non-Asian industrial nations.

Problems are to be found in two areas. First, in recent years a very large proportion of Canada's personal savings have had to be devoted, directly or indirectly, to funding the country's total government budget deficits (including all levels of government, not just the federal). These deficits in turn represent not merely dissaving (the negative of saving) but also primarily consumption-augmenting activities (as opposed to investment-augmenting).

A second problem, and a long-standing one, is that too much of what we save that does end up in investment is not efficiently utilized. Especially in many of our manufacturing industries, Canada has an excessive number of small firms producing an uneconomically broad range of models for a limited and geographically fragmented market.

The result has been a lack of international competitiveness for a large percentage of our manufacturing output (excluding automotive products since the 1965 Canada–U.S. Auto Pact). As prime minister, I would do all I could to improve the productivity of Canada's investments. Trade policy initiatives would be important, but they would not be the only path that might be followed. (Another approach would be the encouragement of pro-competitive joint venture arrangements.)

A major direction in my thinking is that Canadians must become more literate on economic matters. The consumption versus savings/investment dichotomy would be a good place to start, but a real effort should be made to broaden public understanding of the full dimensions of investment. The construction of factories and mines constitutes the most conventional form of investment. But the creation of modern infrastructure—such as transportation and telecommunications networks—is also vital to the dynamic performance of the economy. It is simply wrong to assume that an optimum amount of such infrastructure will be built on the basis of the unplanned free-market mechanism alone.

Along similar lines of reasoning, an increasingly strong case must be made for acquiring and disseminating increments to usable knowledge (also known as research and development, or R & D). We are learning that countries can and do create their future comparative advantages in trade, and as we come to be able to rely less and less on our natural resource endowment for our comparative wealth position, Canada will be forced to participate more effectively in this process or to suffer a loss in its relative income ranking among the nations of the world.

The final dimension of investment is quickly becoming the most critical. As the so-called Information Age gradually supplants the Industrial Age in determining evolutionary dynamics in our society, the role of human capital formation is growing in importance relative to traditional physical capital formation. This transition is not going to be an easy one to achieve, one primary reason being the difficulty in measuring effectively the investment portion of education, broadly defined. Physical capital formation results in tangible things that we can see and touch, such as machinery. Human capital formation produces people who have more skills, more flexibility, and a greater capacity to engage effectively in the rapidly changing Information Age. This type of investment is not very tangible by conventional means of observation.

The key to this whole issue is that technological progress is taking on fundamentally new forms. In the past, the progress we achieved came largely from new capital equipment to augment the physical attributes of men and women—strength, speed, and manual dexterity.

As the Information Age continues to emerge, technological progress is observed much more in augmenting mental attributes—memory, data manipulation, and decision-making.

Not everyone will share equally in the capacity to benefit from the potentialities that the Information Age will create. And everyone need not do so in order to have a useful role in the social system that we see developing around us. But education is taking on a very critical role in the investment process, and I am convinced that this trend will accelerate in the medium-term future.

To conclude, one might well ask, "What have future generations ever done for me?" Fair enough. Our ancestors did not save solely—or even largely—in anticipation of the gratitude of future generations. But if we are encouraged to think more of what we are leaving to the as yet unborn generations of Canadians, we will save more, invest it more effectively (including on the upgrading of our own skills), and will perform overall as a more "high class" nation.

Ruben Bellan

Mr. Speaker, I rise to announce a major new economic policy. My government's overriding priority will be to lower Canada's unemployment rate. For over a decade now, this country has been losing the potential output of more than a million idle Canadians and has been suffering an enormous number of social problems as a consequence of their idleness. Their unemployment has generated crimes, suicides, physical and mental illness, marital discord and breakdown. It is absolutely imperative, Mr. Speaker, to put in place policies that will end this massive economic waste and social harm. From now on, our primary objective will be to arrange that the Canadian economy generates such a number and variety of job opportunities that anyone who seeks work will be able, in short order, to obtain employment that is reasonably related to his or her skill, training, and experience.

In practical terms, Mr. Speaker, this does not mean an unemployment rate of absolutely zero. In a dynamic, free-enterprise economy such as ours, we must expect that at any given time there will be some workers who have just been laid off because public demand has switched to other products, or who have been made redundant by new technology, or have quit their jobs in the hope of bettering their condition by changing their employment. In a prosperous economy, those who lose or leave their jobs will be able to find work in a matter of days or weeks, so that the number of jobless at any given time will be small. During the 1950s and 1960s the unemployment rate was never more than 3 to 4 per cent. Our aim is to re-establish that norm.

To achieve and maintain a prosperous Canada, Mr. Speaker, we shall follow procedures that derive from simple common sense. Workers are employed in the private sector because business firms expect to sell what they produce; the total number of these workers therefore depends on the amount of money spent in the country to purchase goods and services. In the public sector, the number of persons employed depends on how much taxation the public is prepared to bear in order to pay for public works and public services. Unemployment occurs when the total number of jobs offered by the two sectors is less than the number of persons seeking work.

The federal government can take action to generate employment in both sectors. It can reduce its rates of taxation, thereby enabling the public to purchase more privately produced goods and services. It can increase public-sector employment by increasing its spending on goods and services and by enlarging its grants to other levels of government so that they too can improve their public works and provide more public services. The federal government—and only the federal government—has the financial capability to generate the expansion of job opportunity on the scale required, and it alone therefore has the responsibility.

There are a good many people, Mr. Speaker, who will insist that we "cannot spend our way to prosperity." This claim is flatly contradicted by the factual record. In the 1940s, the Government of Canada spent its way out of the worst depression in history and into a five-year period of dazzling prosperity, during which the unemployment rate was less than 1 per cent. The spending, unhappily, was on military goods and services—on bombs, bullets, and shells; on tanks and fighter aircraft; on soldiers, sailors, and airmen. But Canada can have full employment in peacetime if the government spends—at only a fraction of the wartime scale—on the provision of more and better food, clothing, and housing, more and better recreational facilities, on improvements to our harbours, highways, and streets, our water supplies and sewage disposal systems, and to reduce environmental pollution, to replant our forests, to research new products and new forms of energy, and to improve the education and training of our young people.

I am of course fully aware that a reduction in tax rates and an increase in spending will, at least temporarily, widen the gap between the government's receipts and its outlays. (However, in the long run, the effect may be to narrow the gap. The various types of expenditure the government is obliged to make because of high unemployment will be greatly reduced. Meanwhile, a more prosperous economy and a more fully employed work force will increase the government's tax revenues.)

The shortfall of revenue, whatever its degree, will be financed in three ways. In the first place, a growing economy requires constant additions to its money supply in order to finance an ever-larger volume of transactions and to satisfy the need of people to hold ever-larger amounts of cash. My government will create the new money required for these purposes and, in the process, will cover part of its revenue shortfall. Secondly, the government will, as in the past, sell its bonds to Canadian business firms and individuals. These bonds play a key role in the Canadian financial system. They constitute the highest grade of financial asset in the country and are indispensable in the portfolios of banks, insurance companies, and pension funds. As well, they are the rock-solid form in which a great many Canadians wish to keep their savings. A growing economy will require an ever-larger amount of these bonds. Thirdly, the government will obtain money by a novel method. It will sell tax certificates that entitle the purchasers to a series of future tax reductions; the amount of these tax reductions will correspond to the interest payments the purchasers would have received had they purchased bonds. The net result will be exactly the same as that produced by the sale of bonds, though with a considerable saving in clerical and handling expenses. At present, the interest on government bonds is paid with money obtained through taxation—in effect, the government is taking money out of Canadians' left-hand pockets as taxation in order to put it in their right-hand pockets as bond interest. By selling tax certificates instead of bonds the government will, through the addition of a single line in its tax forms, eliminate the costly rigmarole of taking money from Canadians in order to give it back to them.

Mr. Speaker, there is another critical economic issue with which this government will deal, and that is inflation. In the nine years from 1973 to 1982 the inflation rate in Canada averaged 10 per cent, severely eroding the real value of Canadians' savings and threatening an eventual economic convulsion. Although the inflation rate has now declined to about 4 per cent, this is still unacceptably high; and, what's more, it may rise again.

A great many people have claimed, Mr. Speaker, that government spending and budget deficits have been responsible for inflation. This is blatantly untrue, as the factual record attests. The real cause of inflation has been increase in wages and profits that exceeded the country's productivity growth. We had inflation of 8 to 12 per cent because, in years when the country's output was growing at rates of 2 to 3 per cent, wages and profits rose by 10 to 15 per cent. By contrast, in the years when the increase in wage and profit rates was small, the inflation rate was low, regardless of the size of the federal deficit. Thus, during World War II, when the federal government's deficits were equivalent to $100 billion in today's figures, the price level was virtually stable. This was because the real cause of inflation was held in check: wage and profit rates were frozen. Between 1981 and 1985, the inflation rate fell from 12 per cent to 4 per cent, despite a near-trebling of the federal deficit from $12 billion to $35 billion. This was because the real cause of inflation—an excess of wage and profit increase over productivity gain—was much smaller in 1985 than it had been in 1981.

Firm controls mandated by parliament kept wages and profit rates from rising during World War II and thereby assured price level stability. The inflation rate fell in the 1980s because high rates of unemployment intimidated workers into keeping down their wage demands. In negotiating new contracts, trade unions have emphasized job security rather than pay increases; a good many contracts have provided for wage increases of only 3 to 4 per cent; others have provided for no increases whatever; some have actually called for reductions. Let there be no misunderstanding or pretence here, Mr. Speaker. It is high rates of unemployment that have brought down the inflation rate in the 1980s. Restrictive fiscal and monetary policies have curbed inflation only because they imposed unemployment, which in turn has caused workers to lower their wage demands.

In peacetime, Mr. Speaker, we cannot apply wage and profit controls of the kind that were imposed in wartime; they constitute a harmful strait jacket on the economy and are tolerable only during periods of drastic emergency. It is equally intolerable, Mr. Speaker, that we should continue to use the cruel, economically wasteful, and socially harmful instrumentality of large-scale unemployment to prevent inflationary increases in wages and profits. To combat inflation, Mr. Speaker, we therefore propose to ensure that the national increase in wages and profits corresponds to the national increase in actual output. This will be achieved in the following manner.

All wage contracts will be for one year only and will be for the same twelve-month period. All contract negotiations will be completed prior to the beginning of the year to which they refer. Following their completion, the average of the negotiated increases in pay rates will be calculated. If this average figure is higher than the anticipated increase in national output, the government will order that all the proposed increases be scaled down so that the average corresponds to the expected increase in national output. Thus, if the average negotiated wage increase turned out to be 15 per cent when the anticipated increase in national output was only 3 per cent, the government would require that every actual increase be only one-fifth of the negotiated figure. This procedure would prevent an inflationary increase in wage rates, while fully respecting the principle of collective bargaining and preserving the distribution of income produced by market forces. For instance, a union that had managed to obtain a 20 per cent wage increase would get an actual increase of 4 per cent—double the increase gained by a union that had been able to negotiate only a 10 per cent wage increase.

In terms of real income, all workers would in fact get exactly the same increases that they would have had without the program, since there would be no offsetting distortions caused by inflation. Thus, instead of getting a 15 per cent pay increase whose real value was reduced by a 12 per cent inflation rate, the average worker would get a 3 per cent pay increase but in a regime of price stability. Meanwhile, if the GNP and the average wage both rose by 3 per cent, the average profit would also be bound to rise by only 3 per cent.

Some people no doubt will claim that this procedure will not work because trade unions, anticipating that the negotiated pay increases will be scaled down, will insist on larger increases to start with. This argument has no substance: it assumes that trade unions have reserves of bargaining power which they do not currently apply. It assumes, equally falsely, that employers would readily grant pay increases which, even in their scaled-down form, could leave them at a competitive disadvantage. Finally, it overlooks the simple fact that however large the negotiated increases may be, they can be scaled down to whatever final figure is appropriate.

This, Mr. Speaker, is my economic statement. I now invite comment and criticism. But before I sit down, let this be clearly understood. I will listen with very little patience to arguments contending that inflation can be prevented without imposing limits on the size of wage and profit increases. I will listen with even less patience to insistence that in order to prevent inflationary increases in wages and profits, it is necessary to abrogate the principle of collective bargaining; or that, in the determination of wages and profits, it is necessary to substitute government fiat for market forces. And I will listen with still less patience to the claim that, to control inflation, it is necessary to apply policies that cause unemployment. Finally, I will listen with no patience at all, Mr. Speaker, to Marxist dogma which proclaims that our free-enterprise system is so viciously perverse that the government can procure full employment only in wartime by spending on destruction—and that spending on useful goods and services, in order to achieve full employment in peacetime, is bound to bring on disaster.

NANCY J. BETKOWSKI

What would I do if I were prime minister of Canada? It sounds like such a simple question, a topic for a high school essay in social studies. But to discuss the matter fairly requires careful consideration of how one views this sprawling and disparate country. It requires coming to grips with what is the fundamental nature of Canada. It requires an answer to an even more basic question, namely, what is Canada and what direction should we take now to set the course for this country for the twenty-first century?

Clearly, we must build on our strengths. To some, we are still seen as "hewers of wood and drawers of water," but fortunately our natural resource abundance has given us the commodities we need to enter world markets. But our non-renewable natural resource base is finite, and the continuing challenge is to upgrade these resources and to market not only the end product but the technology and services.

We live in the world's second-largest country but our population is among the most sparse. The transportation and communications challenges we have faced since Jacques Cartier first ventured up the St. Lawrence River are with us still. Technological advances in both transportation and communications have to be applied and expanded by Canadians in creating the linkages necessary to hold our country together.

We are among the youngest, most highly educated work forces in the world, and our future depends on continuing to ensure that our education system is the very best we can possibly provide. In times of fiscal restraint, resources are scarce, and education and research will be expected to provide some of the easing of expenditure as we grapple with the problem of the national debt. But education cannot and should not be sacrificed.

Canada could be the training, research, and educational centre of the world. Our industrial policy now should be towards the goal of advancing technology and research. We have the physical facilities and economic capability to accommodate such a goal. We have the individuals with the entrepreneurial initiative, and we certainly have the intellectual capacity. We should avoid the mistake made by other industrialized countries of building soon-outmoded industries. The future should see us marketing our education system and our advanced technologies in transportation, communications, winter habitat, and energy. Our industrial strategy today must be towards this goal or we will be outflanked and unable to compete in the global market.

Thus, I believe that an essential and immediate task should be to create, develop, and communicate a vision of Canada as a nation comprised of a variety of people and cultures living in a broad range of political, economic, and geographic regions. I believe that, as Canadians, we suffer from a lack of vision about our own country. We have pride in our history, pride in our multicultural heritage, pride in our rugged and beautiful country, and pride in our values and lifestyles. But we have a collective habit of stressing our differences and our disparities, rather than our similarities and our national goals. It is essential for the future of this country that we begin to develop a vision for Canada that helps Canadians to see themselves as Canadians first, sharing in the greatness of this country and also sharing in the resolution of major economic, industrial, employment, and social challenges. We need to promote greater awareness and understanding of each other and of the contributions that each of us has made and can make to the future of Canada.

I am concerned that addressing major issues of regional disparities has become overly politicized. Decisions to provide federal assistance to companies or industries in particular regions are too often made, or are seen to be made, for political reasons—to help address falling results in polls, or to bolster the image of the governing party or a particular member of parliament. The public has come to question the ability of politicians to make judgements and policy directions that are in the interest of Canada as a whole. They see only political favouritism: if a contract is awarded to a company in Quebec, it's to help Quebec MPs; if the federal government decides to help our ailing oil industry, it's because Alberta MPs have been lobbying for that assistance. What the public doesn't see is any long-term plan of how this type of decision may be in the best interests of the entire country.

The concept of sharing is important from another perspective as well. As prime minister, I would place priority on a careful re-examination of the way in which Canadians are represented and consequently involved in major policy decisions. I sense in many parts of this country a feeling of powerlessness, of anomie. This is particularly true in the smaller provinces more remote from central Canada. In Canada, we suffer from great distances and we suffer from having our population concentrated in only a few areas. The concept of representation by population is fundamental to our democratic system, but unfortunately it makes it difficult for provinces to see themselves as equal partners in the Canadian confederation. Giving the majority of representation to the highly concentrated population areas, with no countervailing balance, is perceived as leaving the smaller provinces at the mercy of central Canada. An elected rather than appointed Senate would be one important way of providing a more effective balance of power across the country.

One of the primary functions of the federal government—and of the prime minister as leader—must be to ensure that equitable resources are available across Canada to provide for essential public services. At present, Canada is faced with a significant deficit problem. It is a problem that must be addressed, since it has a direct impact on all Canadians through the taxes they pay and the quality of services they receive. It also is a difficult problem to address from a public perspective, since many members of the public have little understanding of the significance of the deficit and are therefore dismayed if programs they benefit from have to be reduced or eliminated entirely. They support in principle the need to reduce our debts, but only if this can be done without reducing the government services they see as a direct benefit to themselves.

As prime minister, I would initiate a major reconsideration of our revenue and taxation system as a means of re-establishing our priorities and attacking the deficit problem. A complete overhaul of our taxation system is essential. I believe we need to return to a less interventionist, freer-enterprise system. In the past, governments have tinkered with our economic system and have believed that providing incentives and concessions to business and industry would stimulate the economy and create jobs. The record of success from this approach has been dismal and disappointing. At the same time, we have shifted an enormous tax burden onto the backbone of Canadian society, namely the middle-class, middle-income workers in secure employment positions. These people are being taxed excessively while the contribution of others is minimized. I believe we have gone too far in expecting corporations and business to solve our economic problems. We have created a private sector that is overly dependent on government support. And we have destroyed the capability of individual Canadians to use their spending power to invest, to create, and to stimulate the economy. It is time for a complete rethinking of our taxation and revenue picture and time to develop a system that is more progressive and more reasonable.

Finally, I believe that one of the most important roles of government is in the area of social policy. As a Conservative, I believe that government must play a leadership role in public policy and social programs. To some extent, governments have been too preoccupied with issues that could be left to the private sector. They have interfered, directed and, in some cases, taken over functions that should be left to the private sector. As a result, we lack clear direction and clear policy in addressing social issues—an area that is a prime function of government. Canada, like all other major developed countries, is facing significant social issues in the areas of social welfare, unemployment, health, and the family.

We need strong leadership from a prime minister in addressing such issues from a longer-term perspective. In my opinion, for example, we are misguided in focusing our priorities and energies on issues like capital punishment if at the same time we do not address in a significant way the underlying issues of family violence and violence in our society. We should not continue to pay enormous costs for health care without also emphasizing preventative medicine and research.

Each of these areas is difficult. They are complex and sensitive because they go to the heart of our society. But they have been virtually ignored for too long. It is time to establish clear policy directions, to relate them to a vision of Canada, and to communicate with the public so that they can share in understanding and addressing these important issues.

Finally, I would like to address a key element that pervades all of this essay: the need for the prime minister to be a leader.

A leader is the one who works harder than any other member of the organization. A leader is one who looks for ideas beyond those that come up through the political structure. A leader is one who sets out the goals and sets out the steps that have to be taken in meeting these goals. A leader is one who can deal with the criticism when a particular step is seen to be inappropriate, because a leader has an objective in mind and can always speak to that long-term objective. A leader is the one with the vision of where Canada will go under her or his leadership. And a leader is one who defines the vision before standing for public office and who steps down when that personal vision for change has expired.

Being prime minister requires discipline and personal, intellectual, and political integrity of the highest standard: it is not a job for the weak of heart or mind.

SHIRLEY CARR

If I were prime minister.... What a thought! And the amazing point I want to make first is this: Anything is possible in *this* country!

In my travels around this magnificent country during the past twenty years, I have found that there are not enough people thinking about Canada as a whole. It seems to be very difficult for us to realize that our parochial differences and ideas have to be set aside from time to time so that we can think through what we can do for our nation as a whole. This means that we must leave our own problems at home for a spell and deal on a different level about Canada as a sovereign nation. What a lot we could then do together to help it grow, to produce wealth, and to share in that wealth! Though, at the same time, we must be extremely conscious of the multifaceted character of our nation and of how we fit into the international scene. This, of course, is particularly important in view of our well-known generosity and the fact that we are a caring nation, even though we truly are still a developing nation.

Having said this, I also feel that there can be no argument about our overall endeavour for world peace and the working towards a better and more harmonious exercise with our world leaders. It obviously would be a major failure to all humanity if this world of ours were to blow itself apart because of the failure to resolve conflict between nations or groups of nations. We have to attempt to understand these factors so that we can act in the international councils, recognizing the forces of change and also the forces of conflict in our world operating today.

We all have contributed to the building of Canada into a strong economic unit among the nations. We have worked out the form of government that suits our condition. We have ridden the storms of two world wars. Yet we ask ourselves one earnest question: Have the people who live in Canada become Canadian people? Have we become a people for whom the word "Canadian" outweighs differences in race, creed, colour, equality, and language? Can our leaders rise and speak in the councils of the nations with the assurance that they speak for all Canadians? No country ever reaches a perfect harmony, naturally, but can we come close to it? I say yes we can, we have done so and will continue to do so.

Canada must play its role from all perspectives in finding a better and more harmonious society. Future generations will expect us to have given this leadership. The Third World countries must have opportunities, certainly freedom from poverty and, in many situations, freedom from the control which currently hinders their development. I am convinced Canada can and will continue to play a role in these areas. We are born conciliators, born negotiators and initiators of new ideas. These we can share honestly and naturally.

Of course, I feel that in order to achieve my ideas, my strength and my commitments, there must be the acceptance of the labour movement in this country with full rights to freedom of association, organizing, and collective bargaining and all it entails. Inherent in this proposition is the attainment of labour's economic, social, and legislative objectives through the organization of Canadian workers in free trade unions and the promotion and advancement of their interests in all fields of common endeavour by the utilization of their collective strength, abilities, and resources.

The trade union movement in Canada was founded to contribute to the realization of the legitimate aspirations of those who toil for a living, and it will not deviate from the pursuit of the cause of peace, freedom, and security for all peoples. We must, at all times, hold true to the high ideals and principles of social justice on which we thought this country was founded.

With a keen appreciation of the tremendous responsibilities which the prime minister must assume, the challenge is clear with respect to fostering and defending the principles of democracy in the economic, social, and political life of the nation.

Having indicated my dream, I wish now to comment on what I see has to be done.

Unemployment: Canada's Shame
The steady rise in the rate of official and unofficial unemployment figures is clearly the single most outstanding failure of Canadian public policy. Successive federal governments have acknowledged the problem but have failed miserably in adopting fiscal, monetary, taxation, and investment policies that would reverse the trend. Full employment as a stated goal of government policy objectives has been all but forgotten. The politicians have taken the easy way out. They have been content to accept the view of "economic experts" that we have entered a period in our economic development where the "natural rate" of unemployment has risen from 5 per cent to 7 per cent to 9 per cent and that nothing can be done about it. The Canadian Labour Congress does not and cannot accept that one and a half million

Canadians will never work again. We will not accept the human misery that flows from these jobless figures.

The real issue for Canada is to provide more jobs and better-paying jobs for all those who wish them. All economic policies should be judged in terms of their impact on jobs, whether they concern taxation, investment, fiscal, monetary, trade, or government procurement. The single major concern of all economic pursuits is an increase in real wages, real economic growth, and a higher standard of living for everyone. There is nothing else! Unfortunately, successive governments have seemingly forgotten these simple but basic truths.

Since the early 1980s Canada's official unemployment rate has been averaging 10 per cent. In the regions it is much, much higher, reaching 40, 50, or 60 per cent in some areas. Only the unemployment insurance program and social assistance we fought for after the Great Depression have prevented civil disobedience and demonstrations by workers and their families. Unfortunately, a by-product of our social policies has been to hide the misery so that the poor and the unemployed are "invisible." Their voices have been silenced and their plight ignored. To their eternal credit, the churches, farmers' and women's organizations, and other social groups and agencies have taken up their defence alongside the labour movement to challenge the economic orthodoxy of present governments, which is rooted in the nineteenth and early twentieth centuries. These policies did not prevent the Great Depression and they don't work now.

The old economic myths have been:

– that government borrowing and spending crowds out private investment (yet all our experience tells us that this has not been so since Keynes);

– that only the private sector creates wealth (yet we have witnessed all levels of government expenditure on roads, sewers, manufacturing plants, crown corporations, etc., which are the underpinnings of our industrial society);

– that governments cannot create jobs, that only the private sector can do so (yet during and after World War II hundreds of thousands of jobs were created by governments);

– that governments are by definition wasteful and badly managed (yet we see hundreds of bankruptcies in the private sector as a result of these very same causes, while companies feed at the public trough);

– that government cannot afford increased expenditures to create jobs and put people back to work (yet unemployment represents lost revenue and production which, once gone, is lost forever).

These are the myths of economic orthodoxy which form the basis for present economic thought. It is little wonder we continue to have high unemployment levels, because these are the same policies the country was pursuing prior to the Great Depression. The overriding national concern today is to rid ourselves of these outmoded and useless myths and to come to grips with a Canada which has moved far beyond this period of our history. It is time to deal with the realities of our time.

Trade

The United States is Canada's major trading partner and best customer. Likewise, we are the United States' major trade partner. This has increasingly been the case; 78 per cent of all our exports are to the U.S. market.

The Canadian Labour Congress has long been concerned about Canada's overdependence on this single market and has advocated reaching out to other nations of the world with which we should be developing closer trading links. We should be putting a greater effort into the GATT and into freer trade through multilateral negotiations, rather than seeking a comprehensive bilateral trade arrangement with the United States, which will certainly cost Canadians jobs and will cost our governments a diminution of sovereignty.

Canada has survived and prospered because it is a trading nation. We need our export markets. These markets have traditionally meant jobs for Canadians and a higher standard of living. It is our position that we should continue our efforts to increase exports to the EEC, to Third World countries and the Pacific Rim, and particularly to China and Japan. Nor do we agree that Canada should continue to be an exporter of raw materials and an importer of finished goods. To us, exporting raw materials is the same as exporting jobs.

Labour Adjustment

Not only have new patterns of trade—with their impact on traditional industries in terms of job losses—underlined the complete inadequacies of Canada's labour market policies, but so have changing international patterns of investment, the computer and new technologies based on knowledge and information transmission. Jobs have disappeared in the resource and manufacturing sectors, which were once the backbone of Canada's wealth, and have reappeared in the service sector as low-paying and largely part-time employment. Whole communities and regions of our country have been decimated in the transition when the local economy collapsed.

Since the 1981 recession, it has become trendy to undertake exhaustive studies to look at part-time work, work-sharing, flexible working hours, unemployment insurance, early pensions, more education, social programs, and so on and so forth, and to examine them as we would the entrails of a chicken to show that the real issue is anything but lack of jobs. All of this self-examination is pure and utter nonsense until we come back to the basic issue of creating jobs.

There can never be effective labour adjustment policies until there are jobs. It's impossible to manage effectively in a shrinking labour market. Training for unemployment is dishonest to workers. Promising them jobs that don't exist is abhorrent, and cutting off their unemployment insurance or social assistance or putting them on work-for-welfare schemes verges on the criminal.

Active labour-market policies lead economic and social change; they don't follow it. Full-employment policies are the pivotal point for developing training programs, mobility allowances, severance pay, early retirement, continuing education, and shorter working time. Canada does not even have the basic data on the needs of the labour market. Companies and employers should be made to register all vacancies with the local Canada Employment offices. We need sector profiles of our industries and services so that we have a good fix on how many people we need to train for our future requirements. None of this we now know, and neither does industry.

The world has changed and is changing rapidly, and we are not prepared for it. Consequently, working people are paying the full cost of this change because government has abdicated its responsibilities. The cry is "Let the private sector do it!" History tells us it never has and it never will. The private sector's only obligation is to the "bottom line." The workers can shift for themselves. This is no longer good enough. The price is too high for workers; for business; for Canada.

Fiscal Policy
Where the prevalent economic orthodoxy deludes politicians into acting on the false premise that the best government is no government, that everything from garbage collection to nuclear power should be done anywhere but in the public sector, the labour movement would pursue the exact opposite. It would take the view that government activity is absolutely crucial to how this country develops. There is a legitimate role for government, along with the private sector, in developing and forging a more productive, humane, and happy society.

The deficit has become the shibboleth of our economic underpinning. It is paralyzing economic thought and action, and is rooted in the mists of economic dogma that equates government balance sheets with those of a business firm. Where a business pursues the bottom line, it can lay people off, do away with jobs, and make great profits, but how is this good for Canada? True, the firm still employs people, but if many firms have been doing this (as they have), what happens to those unemployed? What happens to the government's tax revenue, and how does this help the deficit? Not only is the tax revenue reduced but so is our productive capacity. On the expenditure side, unemployment insurance and welfare costs rise. Yet the orthodox economists argue that government should cut back on the expenditure side by slashing social programs. What utter nonsense!

Government has a responsibility to increase its expenditures both in upgrading capital infrastructure and in active labour-adjustment policies, while at the same time maintaining spending on social programs. The deficit is a result of lost revenues, not of overexpenditures or wastefulness.

Conclusion
Economic policy-making and the thinking on which it is premised are sadly out of whack with Canada's needs. It finds its source in an earlier time and age, when it was ineffective, and it is still suffering from the same affliction today. Government procurement, taxation, investment, trade, social and labour adjustment, and fiscal policy must be directed and planned in such a way that they all mesh harmoniously in creating a full-employment and efficient economy. Canada cannot afford a society in which the rich become richer and the poor, poorer. This was the way of the past, and Canadians deserve much better.

DIAN COHEN

First of all, you have to understand that the only way I would be prime minister is if I were universally appointed for ten years and I didn't have to worry about kissing babies, raising money, or getting elected. But if that unlikely set of circumstances did come to pass, what temptation!

First of all, I'd abolish those silly bearskin caps on Parliament Hill. I mean, have you ever been there on a summer day when one of those poor kids faints from the heat? Shocking, uncivilized. I don't care how much tourism brings in to the National Capital Region. In fact, I might even consider abolishing the National Capital Region. After all, we all have computers and modems now, don't we? Why couldn't we all stay home, where we can brew ourselves a cup of tea when we feel like it, and get some real work done? This would drastically reduce spending on office space, and the price of psychiatric counselling for the civil servants who couldn't handle this would be peanuts in comparison.

Come to think of it, maybe having a federal government isn't such a great idea. I mean, the very first thing I wanted to do was abolish all the schools that don't teach kids how to think. (Is that a big job!— Finding all the ones not to close, I mean.) But then I realized that if I wanted to do that, I'd have an enormous federal-provincial fight on my hands. Who needs it?

If there were no federal government, we could ask the Canadian Institute of Chartered Accountants to administer a really dandy guaranteed annual income. There'd be so much money we could all sit back and think about what we really want to be when we grow up.

I would, of course, institute a national deficit reduction lottery, which would have the whole country in the black with a good social safety net by the end of my term as prime minister.

I would settle with the native peoples by letting them govern all the territories that they claim are theirs. After all, they can't do much worse than we have, can they? And it's their turn to have a crack at it.

I would put the CBC on a user-pay basis. If everybody is willing to give 6 or 10 cents a day to receive it, then that will be just fine. I would also free up the entrepreneurs within the CBC to sell lots more programs in other countries, and I would make both the CBC and the

National Film Board technology transfer centres for Third World countries who want to set up their own television and film production facilities.

I would try to get all Canadians to understand that in an information economy they have to think upside down. Money is kept in investments, where it earns interest. Information, the new currency, has to be shared to create wealth. Information that is hoarded carries a negative interest rate: the longer you hoard it without acting on it, the less it's worth. This is a tough one and would take up a lot of my time.

One of the things I really do want to spend some money on is setting up the Great Canadian Software Bank. This is a pet scheme I've had for years, under which we would buy universal Canadian rights to all kinds of computer software. We would then make it available to all Canadians free of charge. This would create an opportunity for the millions of Canadians who are no longer needed in the industries that still generate wealth but don't need people any more.

For those people, the Software Bank would give them a resource base that would allow them to generate their own jobs. The idea of all those people thinking, exchanging and dreaming up new ideas is really exciting, and the cost would only be a fraction of any of those megaprojects that use brawn for a few years, then throw people back onto unemployment insurance.

Since information is marketable only within a context, and since people come from all over the world to see how well we count, I've decided to keep Statistics Canada. But what Statistics Canada is good at is counting tangible things—and now, two-thirds of us are involved in intangible things like services. So I would give Stats-Can some help, attention, and money to help it figure out what it should be measuring.

I'd be tempted to turn it into two divisions: Data On (or about sectors of the economy, population, demography, trends, whatever, the kind of information you need to make policy); and Data For (information designed for the people being measured to use in their day-to-day business and planning). I'm sure the wags will eventually call these divisions One and Four. One will provide the basis for big decisions such as social policy. Four will serve customers with specific needs. For example, you would call up Four's publications if you wanted to know whether or not it's a good idea to try to peddle your particular brand of coffee machine in a given city and market niche. There are no limits to how useful this could be—and it could even make lots of money.

I would invest a lot of money into a cheap, widely available self-confidence extract that could be injected into Canadians on a regular basis—preferably voluntarily. This would help them deal with the fact that even though we produce lots of natural resources really efficiently, the world has gone funny on us. True competition has gone out the window, as managed trade, subsidies, and desperate foreign exchange needs have replaced the competitive market place. (Never mind being prime minister, I just tried to put together an Economics 101 course and I couldn't find an example to replace wheat farmers as classic participants in the "supply and demand sets the price" process.) This is a Brave New World where Canadians have to be really creative, and that means breaking all the rules. No, I'm not thinking of setting up a Royal Commission on How to Break the Rules for Fun and Profit. I want to train Canadians to figure it out for themselves.

The Canadian Armed Forces, which everybody says are terrific but don't have enough money to do a good job, would be freed to do consulting work for Other Approved Armed Forces (NO KHADAFY WORK). With the money generated from their consulting work, they could then do a good job of maintaining our boundaries.

I haven't yet figured out how I would dig out the underground economy. From what I can see, it's a real going concern. Everybody has two price lists now: cash, it's $400; with bills, receipts, and sales tax it's $750. I figure at least some of this money would go to purchase deficit lottery tickets, but I still have a nagging feeling that we could do better.

I guess if I were prime minister, I'd send a few of my most trusted researchers underground to figure out how the whole thing works, what should be left alone, and what could do with some light and air. I'll admit this is going to be a tough one—to get the right balance between an earthquake and a dust storm—but I'm convinced there's a lot of potential here. After we had figured out what's really successful in the underground economy, we could do two things: we could fix Statistics Canada's measurements, and we could have real tax reform.

I figure this is as much as I can do in ten years, so if you want any more, you'll have to appoint me to another term.

MARJORIE COHEN

My original intention in writing this was to say that it would not be possible to change things much—no matter what my convictions—if I became prime minister. The reasoning behind this pessimism is the recognition that power is a prison and if anyone wants to maintain power there are severe limits to what can be done; that is, structures are so entrenched to serve the interests of the rich and powerful that all efforts towards real change, no matter how concerted or heroic, will be thwarted.

Examples abound of political heads of state who have tried to make a difference but have failed miserably. Look at what happened to Machel's efforts in Mozambique, Allende's in Chile, Mitterrand's in France, Ortega's in Nicaragua. Even J.F.K., who was fairly modest in his endeavours, found enormous resistance to change. He likened being president to being the driver of a ten-ton truck racing down a steep hill with the steering and brakes gone.

But it wasn't simply seeing what has happened elsewhere that put me in such a cynical mood when I contemplated what I'd do as prime minister. There has also been my own experience in this country, with what looks like and passes for progressive change but is really more akin to a dynamic petrification of the system. I have seen truly monumental efforts to improve the lot of the disadvantaged. Groups and individuals have worked for years, decades even, for new laws or government regulations; and in spite of fatigue, burnout, and disillusionment, sometimes the efforts have been successful. But the results are almost never what was intended. The case of the Charter of Rights immediately leaps to mind. On paper it looks great because it guarantees our freedoms and ensures redress for groups who are the object of discrimination. But it is not the disadvantaged who are benefiting from it. Of the nineteen writs issued so far regarding native rights, none has been won by native people. Of the fourteen writs issued under the equality clause (the one that was supposed to benefit women), twelve have been brought by men; and of the nine that have been decided, eight favoured the men.

There is a dialectic of law which operates so that any change, no matter how potentially radical, will occur slowly and will not drastically alter the status quo or the interests of those in power. Another good example of this dialectic at work is the legislation on equal pay for work of equal value. Employers in Ontario have been frantic in their opposition to this legislation, claiming that it would ruin them because they would become uncompetitive in trade. But recently, in the *Financial Post*, there was a calming note in all of the hysteria. The *Post* pointed out that although employers were worried, this was needless, and it gave the example of the federal government which has had this sort of legislation on the books for ten years without severe repercussions. So far, it hasn't altered the way either the government or firms who do business with the government have treated their female employees.

I think I could make a fairly convincing case for the impossibility of the job of prime minister being held by anyone who wasn't content with only minor modifications. But ultimately I decided this approach was just a little too easy. It does make a difference who is in office and what their vision is. Also, I was inspired by I. F. Stone's optimism about politics. His point is that no matter how constraining a situation, "someone with courage and ingenuity can do more than one who's lazy or a coward. Find out what can be done and judge on that: you must always have a sense of the possible." What also occurred to me was that if I were prime minister, some fairly significant changes would already have occurred—at least in the attitudes and expectations of the people. This would give me the leverage I would need.

So here are some excerpts from an interview I expect to have with Barbara Frum on a special edition of "The Journal" the day after my election.

BARBARA FRUM'S PREAMBLE:

Our special feature tonight is an interview with Canada's first female prime minister and is the first segment of a three-part interview. This election has been one of the most contentious in the history of the nation and the results the most surprising. Some refer to it as the feminist revolution, but whatever we call it, clearly the political climate has changed. Most analysts attribute this political revolution to the dramatic reversals to the economy and our social programs resulting from the last government's attempts toward greater reliance on market forces. The most significant changes are a widening of regional disparities, tremendous unemployment among women and youths, greater racial inequalities, and poorer working conditions for those remaining in the labour force. Because of privatization and deregulation, transportation from the North is now virtually nonexistent and even telephone communication within urban areas has become so expensive that most families have had their telephones removed. While some feel these consequences are temporary and are the price Canada has to pay to become stronger in the long run, the general response has been more militant, as is obvious from the results of the election. We are pleased the prime minister could talk to us tonight.

FRUM: Prime Minister, isn't your election the nightmare come true for the men of this country?

COHEN: Perhaps, but I think the results have been most nightmarish for the traditional parties. They did not expect my party to win at all, much less with such a huge majority in parliament.

FRUM: But do you have any words to reassure the men of this country?

COHEN: I think reassurance is unnecessary. Clearly, a large portion of the male population supported women candidates in constituencies throughout the country. But I do want to remind you that we are not a separatist party and while women make up half the members of parliament, men are not without a voice.

FRUM: Let's move on to your program. It is rumoured that you are drastically reducing the size of your cabinet. Is this true?

COHEN: Not entirely. It is true that some cabinet positions are no longer necessary. We will not need a minister for privatization and deregulation, nor a minister of defence, and of course we will no longer need a minister responsible for the status of women. But we do intend to create some new cabinet positions and to change the focus of some old ones. The plans for the total reorganization of cabinet have not been completed, but so far we have decided that the new cabinet positions will include a minister responsible for child care and a minister responsible for the equal distribution of income. We are seriously considering elevating the housework bureau within the Ministry of Labour to a cabinet position. We also intend to change the focus of the ministry that deals with employment—this will be called the Ministry for Full Employment.

FRUM: These are fairly radical changes. Do you think the country will support you on these issues?

COHEN: None of these plans was kept a secret during the campaign. All of them were spelled out in great detail, including what the focus of each ministry would be. As I have gone to great lengths to explain....

FRUM: Excuse me, Prime Minister, I want to go back to your Ministry for the Redistribution of Income.

COHEN: That's the Ministry for the *Equal* Distribution of Income.

FRUM: Surely this is not possible. The wealthy will have no incentive to invest and will simply leave the country. As an economist, surely you realize that we have to stimulate business confidence and do all that we can to ensure a better climate for business in this country.

COHEN: Canada has operated on that assumption for some time, but all of the recent emphasis on the "free market" has turned out rather badly. We've seen a massive flight of capital. Not only have we lost our international markets, but we've lost our domestic ones as well. Production has moved away from Canada, since multinational companies have been able to serve this market from outside the country. And, I must add, it is no accident that production has moved to countries which have the most repressive governments where there is no concern about—or little ability to control—the health, safety, and income levels of their people.

FRUM: How does this relate to equal income distribution?

COHEN: I was getting to that. Your assumption is that a successful economy requires great inequalities in wealth to generate appropriate motivation for investment. Our experience has proven quite the opposite. Improving things for business did not translate into benefits for the people of this country. Business is doing fine, but we have massive poverty, unemployment, and greater inequalities than ever before.

FRUM: What would you do to redistribute income?

COHEN: First of all, we need to make full employment a reality. Then we need to ....

FRUM: O.K., let's talk about that. Hasn't that been the objective of government programs in the past? Isn't it clear that job-creation programs simply don't work?

COHEN: I am not talking about job-creation programs. They have been pathetically inadequate measures to deal with a real disease.

FRUM: Band-aid treatments?

COHEN: Worse than that—more like lick your wounds. The point of these programs has never been to get everyone working at jobs which are really needed. Their point was to make governments look as if they were doing something. We will not solve the problems of this economy if we simply create jobs. Most jobs are meaningless, purposeless, and performed under boring, stupefying conditions. No one should ever have to create something or do something useless or harmful. The goal cannot be just to get everyone a job, although even this endeavour would be quite novel in Canada. My point is that we need to recognize that the work we do—and the conditions we work under—are crucial. The problem is not that there isn't enough to do. Our problem is how to organize work so that what needs to be done gets done and what is not needed is avoided.

FRUM: Isn't this all very philosophical? It's a nice idea, but surely you need a plan!

COHEN: That is precisely the point. There is so much waste of labour and resources and so much unnecessary production because we do not plan. Too much is left to the off-chance that the general scramble to get rich will somehow provide people with the things they need.

FRUM: It is often argued that full employment isn't a necessary objective any more. If we can produce enough for everybody with a smaller labour force, shouldn't we rather be putting our energies into devising social programs that will take care of those who don't have jobs?

COHEN: This argument has surprisingly widespread appeal in certain intellectual circles—the "post-industrialists" on both the right and the left. But I notice that those who are likely to be among the unemployed find it has considerably less charm.

FRUM: But hasn't technology advanced to the point where we can be freed from the necessity to work?

COHEN: Only if you are considering work involved in the production of things. It is true that we require much less labour to produce food and other tangible items that people need in order to live. However, there are great needs which are not tangible and which require human labour.

FRUM: Such as?

COHEN: Almost all of the social services. The service industries have taken a terrific beating in the last few years as a result of free trade and budget reduction efforts, and the consequences to the economy and people are obvious. We need to realize that producing services is just as significant as any other form of production.

FRUM: What are you talking about specifically?

COHEN: Health care, education, child care, care of the elderly, transportation, communications.

FRUM: These are all items that will be extremely costly to government. While promises to improve these kinds of services are always popular during an election, they are an enormous drain on government resources.

COHEN: We have to stop viewing services as unproductive activities. A child-care job is just as significant as a job in manufacturing. It adds to our general well-being and stimulates the economy. We must remember that when one person spends, someone else has an income. How the income of the spenders is generated is less significant than the fact that they have the money to do it. But in the process, it makes enormous sense that necessary work gets done.

FRUM: We are just about out of time. Could you very quickly tell us what you will do to restore transportation, communication, and postal services?

COHEN: The privatization of Air Canada and the post office has been a disaster. My campaign promise was that transportation and communication facilities would become public enterprises. I intend to do this immediately.

FRUM: Another quick question. Many fear you will introduce legislation to impose minimum hiring quotas for disadvantaged groups in the labour force. Do you intend to do this?

COHEN: Yes.

FRUM: There is so much we have not covered today, but before we go I would like to ask one last question. Why do you think you will succeed?

COHEN: I am under no illusion that any government will solve all the problems of a society. I have no doubt that we will fail—but I think that we can fail better.

FRUM: Prime Minister, it has been good talking to you, we look forward to our next two interviews. I thank you.

COHEN: You're welcome.

SHEILA COPPS

Ain't democracy grand? How else could sixty assorted political/social/community/religious types be asked to give their version of "If I were prime minister" in about two thousand words?

Let us examine the premise of the title: If I were prime minister.... This question cum statement appropriately tails off with all the forcefulness of Wayne Gretzky at a curling match. Perhaps that is as it should be. The time is long gone when we can look to our political leaders to provide the definitive answers. No prime minister can be expected to hold the key to all our social and economic problems. At the same time, no citizen has the right to expect the prime minister alone to shape the direction of the country. Perhaps this inflated expectation that a prime minister can provide all the answers is what makes me shudder even to contemplate the question at hand.

Is it a blessing or a curse to be elected to govern one's country? As long as the public continues to indulge its schizophrenic perception of politicians, I daresay it is the latter. On the one hand, people believe that politicians generally and the prime minister (in the generic sense) particularly are up to no good. At the same time, they confer on the politicians the responsibility for everything, from the stability of world monetary systems to the strength of local economies. Where can the politician find the equilibrium to develop a sense of balance between expectations and achievements?

It is critical that we politicians ourselves do not inflate the expectations of the public beyond any measure of reality. The Conservative election campaign of 1984 provides a chilling contrast between prime ministerial expectations and reality. It was the prime minister himself, in his heated pursuit of the Holy Grail, who massaged public expectations beyond any achievable level. Aided and abetted by a campaign strategy and press expectations that gave new meaning to the notion of high bridging, like Humpty-Dumpty he set himself up for an inevitable fall.

Above all, the prime minister must have some sense of the why of politics. If one's goal in life is the act of becoming prime minister, the achievement can only be anticlimactic. If, however, one seeks the position because some basic questions are not being answered, the job enables the pursuit of those questions. Hence, having a sense of our country is critical to the success or failure of any prime ministerial mission. As the world shrinks, so will grow the importance of a strongly imprinted national identity. As international boundaries are blurred by diminishing distance and proliferating communication links, the paramount question becomes "Why Canada?"

Current bilateral trade discussions with the United States foretell greater questions surrounding the survival of our nation. Perhaps the ethereal "If I were prime minister" could best be addressed by asking ourselves, "Why have a prime minister?" The extension of this thesis begs the further question, "Why have a separate country at all?" Why not take the proverbial leap of faith into uniting the North American continent under one sociopolitical regime?

The question that must be answered by any prime minister is "Why not?" What makes the uniqueness of Canada and how can we strengthen and nurture that uniqueness through the political process? Politics alone cannot guarantee the survival and flourishment of a nation. But certainly a strong prime ministerial sense of our nation is critical to any attempt to govern.

The north-south magnet which has drawn most Canadians to settle down within a hundred miles (oops! kilometres) of the American border must be attenuated by an east-west counterbalance which persuades us of the necessity for a separate nation. Nonetheless, if we examine the counterbalance, it seems to run more counter than balance.

Are we, as one former prime minister said, simply a community of communities? Or is there a tie that binds beyond the regional questions that seem to pit province against province and language group against language group?

If we examine our growth over the past two decades as a bilingual, multicultural nation, we have much to be optimistic about. Who would have imagined, even ten years ago, that French immersion classes in Vancouver would be so popular that people would line up overnight for enrolment? Who would have dared to dream, twenty years ago, that white Anglo-Saxon Toronto the Good would be enriched by a polyglot influx of people creating a cosmopolitan flavour unrivalled in our country? Who would have believed that the Quiet Revolution of the sixties would underscore the brash confidence of the eighties in Canada's new bull market in Montreal?

What has all this to do with being prime minister? It was the historic vision of Lester Pearson, followed by the Gallic determination of Pierre Trudeau, that helped realize the dream of Canada.

How many of us remember where we were on 1 July 1967 when this country came of age? How many rejoiced that Canada was a world-class country when, that same year, we hosted an Expo to rival all expositions? And how many countries saw Canada coming full circle last year with the British Columbia showcase in Vancouver, which tied us together from east to west? The role of a prime minister is to square that circle, to create a climate where easterners and westerners have an equal stake in the betterment of our country, where the oil rigger in Alberta believes, with the same vigour as the worker in the industrial heartland, that Canadian policies include him. The prime minister must instil that sense of belonging, that notion of unity and the appreciation of our shared uniqueness.

Know thyself! We are not simply an appendage of the continental United States. We are a unique country with a history of Canadian solutions to Canadian problems, with a commitment to cultural plurality, a country with unique political traditions and a strong sense of social justice. To fire the imagination of Canadians, the prime minister must first understand us and at the same time remain committed to embracing our individuality. Rather than seeking to copy our neighbours to the south, the prime minister must forge and strengthen a unique Canadian identity. A made-in-Washington economic and social policy is not a panacea for Canada. The only panacea is pan-Canadianism of the kind that Lester Pearson and Pierre Trudeau sought. Pan-Canadian political strategies reinforce a united yet individuated country from coast to coast. It must be the goal of any prime minister to reinforce this pan-Canadianism while ensuring that we can play a unique role in the world's collective well-being.

Blinkered continentalism is not our answer. Sir Wilfrid Laurier predicted that "the twentieth century belongs to Canada." The current prime ministerial challenge is to ensure that Canada opens its heart and soul to the world: its heart, with a social framework that ensures a safety net for all those Canadians who cannot help themselves; its soul, with an independent foreign policy led by a prime minister who understands what makes us unique.

Without that abiding belief in the sovereignty of our nation, without that commitment to safeguard Canada's international role as an honest broker, any prime minister risks the ignominy of going down in Canadian history as "Madam President."

DAVID CRANE

As we move out of the twentieth century and into the twenty-first, we face dramatic choices that will be decisive for our future. At home we must build a new economy in which thoughtware—information, knowledge, creativity—becomes the critical force for economic progress, replacing the old hardware of a resource-based, mass-production society. Looking beyond our borders, Canadians can and must provide leadership in promoting world development and preserving a life-sustaining planetary environment.

As prime minister of Canada, my fundamental goal would be to provide the necessary leadership and direction as we approach this new age of the twenty-first century, recognizing that if we continue our current path of inaction we could easily become one of the has-beens of the world stage.

We know we have many economic problems in Canada. We lag in innovation and entrepreneurship. We spend too little on science and technology. We aren't great in exploiting and marketing what we do develop. We're too dependent on the United States. We seem frightened of change. We spend too much on preserving the status quo and not enough on building for the future. We save a lot of money, but too little of it finds its way into new activities and new people.

Yet we cannot escape the future, even if we fail to help shape it. New technologies are changing the world. One example is the information world of computers, software, microelectronics, and telecommunications. Other critical "core" technologies include biotechnology, space, and new materials to replace traditional materials such as steel, aluminum, and copper. The content of what we consume is changing as well, away from natural resources and assembly-line labour and towards greater creative content, such as research and development, design, testing, and marketing.

Looking beyond our own borders, world development is the great global challenge. Between 1950 and 1986 the world's population grew from 2.5 billion to 5 billion people. By the year 2000 there will be 6.2 billion people. Over the next generation the developing world must find jobs for 3 billion young people reaching working age. This is an unprecedented test for economic development. But population growth of this dimension, accompanied by expectations of social and eco-

64

nomic progress, will bring in its wake unprecedented pressure on the world environment. Our task will be to find ways to reconcile the urgent need for global economic progress with the even more compelling need for a life-sustaining environment.

As prime minister, I would see my overriding task as guiding Canada through a period of intensive, often painful, but ultimately rewarding change. To help accomplish this I would have four key goals:

- build a new economy capable of providing Canadians with meaningful jobs and a decent standard of living;

- extend social progress through special attention to the problems of adjustment in a fast-changing economy and the needs of an aging population;

- commit Canada to an international leadership role to manage the world economy better, to ensure the funding and other policies necessary for world development, and to provide a life-sustaining environment for future generations;

- strengthen Canadian identity and unity in a positive way, not only by encouraging our cultural industries and making our political institutions more responsive but also by bringing Canadians together through positive domestic and international challenges.

It was the European statesman Jean Monnet who said, "People only accept change when they are faced with necessity, and only recognize necessity when a crisis is upon them." My underlying message as prime minister would be that events are moving too fast for us to wait until a crisis hits and forces us to action. By the time a crisis hits, it's already too late. One of the most important responsibilities of political leadership today is to provide direction so that we have the opportunity to avoid crises and the chance to take advantage of opportunities.

For Canada there are a number of key developments we can no longer ignore. One is the changing role of natural resources, which in the past were so vital to our jobs and growth. They will continue to be important, but we cannot count on our resource industries as an engine of growth in the future. Manufacturing is in the midst of similar sweeping changes as robots and other forms of new manufacturing technology eliminate jobs and transform old industries. Fortunately, this new technology also provides new opportunities for Canada. Unlike old-style mass-production industries, which needed access to markets of 100 million or more, new technology will make it far easier for Canadian companies to develop world-competitive products with much smaller production runs.

But most of our future jobs and opportunities will occur in service industries, such as finance, engineering, marketing, design, culture, and science—so-called knowledge jobs—and in the entrepreneurial start-up of new manufacturing based on new technology. Most of these jobs will be in our cities.

The natural resources for this new economy will be knowledge, creativity, and human capital. Canada's future depends on mobilizing these human skills—in science and technology, in culture (including design, filmmaking, architecture), and in entrepreneurship. Yet although Canadians have demonstrated world-class creativity, it is not firmly entrenched in our culture. We must also recognize another aspect of the new economy: the declining role of large organizations and the growing role of small enterprises. This means the end of the lifetime career, and a world with much less personal job security. Canadians will have to assume greater personal responsibility for staying abreast of new thinking in their areas of work.

My principal economic goal as prime minister would be to build an industrial base in goods and services that is global in outlook, innovative in technology and marketing, and is based on the importance of entrepreneurship, science and technology, and culture, including design, fashion, and marketing. Since this new economy would depend on the brainpower of Canadians, my government would work with the provinces to build a world-class educational system in Canada, from kindergarten to college. We would provide strong levels of support for our scientific and cultural communities, accelerate technology diffusion, and improve the opportunities for entrepreneurial success. Research and development spending would be raised to a level in line with that of our industrial competitors, which would mean doubling Canada's R & D effort as rapidly as possible. Larger foreign-owned companies in Canada would be required to carry out R & D or dedicate a portion of their sales to a national fund for basic R & D. Our financial institutions under federal jurisdiction would also be directed to allocate a minimum lending level in support of science and technology in Canadian industry. Government would also establish a risk-sharing entity to help companies adjust to change or expand. But it would only provide equity or other financing when companies could raise up-front private capital as well.

We would pursue Canada's trading interests through the new round of multilateral trade talks under the General Agreement on Tariffs and Trade (GATT). My government would use the Canada–U.S. free-trade talks to resolve outstanding irritants, but we would not proceed with a free-trade treaty. It is not in Canada's long-term interest to lock itself even more tightly into a continental Canada–U.S. economy. A Canada–U.S. free-trade agreement would lead to the harmonization of

Canadian and U.S. policies in a wide range of areas, would take away the option of increased Canadian ownership of our economy, would tie our hands on industrial and resource policies to develop industries and jobs, and would weaken our cultural industries, which are fundamental to our political independence.

Our long-term interest lies in greater trade diversification into other markets. A major objective of my government would be to expand Canada's trade relations with the rich markets of Japan and Europe, as well as with the expanding markets of the developing world, from Brazil, South Korea, the Philippines, and Mexico to India and China. Canada made a half-hearted effort at trade diversification in the early 1970s through the Third Option. But that effort lacked a strategy and long-term commitment, and limited itself to Europe. My government would take a global approach and would back this up with a coherent strategy and a long-term commitment.

A commitment to economic progress—including full employment—would be matched by a commitment to social progress. Without improvements in social programs, many Canadians will continue to resist change. But as new technologies and other forces of change make themselves felt, growing numbers of Canadians will be forced to adapt, whether through skills training, shorter working hours, early retirement, or some other way. To cope, we will need a new age of social innovation, much like the period of the Great Depression and the aftermath of World War II. In addition to a guaranteed annual income and an expanded role for the Canada Pension Plan, we will have to provide for lifetime education and perhaps even offer tax incentives for education and creativity.

Regional economic disparities also require urgent attention. But new and much more selective approaches are needed. The federal government must help slow-growth regions, but this help should be targeted mainly on regional cities and should be tied to local leadership—business, labour, academia, and government—coming up with city development plans. Jane Jacobs is right to focus on cities as the focal points of dynamic growth.

Canada's foreign policy under my government would give priority to the two areas where I believe we can do the most good: promoting world development, and working for a sustainable environmental system.

World development is at a critical stage. Economic gains of the past fifteen years are being lost, and young democratic regimes are under siege because developing countries are losing their capacity to grow. The debt crisis, protectionism, depressed commodity prices, and the pressure of spiralling populations are all threatening the economic future of the developing world. To avoid an economic and political crisis of global proportions, we must find ways to provide development finance and access to export markets for developing nations. The resources of the International Monetary Fund and World Bank must be significantly increased, and foreign aid budgets must be raised. This is one area where Canada should lead.

There is an ethical reason for doing this: Canadians care about the plight of other human beings. But there are long-term strategic reasons as well. The developing world should become increasingly important as a trading partner, with economic growth rates in excess of those in the industrial world. Moreover, the process of economic adjustment and change can be better handled in an environment of strong world economic growth. Within the developing world, economic growth is important to facilitate change without radical violence or military rule. Emerging democracies—in Brazil, the Philippines, South Korea, and India, for example—have a better chance of success with stronger growth.

My government would bring a similar sense of urgency to world forums on environmental issues. The thinning of the ozone layer threatens both human health and agricultural production. The increased layers of carbon dioxide in the atmosphere—the greenhouse effect—could precipitate calamitous changes in the world's climate. The destruction of tropical forests threatens the future of many living species, the supply of water, and the availability of useful agricultural land in many developing countries. Acid rain, toxic wastes, excessive pressures on environmental systems from overpopulation are among the other environmental concerns. No country alone can solve these problems, and all countries must participate in their solution. But world environmental issues are not receiving sufficient attention, in spite of the huge human and economic costs of environmental breakdown. My government would provide world leadership on these issues, just as it would on world development.

All of these actions—building a new economy and enhancing social progress at home, and providing committed world leadership on development and the environment in foreign policy—would, I believe, have a powerful unifying effect among Canadians, giving the country direction and purpose for the future. This, in turn, would do much to enhance Canadian self-confidence and identity. My government would build on this motivated Canadianism by supporting our cultural industries, strengthening our political process, seeking new ways to expand the participation of Canadians in their future, and pursuing new forms of consensus-building activities. Just as the Canadian flag and the celebrations of centennial year and Expo 67 galvanized positive and creative feelings, a determined country with a sense of direction could recapture that energy.

The fundamental challenge in political life today is to provide direction and leadership. This is what Canadians lack today. But with a new commitment to change and policies based on moral purpose, I believe we can get this country moving again—and in a way the entire world will cheer.

JOHN CRISPO

It is difficult for me to imagine assuming any elective office, let alone that of the prime ministership, because of my propensity to offend just about everyone on everything simply by stating my version of the truth. Assuming I was so fortunate—or unfortunate—I hope and trust that I would not succumb to the usual political temptation of simply saying what the electorate apparently wants to hear. Instead, I would prefer to be honest enough to level with the people of Canada about the challenges which confront this country and what we all must do together to rise to these challenges.

My first and foremost action as prime minister would be to insist on a high standard of ethics and integrity in my administration. This is an indispensable prerequisite if we are to restore a meaningful degree of public confidence, faith, and trust in our government institutions. This would be the premier item on my political agenda. That agenda would include several other major priorities, as would my economic and social agendas.

My Political Agenda
Reform of the widely abused patronage system would top my political agenda. Since patronage is unlikely ever to be entirely eradicated, I would attempt to minimize its negative effects by redirecting it in a more positive direction. Thus, in the case of all agency, board, and commission appointments—just to illustrate my general approach—I would introduce a procedure whereby these appointments would be made by the two major political parties proportionate to their representation in parliament. This would have two decided advantages. In the first place, both parties would undoubtedly seek out more competent candidates, rather than risk losing out to the other party by relying on their usual collection of bagmen, cronies, and hacks. Secondly, public bodies so constituted would be much more likely to serve the interests of parliament and the people as a whole, rather than just the incumbent government and the party in power.

Reform of the House of Commons has begun but has a long way to go. Central to such reform is the need for influential standing committees, which serve as the initial focal points for gathering facts and opinions on the important issues of the day. The budgetary process, for example, should begin with an appearance by the minister of finance before the House finance committee, when he or she would review the current constraints and options as the government saw them. Next, the committee would hear from expert witnesses, from representatives of major interest groups, and from spokesmen for influential think tanks. The committee would then report out its views—presumably in a majority and minority form—before the minister finally brought down the official budget.

If the Senate cannot be abolished, it must be radically restructured if not transformed, and this would be another of my priorities. To ensure a more representative character and more regular turnover, one half of its members would be appointed by the two major federal parties, proportional to their vote after each federal election (and presumably on the basis of party lists they would announce before the election, as with West Germany's second house). The other half would be appointed on a similar basis by the two major provincial parties in each of the provinces following each of their elections. To avoid deadlocks between the two houses, the new Senate—which might well be renamed the House of the Provinces—would have only varying powers of delay with respect to legislation passed by the House of Commons.

My Economic Agenda

My economic agenda reflects my view that the number-one challenge confronting Canada is to become more competitive by becoming more efficient, innovative, and productive. Only by these means can Canada achieve full employment, grow more rapidly, significantly increase its people's standard of living, and generate the wherewithal—without social friction—to do better for the disadvantaged and downtrodden within our midst.

A necessary but not sufficient condition for Canada to become more competitive is to achieve a free-trade arrangement with the United States, and I would pursue the matter vigorously. No other trade deal makes anything like the same sense for Canada, because the United States represents the single wealthiest market on the face of the earth and the one market in which Canada can still compete effectively, even in manufactured goods. The United States now takes almost 80 per cent of our exports, and we have no alternative market for these goods. The real choice confronting Canada in terms of its trading relations with the United States is not between free trade and the status quo but rather between free trade and growing U.S. protectionism, something which could prove devastating for this country.

Carried by the CBC and other nationalist media outlets, the opponents of free trade are throwing up every conceivable red herring and engaging in every form of scare-mongering known to man. What they are telling Canadians is that free trade will cost them their jobs, their culture, their medicare, their pensions, their sovereignty, and ultimately—as if there is anything else—their country. Their emotional nationalistic rhetoric is discouragingly effective, but it totally fails to come to grips with the trading reality which confronts this country. The fact of the matter is that the very things they say are threatened by free trade are more likely to be threatened by the failure to achieve it.

Canada must also come to grips, on a sustained basis, with its massive government deficits. Combined federal-provincial deficits proportionately amount to over twice the combined federal-state deficits south of the border. These deficits not only incur huge servicing costs but reduce the scope for effective contracyclical fiscal action in any ensuing period of recession.

As prime minister, I would introduce two major measures to reduce the federal deficit. In the first place, every so-called tax expenditure available to corporations and individuals (such tax expenditures actually range from useful incentives to flagrant loopholes) would be rescinded unless it could be demonstrated that the tax expenditure in question was serving a worthwhile purpose in an effective manner. In the second place, every type of social security payment would be subjected to a clawback after the recipients' gross annual income reached a specified level (thereby retaining the principle of universality while introducing a non-degrading and non-demeaning means test).

Tax reform is also essential in Canada, although only one neglected aspect of this need for reform will be dealt with here. It concerns the need to switch investment incentives away from the paper and property shufflers—with their ill-gotten capital gains, based largely on one conflict of interest or another—and towards real capital investment, which produces new enterprises, goods, services, and jobs. I would generate this change in the only way possible—by placing a very high tax on short-term capital gains and placing little or no tax on long-term gains.

Canada must also re-examine its research and development incentives. There is mounting evidence that the real pay-off from advancing technology arises more from the rapid adoption and diffusion of new technology than from its actual discovery. Except in a few areas where Canada has an obvious comparative advantage in basic research, my administration would place less emphasis on the latter and more emphasis on the application of new scientific and technological breakthroughs.

More privatization and deregulation also have a place in Canada in order to ensure that the bottom line and market forces play their proper role in as many areas as possible. This should all be an integral part of a vigilant competition policy which protects the public as much as possible from monopolistic groups of one kind or another. Mind you, especially when it comes to deregulation of transportation industries, everything possible should be done to ensure that this does not result in any compromising of safety standards.

Canada should also have in place more effective anti-inflationary measures aimed at cost pushers of all kinds. I have long advocated a cost and income review board, with the appropriate acronym CIRB, to monitor all cost and income movements with a view to singling out for attention any untoward upward cost and/or income movements that are not explained by an economic shortage or by social inequity. Any group extracting undue gains from the system would know that if it continued to do so, any special powers, prerogatives, or privileges that had helped it make such gains would be curtailed or removed.

My Social Agenda
The first item on my social agenda might just as easily have been the last on my economic agenda. I refer to the need for more effective retraining, upgrading, relocation, and income maintenance programs for those disrupted by the many changes this country must undergo as it strives to adjust to an ever more competitive environment. It is vital that we have more effective manpower policies in place in order to avoid undue resistance by those caught up in any change process, since it is totally unfair to expect the few to absorb the costs of progress while the rest enjoy only the benefits.

One cannot mention manpower policies (or should it now be "person power" policies?) without raising the issue of women and minority rights. What is needed more than anything else in this area is equality of access and opportunity for all individuals in our society. With this priority in mind, I would place a legal reverse burden of proof on all institutions to demonstrate that they do not discriminate in their intake, education, promotion, compensation, or related policies when charged with having done so. Such an approach would obviate the need for such symptomatic measures as affirmative action and quotas, not to mention equal pay for work of equal value, with all the distortions they cause.

As already indicated, the clawback approach I would take to social security would move us in the direction of a guaranteed minimum income, or perhaps two guaranteed minimum incomes: one generous for those permanently disabled or retired, and the other less generous for those temporarily out of work because of injury, sickness, or unemployment. The rationale for moving in the direction of a guaranteed minimum income through a negative income tax should be obvious. It is simply that we cannot do better by those who are really in need if we insist on doing the same thing for everyone.

A similar rationale underlies the approach I would take to the rising costs of medicare. If we are to cope with the medical costs of our aging population, the costs of medicare must be subject to meaningful restraint. The only way to achieve this is to make people conscious of the fact that it is not a free service—yet to do so without introducing a crude means test. To this end, each taxpayer's annual medicare costs up to a reasonable maximum would be added to his or her taxable income. Thus, the poor would pay nothing for medicare, and those with the ability to pay would pay their proportionate share of the costs. This is a principle that may eventually have to be applied to other costly areas of public services, such as higher education.

Even now it would seem appropriate to consider an income-based voucher system to ensure that there is more equitable access and choice with respect to all levels of education. Such a system, which should at least be tried on a pilot basis, would ensure the most qualified students readier access to the educational institution of their choice, regardless of their income. In addition, it would put all such institutions on a more competitive footing, since these vouchers would constitute their major source of income until they learned to tap other sources of financial support more effectively than they have done to date.

Other Issues

In a short essay such as this, one cannot begin to do justice to all of one's socioeconomic-political concerns. Yet, two other areas—defence and foreign policy—command attention.

Canada's defence policy, in my administration, would remain anchored to its NORAD and NATO commitments. If anything, we should be increasing our contribution to these alliances, since in neither alliance are we doing our share. Commitment to our U.S. and Western European alliances should not mean that we blindly follow the U.S. line on everything; but in the final analysis, we should recognize that it is primarily the United States which deters Russia from subjugating even more countries and peoples than it already has. Two world wars should have taught us that appeasement is no way to deal with aggressive totalitarian regimes.

As for foreign aid, I would have Canada concentrate most of its aid on the Third World countries which are trying to respect democratic principles and human rights. I would also concentrate more of the aid on support for responsible and voluntary population-control policies in those countries where this is the crux of the problem they face.

None of this emphasis, of course, would preclude humanitarian aid to any country confronted by a natural disaster.

To conclude, this was supposed to be Canada's century; and in many ways it has been. Yet the country has still not begun to realize its full potential, which now may only be attained in the next century. It will not be realized even then, however, unless Canadians face up to the harsh facts of life.

If I ever found myself prime minister of Canada, I would give Canadians a dose of reality therapy as fast as I could. I am convinced that they would begin to see the benefits before my first term of office expired. Even if the benefits were not yet *that* visible and the voters threw me out, it would still have been worth it, because I would know I had done what I thought was best for the country.

KEITH DAVEY

I would do sixteen things if I were prime minister of Canada. I would enact the following liberal program:

- The single most important issue in the world today is the threat of nuclear conflict. Not only would millions of Canadians be killed, but the world as we know it would disappear. I would therefore declare Canada a nuclear-free country. There would be no nuclear weapons or delivery systems permitted on Canadian soil. We would remain in NATO but would withdraw from NORAD.

- Investment Canada would revert to its proper role as a Foreign Investment Review Agency. Canada would no longer be for sale. American investment would be welcome in Canada, but only when it was in the Canadian interest and never on an equity basis. Canadian cultural integrity would be maintained and expanded.

- The deficit would be reduced by heavily taxing corporations and wealthy Canadians.

- The government would implement a program of quality day care for all working mothers.

- The government would fully implement a program of pay equity. Legislation would force employers to pay women the same as men for doing jobs which required similar skills.

- Instead of seeking free trade with the United States, the government would aggressively seek an expansion of worldwide international trade, which would, of course, include the United States.

- The government would create a one-year job of last resort for every unemployed young Canadian. Extensive training programs, with particular emphasis on high-tech skills, would be mandatory throughout the school system.

- The government would embark on a public information campaign, as well as declaring war on drugs and alcohol abuse.

- Every woman would have the freedom of choice about abortion.

- The Senate would be elected and the role and function of the Senate would be upgraded.

- The long-standing Canadian ideal of a mixed economy would be maintained and expanded. Privatization for its own sake would disappear. There would be far less deregulation.

- Tough environmental laws would be enacted at all levels of government.

- Open immigration would be encouraged. So would multiculturalism, though there would be a concerted attempt to bring more and more immigrants into the mainstream of Canadian life.

- Canada would strengthen its commitment to the Third World and the United Nations.

- Canadian research and development would, in fact, be tripled.

- The alarming concentration of wealth in all sectors of our economy would be reduced. Further mergers and acquisitions would involve the public interest. Some monopolies, including media monopolies, could be dismantled. More and more Canadian entrepreneurs would participate in building our economy.

GEORGES ERASMUS

If I were prime minister of Canada I would, of course, have to prioritize the challenges facing me in every area of the government's activity. I cannot attempt to cover all of these in a short article; but from my point of view as a Dene (and a so-called Indian) who is familiar with the North, I have certain personal priorities which blend well with the challenges facing any prime minister of Canada today. (By the way, I say that I am a "so-called Indian" because like many citizens of the First Nations of Canada, I find the historical misnomer "Indian" to be a remnant of European imperialism and a pejorative term.)

If I were prime minister, top of my list of personal and governmental priorities internally would be social justice, economic recovery, and national reconciliation; externally, peace and environmental concerns. Until recently, when most people in Canada talked about social justice the aboriginal peoples almost always were a footnote. I am glad to see that this is changing for the better, largely because of the attention being given to aboriginal and treaty rights since the renewed constitution came into effect.

Yet the aboriginal peoples are still far from their rightful place in Canada. When the constitution was proclaimed in 1982, a revered elder of a First Nation in Ontario said that once aboriginal rights were securely protected in the Canadian constitution, he would give his life to defend it. He was articulating the thoughts of thousands of aboriginal persons. For over two centuries, aboriginal peoples were bereaved peoples (and I'm using the word "bereaved" in its proper sense of having been dispossessed or robbed of something belonging to them). They were dispossessed or robbed of material things such as their lands (together with the resources) and of non-material things such as their self-esteem and their pride in their rich cultural heritage. Again, I am glad to see that this is changing for the better—but we still have a long way to go before complete restitution is made.

Aboriginal peoples all over the world have a deep sense of history and of their continuum on this earth. It is no different here in Canada. Their history is precious to them, especially their historical links with the French and British crowns—now the Canadian crown—going as far back as the fifteenth century and landmarked by the Two-Row

Wampum (an agreement in 1650 for mutual respect and peaceful coexistence between the First Nations and the crown) and the Royal Proclamation of 1763 (which set out the ground rules for the colonial settlers), as well as the treaty-making process that followed.

If I were prime minister, therefore, I would want a very progressive aboriginal land rights policy. (Here again, the government mistakenly calls this "land claims" by the Indians!) My policy would be aimed at facilitating the ability of First Nations to become self-reliant and self-governing. If they are to deal directly with developers, they must have ownership and control of subsurface resources. We have to introduce new, maybe unique, systems of land tenure and land management in Canada; in other words, create the laws that would respond to the legal and moral demands of aboriginal title. Does this mean that a government under my leadership would "hand Canada back to the Indians"? The question is mischievous—there is enough land in Canada (which is the second-largest country in the world, with only about 25 million inhabitants) to satisfy legitimate and just aboriginal demands!

What if certain provincial governments resisted the restoration of fair land bases for the aboriginal peoples? My government would have to play a strong leadership role consistent with the obligations passed to it by the historic French and British crowns. Thus far, nothing has prevented past federal governments from moving forward to assert their authority, their jurisdictions, and their sovereignty vis-à-vis the provincial governments, as well as on the international level. We have the ability to expropriate, but I see no reason why a fair land and jurisdiction arrangement should not be worked out with the First Nations. As prime minister, I would move very quickly with like-minded provincial governments—would create a momentum, create positive precedents, and demonstrate to the public that it is in everyone's interests if the First Nations could be "helped to lift themselves up by their own bootstraps" so to speak.

The tougher areas would be left for a second stage, but I would move immediately to rectify matters with the First Nations in those areas under federal jurisdiction, such as parks activity, fisheries, inland waters, and so on, where there is a direct impact on the First Nations and their ability to flourish in a revitalized Canada. I would offer no apology for the emphasis I would give to the fledgling First Nations governments, since their economic progress would be a major contribution to the overall Canadian economy.

At present, the majority of federal funding to the First Nations has the effect of maintaining the welfare structure. A government under my leadership would turn this around. Present government expenditures on economic development and employment projects would be reversed so that more emphasis was placed on them. The primary emphasis would be on the economic development of the First Nations as an investment in the future of Canada; there would be major changes in the tax structure to allow the private sector to play its role in First Nations development; aboriginal lands would be regarded as special investment areas, with such vehicles as tax holidays and joint ventures with aboriginal institutions, whether family-owned, band-owned, or nation-owned. First Nations have to be allowed to obtain revenues either directly from their lands (if these are profitable enough) or from the Gross National Product. However it be done, the deplorable "fourth-world" conditions now obtaining in this vast and rich country of ours must be eradicated.

Strong First Nations economies would, of necessity, contribute to strong regional economies in Canada. My government would develop a long-term economic strategy in which every Canadian resource and commodity would be developed and refined as much as possible in its own local area; this would provide employment locally in many parts of Canada. There is also the need to change our role as a supplier of raw materials and a buyer of finished products. At present, the bulk of Canadian investment is in non-renewable resources. We ought to pay far greater attention than we now do to renewable resources and, at the same time, help restore those resources that are being ruthlessly exploited, such as forestry. Canada lacks a reforestation policy, while we relentlessly denude our mountains and heartland of trees and forests that have taken thousands of years to flourish.

So far as is possible, we ought to banish the welfare mentality and give every citizen in Canada the opportunity for gainful employment. There is an urgent need for long-term planning for permanent jobs. My government would also consider a guaranteed annual income for citizens in areas like the Atlantic region and would institute a system of permanent income to avoid using unemployment insurance as a subsidy. In such a system, our senior citizens, our disabled, our widows, and our single parents would share in the economy and enjoy the social justice we talk so much about.

I stated earlier that national reconciliation would be another of my preoccupations as prime minister of Canada. I would like to see the ordinary person regaining a greater measure of control over his or her own life. In an age of big government, big business, and big labour, the individual counts for relatively little or nothing. I think, particularly, of the elderly, the poor and disadvantaged, and the aboriginal peoples.

My government would create a network for regular consultation with different types of organized interest groups to assist in long-term planning that would transcend political party lines and would focus on the Canada of the twenty-first century. I would involve environmentalists, women, aboriginal people, labour, the churches, the corporate sector, and those whose livelihood was in the renewable-resource areas (fishermen, trappers, and farmers).

I also mentioned earlier the need to do right and justice by the aboriginal peoples, who have generally been materially and nonmaterially dispossessed, and treated like outcasts and strangers in their own native land. If I were prime minister, I would feel it incumbent upon me to restore aboriginal peoples to their rightful place in today's Canadian society.

As well as dealing with issues of land rights and economic development, I would institute a program for the protection, development, and relearning of aboriginal languages. Specifically, every aboriginal child would receive a minimum number of years of schooling in his or her own language. I would encourage writers to publish in their aboriginal languages by granting annual government awards for poetry, short stories, and novels, as well as a special category for accurate historical literature telling the aboriginal side of the story.

There is an urgent need to educate the descendants of the European settlers and the newly arrived immigrants about the history of Canada as it relates to the First Nations. An extensive program of adult education and information would be fostered by my government, and I would urge provincial governments to ensure that school curricula reflected the teaching of the accurate history of Canada and the contribution that aboriginal peoples have made, and can make in the future.

Canada is entering upon a period of rising aboriginal nationalism, which neither governments nor laws can reverse. If this nation-state called Canada really is to come of age, it must admit the historical fact that its original founding nations are the First Nations. A reconciliation of Canada with its aboriginal peoples will add to the richness, the dignity, and the vitality of the nation-state. Canadians must come to terms with the reality that Canada, like Switzerland, is a multinational and multilingual nation-state and not just a multicultural one; our constitution, and the laws that flow from it, must recognize this reality and its consequences. For if one nation or culture is allowed to dominate, the nation-state becomes imperialist.

A government under my leadership would certainly give a lead in nuclear disarmament. I would support a nuclear-free Canada and the prohibition of cruise-missile testing, as well as NATO exercises such as we have had over the territory of aboriginal peoples. I am not persuaded yet that any of these moves would be inconsistent with Canada's membership of NATO.

My government would, in the nature of things, have to adopt a serious and extremely assertive tone with our neighbour and ally, the

United States, on the matter of environmental pollution. Our two countries have to develop long-range planning to ensure, as far as possible, a safe and sound ecological system for future generations.

If I were prime minister, I would strive ceaselessly for a Canada that would be able to hold its head high in a world of peace—and this means that we must have no skeletons in our own cupboard. After all, if peace and harmony do not begin at home, where will they begin?

PETER ERNERK

What would I do if I were prime minister? The idea takes my breath away. Before answering, I must first imagine a world that would lend credibility to the question. The attitudes of most Canadian voters might have to shift before an Inuk leader could attain such a lofty position in federal politics. Since most Canadians are not noted for their revolutionary zeal, particularly at election time, changes in their everyday lives would have to make it appealing, if not essential, to "vote Inuk."

As the earth's capacity to sustain life is eroded, it is all too easy to outline a nightmarish future for Canada and the world, a future in which the planet's population would be decimated by countless self-inflicted injuries caused by the continued senseless abuse of the biosphere. Perhaps I would be elected primarily because I had grown up in the Arctic, in the ancient indigenous culture, and therefore had a different perspective on the tortured course that our country seems to be following.

What do the Inuit have to offer? Well, we have lived in harmony with our northern environment for thirty thousand years, while it has taken less than a thousand years for "Western" values to bring the entire planet's ecology to the brink of collapse. Perhaps a majority of Canadians will not realize that there are better ways of doing things—until more nuclear destruction, more toxic waste, more acid rain, more famine, more incurable diseases, and countless other miseries have taken their toll.

These problems confront all humankind and cannot be tackled by one country, one government, or one person alone. But change must begin somewhere. So why not in Canada? Perhaps a majority of Canadian voters will eventually recognize that the holistic traditions of this nation's indigenous peoples are a viable alternative—and will vote accordingly.

My first act as prime minister would be to bring industry, energy, and agriculture to terms with the environment. Intelligent prerequisites would be established. Just as personal hygiene and sanitation greatly reduced disease in early industrial Europe, so environmental hygiene would help to do the same in the late industrial world. Many Canadians know that the public inevitably suffers when profit margins come before environmental health. Having learned this, Canadian society should stop confusing material wants with real needs; then industry would stop consuming and producing things at a rate, and in ways, that are detrimental to the earth. Emphasis should be placed on non-polluting manufacturing processes, on biodegradable goods, and on decentralized production.

From my experience, the public knows that atomic power plant accidents and atomic waste products are particularly harmful to the environment, and they won't stop being harmful for thousands of years. Under my administration, those nuclear power plants that had not already run down or broken down or melted down would be shut down. The construction of hydroelectric dams, which damage food chains by altering land and river ecosystems, would be curtailed. The exploration, development, and transportation of fossil fuels in environmentally sensitive areas would be stopped. The dependence on burning fossil fuels that poison the air we breathe could gradually be reduced as other energy sources were brought on line. Passive, decentralized energy systems would be implemented, most notably solar power and wind power (two energy sources that cannot be packaged and controlled by unscrupulous energy cartels or power companies). Every building and every community would have solar panels and windmills. Every individual would know the importance of energy conservation.

My government would stop agriculture from growing annual plants that leach the life from the earth. Farmers would stop using unnatural chemical fertilizers and pesticides, which end up in the water and food chains. Factories disguised as fields (agribusiness) and factories disguised as farms (battery farms) would be closed. Much of the Canadian prairie would revert to what it was originally—grazing land for animals. Hunting and gathering would again grow in importance throughout most of Canada.

Decentralization of industry, energy, and agriculture would mean a decentralized population. My government would act on what many Canadians know: that cities are just excessive concentrations of unsafe industries and frustrated people. The creation of small, secure, decentralized communities would provide many solutions to the nation's ecological and social problems. Overcrowded urban Canada would no longer strain the recuperative powers of the immediate environment—the air we breathe, the lakes, rivers, land, and oceans, which are the foundation of this nation. New ways of looking at work would be established.

The concepts of employment, finance, and usury would be re-evaluated, and the banking system would probably be dismantled. The wage-based economy would evaporate. People would rediscover other ways of justifying their lives. Self-actualization would give purpose and meaning to their existence. Life would no longer be sacrificed to the carrot of economic growth and the stick of economic efficiency.

The processes, products, consumption, and by-products of industry, energy, agriculture, and society should not hurt the biosphere. There should be an intelligent interchange. For decades, Canadians have been told that they can efficiently "manage" or economically "control" their environment with impunity. This is like telling a child that he can control his parents if he just holds his breath for long enough. A more mature social and political philosophy, which places life before economics, must evolve.

My second, and last, act as prime minister would be to bring about the dissolution of rigid, arbitrarily designated, provincial and territorial boundaries so that amorphous, autonomous "bioregions" could develop, based on cultural, historical, geographic, and resource considerations. This would effectively settle land claims issues. All parties would recognize that no one can "own" land, in the truest sense of the word. Land is a resource that nurtures and provides, only as long as it is cherished and respected. It is fatal to treat this planet, and the living things on it, as mere property.

The adversarial political, legal, and labour systems—long recognized as counterproductive to fostering trust, responsibility, and goodwill—would be scrapped. Bioregional councils, appointed and operated by consensus, would emerge. Councillors would be community elders and others whose wisdom would be plain to all, based on the evidence of their daily lives. Being a councillor would not be a full-time job.

Councils would provide a maximum amount of visionary guidance and a minimum amount of interference in the everyday lives of Canadians. The majority of the country's laws—long recognized as extraneous, redundant, or harmful—would be repealed. They would be replaced with traditional, unwritten laws of human social conduct. Since these laws would be intrinsic to the development of each member of society, very little external policing would be required.

The Canadian prison system—long recognized as detrimental to the rehabilitation of criminals—would be eliminated. Each decentralized community would take responsibility for the judgement and correction of its deviant members. There would, generally, be fewer acts of antisocial behaviour, because the alienating quality of anonymous crowds of strangers would be negligible in small, stable populations.

Education would also be decentralized. Most learning already occurs at home and at play. Parents, relatives, and tutors would acknowledge this social educational framework and would start teaching there, instead of submitting children to the artificial structure of the school setting. Schools, colleges, and universities would become libraries and physical resource bases, rather than centres for standardized inculcation. Everyone and everything within a community would be treated by all as an interactive resource base. Learning would be a self-perpetuating lifelong process of encouraging the search for common-sense solutions to problems, instead of being an ossified amalgam of facts and formulas, learned by rote and available for a limited time only.

Travel outside each bioregion would be greatly reduced as people set out to rediscover and appreciate one another and the land. Some travel would continue for the purpose of education and research, but in a secure society it would generally be regarded as an obligation rather than as a privilege or right. Less transient individuals worldwide would reduce the spread of disease and the absorption of cultures through interaction. The growing homogenization of the world's languages and cultures is not necessarily beneficial to humanity. Diverse languages and cultures provide different insights into reality. These different insights are at the heart of human resourcefulness, and resourcefulness is universally recognized as a key to human survival.

Although the above outline gives a radical response to the initial question, I trust it will not be taken for any more than it is: pure speculation. Until the Canadian people can see their way to electing an Inuk prime minister, I shall put all my energy into preserving and promoting Inuit culture. In this way, an ancient blueprint for meaningful human relations with nature and with other people will continue to exist. This is not retrograde behaviour; it is an attempt to validate a traditional social order in the face of modern problems. Someday, the rest of Canada will recognize that the Inuit have something to contribute. Someday, our ways will be recognized as being most sorely needed. But I'm not holding my breath.

JACQUES FRANCOEUR

If I were elected prime minister of Canada, it would be under false pretences. Because I would take the job only on one condition—that I would be a benevolent (hopefully!) dictator, restricted to a single five-year term, and would not be committed to try for re-election. Thus, with a relatively free hand, but limited to five years, I think I could do some good for Canadians, although they might not like it at first—at least, not until most changes were proven right and good, which would probably be after my five years were up.

The problem with politicians nowadays, in a democracy like Canada (and politicians of all stripes, mind you) is that they are always worrying first about the good of "The Party" and, of course, about their re-election in five, four, three, two, or one years. With my limited-in-time benevolent dictatorship, I would be free from the all-consuming passion to be there longer and longer, while doing less and less of what is needed to ensure a better Canada.

My first break, of course, would be that I would not be stuck with incompetent ministers whose only claim for the job was "There has to be someone in the cabinet from Region X" or "Minority Z has to be represented." Thus, I would pick my ministers strictly for their talents, and I could probably run Canada with ten of them. I would also shake up the top civil servants because, being a benevolent dictator, I could force them to play ball rather than letting them run their departments as they please, which is too often the case with weak ministers. As for the rest of the civil servants, I would grant promotions and pay increases on merit—even if it attracted cries of patronage at times—and as the result of periodic exams.

I would revolutionize the Canadian scene by doing away with the present "Canada must be bilingual from coast to coast" policy, which will never work. (Why on earth should a French Canadian expect to find a French-speaking clerk in a small British Columbia post office? Or why should a lost English-speaking soul insist on being served in English in a remote Beauce village?) Instead, I would set up a Swiss-type confederation—which, for a thousand years, has proved to be workable, peaceful, and enriching. In case you don't know, the Swiss have a system of cantons which, except for the capital, are defined as either German-speaking, French-speaking, or Italian-speaking.

Efforts are made to supply services in the other two languages. But often this is not done, since it is not obligatory. Yet no one raises hell, because the shoe is on the other foot a few kilometres away.

I would institute a compulsory public-service period for all youths, male and female, either at age eighteen or when they complete their full-time studies. It could be served in the armed forces, in community work in Canada, or in the Third World as part of a Canadian peace corps. All youths would be paid "military" salaries and all would receive lectures on citizenship, democracy, the constitution, etc.

I would revamp our tax system along the lines of the new tax law of the United States, but I would also order severe penalties for all under-the-table deals and unreported work. This alone might well erase the federal deficit quite rapidly! I would try to restructure unemployment benefits and welfare payments to give more to those who really need it (single parents with children, the unemployable handicapped, etc.), but I would penalize able-bodied recipients who shy away from available work.

I would try to give special help to entrepreneurs, exporters, creators, and others who can do the most to create jobs and improve the Canadian economy. I would try to bring Canadian productivity on par with those of certain other countries by means of a system of bonuses and rewards. As for the boards and commissions which maintain artificially high prices for milk, poultry, and work done by certain tradesmen (electricians, plumbers, etc.), I would eliminate most of them. There is generally no need for these artificial structures, and free-market forces should operate in these domains as in other sectors of the economy. Meanwhile, I would ask one question of the post office: Why does it cost so much more to mail a letter in Canada, for much less service, than in the United States? As the gag goes, a letter in Canada costs 36 cents: 18 cents for delivery and 18 cents for storage!

In international affairs, I would stop pretending that Canada is a major world power. Thus, our military budget could be reduced, because I don't think that keeping a few planes and several hundred men in West Germany scares the Russians, nor would they really be useful in a conflict. But I would use some of this money to upgrade the military forces stationed in Canada so that they could be used more efficiently in cases of disasters. They would also be available for specific peacekeeping missions for the United Nations. Meantime, I would affirm our independence towards the United States by making it clear that good relations are a two-way affair, even if this means a few tit-for-tats in economic affairs.

Finally, I would have to kick myself out of the job for day-dreaming... long before my five years were up!

E. MARGARET FULTON

As prime minister, I would make every effort to see that the Canadian people fully understood the reality that informed my thinking. This reality is rooted in the knowledge that civilization as we know it, and life on this planet in general, is threatened by extinction. Supposing a nuclear holocaust is avoided, there still remains the possibility of total extinction from famine or from environmental or genetic destruction. Consequently, there are many inadequacies in our past systems of thought and in the folly of persisting with cultural, social, and political structures which no longer serve human needs.

We need a vision of a new reality—one based on concepts of sharing rather than on the maintenance of power. We know how to destroy and conquer. Can we now learn how to preserve and nurture? We must image ourselves in an organic state, not a static one. By learning to accept constant change, a dynamic ideal of interactive government can evolve that is more appropriate for an emerging electronic era.

To be meaningful, any new vision must be rooted in the best of past experience. The objectives of former Canadian governments have included four major concepts: humanity, equity, rationality, and participation. The failure to achieve these ideals lies in confrontational and adversarial-style politics, reinforced by strict adherence to rigid hierarchical structures. This vertical vision of government and of society as a whole is no longer viable. All levels and departments of government need to be restructured. Organizational models based on intersecting circles must replace the rigidity of boxes and "envelope" systems. Decision-making policies will thus be altered to avoid limited discussion and secrecy, and to provide maximum opportunities for debate, review, and reassessment. The general public must be re-educated to participate more fully in the total governing process.

Working within the context of Canadian history, my government would review certain legacies of earlier prime ministers which now need modifying so that they can serve the Canadian people more effectively. Sir John A. Macdonald recognized that Canada had to have a national transportation system if it was to develop into a nation independent of the United States and Great Britain. We must refurbish that dream and make it less costly for Canadians to travel in Canada than to travel to Europe, the United States, or other countries. Canadians need to experience personally the vast expanses of this country. They need to understand Canada geographically as well as historically and culturally.

To extend the concept of nation, R. B. Bennett designed two major institutions: the Bank of Canada and the Canadian Broadcasting Corporation. The CBC, in particular, must be given a budget to operate both radio and television programs without advertising. It must provide more Canadian content and serve all regions of Canada more effectively. In short, I would revitalize the CBC in terms of its original mandate: to elevate Canadian culture for the Canadian people.

Mackenzie King kept the nation together during World War II and then through the transition from an agricultural to an industrial economy. John Diefenbaker recognized the multicultural aspects of Canada and tried to convey a vision of equity, while Joe Clark added the sense of Canada being a "community of communities"—a concept which, handled sensitively and with moderation, allows for equity while preserving the richness of diverse cultures. Lester Pearson furthered our sense of sovereignty by giving us a national flag, while Pierre Trudeau awakened us to the bilingual nature of Canada and gave us a patriated constitution with a charter of human rights.

The legacy of previous prime ministers has been one of openness and fairness, with a refusal to cater to the protective instincts of those who want to impose their beliefs and systems on others. I would attempt to maintain this approach, while enhancing it in terms of present realities. We live at a time when fears and fanaticism abound. There are those who thrive on prejudice and bigotry, and demand exclusive religious and educational rights. Our many social problems include crime, pollution, unemployment, inflation, alcohol and drug abuse, and violence. One aim of my government would be to bring about a social transformation in such a way that the wholeness of a pluralistic Canadian society would be maximized and divisiveness minimized.

In achieving these ends, I would draw inspiration from five major movements that have been a seedbed for thought and ideas. The first is the international movement supportive of the United Nations and of the belief that all nations should share one another's ideas and resources. Among other measures, I would strengthen Canada's credibility by affirming its multilateral relationships. Ninety per cent of the world's population lies outside the American and Soviet empires, and it is essential to form a third bloc of non-nuclear nations to provide alternatives to the American-Russian balance of power.

Second is the ecumenical movement of the 1960s, which opened the way for more constructive dialogue among all major religious groups. My government would support the World Council of

Churches and would press for the involvement of religious leaders at international meetings. It is imperative to rid the world of both religious and political fanaticism, and to permit all people to worship as they choose.

Then there are the ecological and environmental movements. I would implement strong policies to protect our total environment and would listen more carefully to the native peoples and learn from their experience. I would also see that ecology programs were taught more effectively.

Fourth is the women's movement, which has demonstrated that all governments throughout the world have discriminated against women—thereby losing the potential of half the world's population. As prime minister, I would have an equal number of women and men on all government committees, and I would implement policies on comprehensive day care, pay equity, pensions for housewives, and so on. Judge Rosalie Abella's report provides a blueprint for government action in this area.

Finally, there is the peace movement, which forms an umbrella for all the other movements, since peace is the central issue of our times. This movement, which has become a growing world force in the past two decades, has exposed the waste and folly of the military-industrial complex. My government would reduce the defence budget and withdraw monetary support from private companies that have arms contracts. The money would be redirected to human services. Just as Mackenzie King mobilized Canada to make an all-out war effort, I would mobilize it for an all-out peace effort.

This can be done, and in fact it is part of the government's mandate as set out in the British North America Act of 1867: "To make Laws for the Peace, Order and good Government of Canada." I believe that the time has come for the Government of Canada to assume its constitutional obligations and to act for the welfare of the nation in the light of present realities.

Building, then, on the work of earlier prime ministers, I would strengthen those institutions that give us our sense of being Canadians—transportation systems, for instance, and especially communications. There is "too little for the mind" in private broadcasting. Only a revitalized CBC, working with the National Film Board and Canadian publishing companies, can create the ideas and images that can help transform society and redefine democracy. Canadians must understand what it means to be citizens in a truly participatory democracy. In the clamour for "rights," many people simply mean licence; they forget that liberty also means responsibility and obligation. The task of government should not be to hold power over people but to empower each adult to take full responsibility for his or her life.

To be effective, the democratization of society must involve all aspects of personal and public life—cultural, social, sexual, moral, religious, racial, national, and economic, as well as political. Many conferences and task forces have been established over the years in an attempt at participatory democracy, and they have produced a wealth of reports with sound recommendations. But the governments of the day have largely ignored these recommendations and have lacked the political will to make constructive change.

As prime minister, I would immediately set up a federal-provincial task force, which would cull through the reports of all royal commissions, task forces, and major conferences since the 1960s, with a view to developing a National Plan of Action. Then, since many of the recommendations in the above studies foundered because of the division of legislative powers between the federal and provincial governments, I would have the task force examine ways of reducing duplication and waste at all levels of government (phasing out the Senate would be an initial goal). Next, it would explore the possibility of phasing out certain aspects of provincial jurisdictions that limit federal-provincial co-operation. A more flexible system is needed, not only for free trade among provinces but to enable professionals such as teachers, lawyers, and nurses to move from one part of Canada to another without being penalized in terms of medical care, pension rights, licences, professional accreditation, etc. Finally, the task force would explore ways of giving more responsibility for decision-making to local boards and municipal governments.

The issue of federal-provincial jurisdiction has been a major problem in Canadian politics. Dr. Richard B. Splane offered a solution in his submission to the Special Joint Committee on the Constitution of Canada, 1980. He proposed that the sharing of powers between the federal government and the provinces should be based on rational rather than doctrinaire criteria. For example, the provision of health services can best be carried out by the provinces, as can some forms of income security measures—though, in general, these should be nationwide and thus federally administered. The federal government, argued Dr. Splane, should be "constitutionally entitled to work closely and continuously" with the provinces in seeing that throughout Canada adequate income security measures and social services are provided.

As prime minister, I would attempt to resolve the jurisdictional problems on the lines suggested by Dr. Splane. Because there are so many injustices in the present system, I would take immediate action on income security. Yet reform can only be successful if it brings together the benefits from income transfer programs with those from tax provisions. "A single, national program called a core income program" was advocated in 1973 by the Canadian Council on Social Development's national task force. In the mid-1970s a federal provincial review of social security made similar recommendations, and in 1985 the Macdonald Commission strongly supported such a plan. I would implement the plan and would make it a top priority to provide a guaranteed annual income for all Canadians. But as with human rights, there would be no paternalism or sentimentality about the program. Because of it, many existing welfare programs would be phased out. Canadian citizens must be educated to the responsibilities that are part of income security.

No segment of human services is more important than the education of the people, yet no segment has suffered more because of jurisdictional problems. Again, there exists a plethora of excellent reports, yet despite numerous commissioned studies of all levels of education, little has happened at the legislative levels. As prime minister, a major goal would be the formulation of a national education system, extending from early childhood and day care to postgraduate studies and special programs for seniors. Indeed, the four major goals set by earlier prime ministers—humanity, equity, rationality, and participation—can only be achieved when all citizens have the opportunity to participate in lifelong learning that will give them a real sense of Canadian identity.

An interactive committee, drawn from all levels of government and working with professional experts, would be set up to design a national system of education that would allow for the equal sharing of costs, powers, and responsibilities. This committee would bring the provincial Departments of Education together with the federal Departments of Labour, Employment and Immigration, Communications, Health and Welfare, and the Secretary of State. It would be charged with the responsibility of changing the envelope system of funding; and of co-ordinating, in a rational way, all provincial school, college, and university education programs with federal rehabilitation and job-training programs. "Learning a Living" (the title of an Employment and Immigration study) must become a reality. Education, work, health, and leisure can no longer be classified as separate activities. Paid study leave must become common practice throughout all branches of society, but the highest standards of excellence must prevail during both employment and study periods. All educational institutions need to be restructured to allow for more flexibility and a greater flow of non-traditional students.

The overall needs of citizens in terms of reaching their fullest potential as human beings and as Canadians will never be met as long as governments continue to classify and separate the different areas of human activity. To achieve our goal of humanity, we must take a holistic approach rather than continuing the present fragmentation of effort, which is wasteful of resources and ineffective with results. Federal responsibility for law and order becomes meaningless if all the government can do is build jails. We should be funding crime-prevention programs and increasing counselling and rehabilitation programs. These will provide many more permanent jobs than the traditional megaprojects do.

As prime minister, then, I would allocate major funding to the education and the social science faculties to do the research and train the teachers to meet the needs of an ever-changing complex society. These professionally trained people are as important in creating a new society for the future as scientists and engineers were in creating the industrial era. Moreover, Canadians would not only be educated for work and self-development; they would also be educated for leisure.

New curricula would be designed to reflect the modern realities outlined in the five new movements now shaping our society. As well as the standard schools, whose primary goal is to provide all students with basic skills in our two common languages and in mathematics, we need boarding schools to provide each student with agricultural, wilderness, and community-living experience. If lifelong learning is to become a reality, schools must be open to all people at all ages and all stages of development. Financial resources must be channelled to community schools and to continuing education departments. Adults, immigrants, and those with special learning needs must be given greater opportunities to learn. We need, then, not fewer teachers but more, and teachers who are trained in a wider variety of disciplines with a wider variety of skills. Similarly, we need more and better-trained health-care workers, more police workers, and more day-care workers. Every segment of human services would benefit from such a national educational system.

Educational institutions in a free society must, above all, provide opportunities for all citizens to examine ideas and to determine how these ideas may usefully contribute to human understanding. Young people must be taught at a very early age how to be rational and objective. A major goal of my national education system would be to develop programs to raise critical awareness and to provide an alternative to the type of socialization offered by the mass media. The work done by our educators and behavioural scientists would be given a prominence equal to that of our scientists, technologists, engineers, and commerce and business entrepreneurs. It is imperative to get an understanding of our environment and our humanity into balance with our understanding of science and technology. Only if we develop an educational system such as the one I have outlined can we hope to create a new mentality for Canadians—one that deals in prevention and nurturing, not punishment and conquering. Moreover, as this national education program developed, it would create a multiplicity of jobs of a lasting nature, which in turn would improve our economic base.

Yet major reforms of any aspect of Canadian life cannot be superimposed by an authoritarian government. Government can initiate ideas and can govern, but changes will only work when there is a sufficient number of citizens who are educated and committed to creating a new society. This vision can become a reality if we use our modern technology to bring about greater communication, both domestically and internationally. Canada could become a leader among world nations. All we need is a new type of political will to legislate for constructive changes. The industrialized world as a whole is undergoing a metamorphosis to a trans-industrial society, and Canada could be one of the first nations to acknowledge and identify this fundamental transformation. In so doing, we could then act in such a way as to reduce the social disruptions which normally accompany such major transition periods.

Canadians are, I believe, among the most privileged people in the world. We live in a country second to none. "To whom much has been given, much will be required." It seems to me that Canadians are now required to cast aside a mode of self-interest, to let go of pragmatic value systems and stagnant traditions, and to embrace a practice of sharing. The future cannot be taken for granted; it must be consciously and conscientiously planned.

JAMES GILLIES

If I were prime minister, I would recognize that in the last decades of the twentieth century Canada must be transformed from a nation whose wealth is based on resources to one whose wealth is based on knowledge and technology. I would realize that unless this transformation was made, it would be impossible to achieve any other goals for the nation—cultural, social or regional—and that the standard of living of Canadians would inevitably decline.

To make this change, however, will not be easy. I know that Canada is a trading nation—almost 35 per cent of the Gross National Product is generated from trade—and that historically most of the trade has been in natural resources, semi-finished products, and agriculture. While John A. Macdonald's National Policy involved the use of tariffs to create a small manufacturing sector in Ontario and Quebec, the basic public policy in Canada for over a century has been designed for other purposes: to expand international markets for agricultural products, raw materials, and semi-processed resources by reducing barriers to international trade; to keep tariffs low on those imports that might increase the cost of production of resources; to avoid anything that would in any way jeopardize trade with the United States, by far Canada's largest market; and, finally and perhaps most importantly, always to encourage an inflow of capital.

Implicit in the policies based on resource development is the assumption that there will always be a great international demand for Canada's products. Unfortunately, in the past two decades the demand for natural resources has declined, not because manufacturing has become less important in the world economy (the reverse is true) but because the amount of raw materials needed to produce manufactured goods has dropped. There is less steel in cars and none in microchips; newsprint is thinner; 50 to 100 kilograms of fibre optics transmit as many telephone messages as 2000 kilograms of copper.

Moreover, at the same time that the demand for raw materials has declined, the supply has increased. Third World countries with modern technology have become major low-cost producers of most resources, and they compete effectively against Canadian suppliers—so effectively, indeed, that in market after market Canadians are supplying a smaller and smaller share of the total demand. In agriculture the story is the same. Canadian markets are declining.

As if all this was not enough, the major market for Canadian exports, the United States, is dramatically changing. The industries that were the backbone for American growth (i.e., assembly-line mass-production manufacturing activities) have moved to what are euphemistically known as the lesser developed countries, the Third World countries. In sector after sector, where U.S. producers once dominated world markets, they do not even maintain their share of the domestic market and in many areas they are not trying to do so. The United States has moved from an economy based on large-scale mass-production industries to one built on knowledge and information, and this is not a change that a nation such as Canada, which derives much of its wealth from the sale of natural resources to the United States, can view with equanimity.

As the twentieth century draws to a close, it is apparent that Canadians can no longer maintain their standard of living simply by selling assets. Our assets are in less demand, they are highly priced (relative to competitors), and the basic economic structure of our major customer has changed. It is clear that the nineteenth-century strategy, which in many ways has served the nation well in the twentieth century, will be totally inappropriate for the twenty-first.

Competitive Advantage and Public Policy
If Canada is to be prosperous in the future, Canadian policy must be built on a recognition of the fact that a competitive advantage in world trade is now based on public policy, not on natural resources. It is public policy that explains why 18 million Taiwanese export four times more to the United States than 75 million Mexicans do, in spite of the fact that they are more than 6000 kilometres farther away from the market. It is public policy, not resources, that explains why Japan is rapidly becoming the wealthiest nation in the world, rather than a major exporter of rice. And it is public policy, not resources, that will determine whether, in the years ahead, Canadians will have an increasing share of world trade, and therefore a continuing high standard of living.

But how can we put in place new policies to take advantage of new conditions? How do we determine what those policies should be? How can an explicit consensus about the goals of the nation (and the policies to fulfil these goals) be created in a federal, pluralistic state? In a governmental system built on the consent doctrine, where policy-making is essentially the task of coming up with the lowest common denominator among competing groups, how can a national consensus be derived about anything? How can the national interest be put ahead of the interest of special groups? These are the central questions that must be answered if Canada is to have a coherent set of economic strategies that will maintain the Canadian standard of living in a rapidly changing world.

Creating a New Consensus

The task of obtaining a national consensus about goals is the task of government; and while, in this nation of many governments and overlapping jurisdictions, the locus of responsibility for doing so may be debated on constitutional and other grounds, as prime minister I would see it as my major responsibility to attempt to develop a new consensus about economic goals. Although I could not create the consensus, I could start the process by which one was created. No one else can do this: only the prime minister has the moral authority to put in place a mechanism whereby new goals for the nation can be specified. But it would not be an easy task. Indeed, in the face of provincial interests, strong bureaucracies, and endless special interest groups, it might be impossible to accomplish.

In a parliamentary democracy such as ours, the only place where a national consensus about economic goals can be created is parliament itself. With its elected representatives in the House, and with its senators (appointed in theory if not in fact to represent the interests of the regions), it is, moreover, the perfect place for the development of a consensus. Indeed, a standing committee of the House and Senate is the only body that has the potential legitimacy and credibility to create such a consensus, for it is the body before which everyone—cabinet members, provincial premiers, industrialists, union leaders, consumer advocates, economists—can appear to make their case as to what the economic goals of the nation should be. Such a committee cannot initiate and enact the policies necessary to fulfil the consensus. That is the task of the executive and the full legislature. But it can create the consensus.

There is a problem, however. In order to be an effective consensus-creating body, parliament must be perceived as having the legitimacy to perform the task. Unfortunately, neither part of parliament, the House of Commons nor the Senate, has at present such legitimacy. In the Commons the legislative arm (as opposed to the executive) has been relatively ineffective in the past half century. It has not adequately fulfilled its responsibilities of reviewing legislation and expenditures. Moreover, the fact that in recent years the national political parties have been anything but national has meant that policy vitally affecting a region has often been made with little representation from the people of that region. Finally, the rise in executive federalism has decidedly weakened the role of the legislature in the entire governing process. Yet none of these problems are overwhelming. They could be resolved without dramatic action.

The legitimacy and credibility of the Senate is another matter. In a democracy, no governmental body has legitimacy unless it is elected. Consequently, as prime minister, I would make the Senate an elected body. I would then charge a standing committee, composed of members of the House and the elected Senate, to begin the process of evolving a new consensus about the appropriate economic goals for the nation. If the whips were removed so that committee members were not bound by party positions, and votes in the committee were not votes of confidence in the government, there would be no reason why a committee made up of members from all parties and all regions could not develop the elusive consensus about goals. These goals would then form the basis of my government's policy.

From Consensus to Action

The introduction of the policies to achieve new goals would bring national gains of great positive proportion, but inevitably it would also bring catastrophically large losses to some people, firms, industries, and regions. It would be improper and politically infeasible that while all would share in the gains from change, only a few should shoulder the burden of the losses. To be certain that such inequity did not happen, I would initiate the organization of permanent advisory bodies with representatives from all groups affected by change. These sector groups would report to a deputy prime minister and would be charged with recommending how gains and losses should be shared.

None of the policies would be designed to pick winners. That is something the market can do. The thrust of the approach would be to get out of the losers—to move resources from ineffective use to productive use. For example, it might be judged better to place $100 million of regional development support per annum into a high-technology university, rather than providing an annual subsidy to keep an inefficient plant in operation. But the realities of modern democracies are such that if the plant was closed, both fairness and politics would require that appropriate compensation (as judged by the groups affected) would be made available to those who lost by the change.

Facing Reality

As prime minister I would view the Canadian situation as a race between institutional inertia and international change, and would understand that institutional inertia has been winning hands down. It may seem undramatic to spend one's time as prime minister in structuring new ways of making decisions and developing consensus. Parliamentary and governmental reform may seem a weak reed on which to rest Canada's economic future. But it is not. If reform does not take place, the Canadian economy will decline, and social programs and cultural aspirations will not be fulfilled—because resources will not be available to support them.

Canadians must face reality. It is almost an axiom that any nation that becomes rich by selling its natural assets—but does not use the product of the sale to restructure its economy—is certain to become poor. The fact is that Canada is in such a situation, and consequently it must create a new economic base for growth and development. To do so requires the elimination of many existing programs and the development of new ones. This can only be done, however, by changing the existing institutional structures.

The fundamental problem in Canada is not lack of economic knowledge; everyone knows that resources must be used efficiently, that research and development should be increased, that certain subsidies should be dropped, that markets should be allowed to work more effectively and that they should be larger, and so on. But we do not have a process in place to get these things done.

As prime minister I would know that I had one overriding and unavoidable task—to put in place the institutional framework that would make it politically possible to transform the Canadian economy from one that is based on natural resources to one based on technology and knowledge. I would appreciate that this is a political and organizational task—not an economic one—and I would therefore dedicate myself to bringing about the requisite institutional changes that would make the transformation possible.

I would realize that this is a monumental task and that it would probably mean that I would be a one-term prime minister. But I would also know that if I achieved my goal, the twenty-first century could belong to Canada.

JOHN GODFREY

A will to participate in history is also, after all, a will to belong to mankind, to nations, to privileged moments... the realm of legend.

André Malraux

The African famine made a community of the world in 1985, a historic fact in itself.

The Globe and Mail,
22 January 1986

I am pleased to announce the Government of Canada's new policy towards Africa. Previous Canadian governments have been very generous to Africa, particularly after world television revealed the extent of the famine gripping the continent in late 1984. But gradually, as world media attention has turned away, Canadians have lost sight of the challenges and opportunities for Canada in Africa in the years ahead.

Why Africa? Because the challenge of Africa remains the challenge of our generation. In 1984 the outside world finally awoke to the fact that Africa was suffering the greatest ecological disaster of modern history. The crisis had been building for twenty-five years. At its height, the lives of 35 million of our fellow human beings in twenty-four African countries were threatened. Millions died before we woke up and intervened at the last possible moment.

That intervention was the most successful effort in international co-operation ever mounted. The financial response from people around the globe was overwhelming. Canada was a leader. The crisis was alleviated, and nature helped when the rains returned. But the underlying problems remain and the crisis will return in force if we do not remain involved. Then how will history judge us?

Canada today faces its own problems. On the global scale, we seem helpless when threatened with the possibility of nuclear annihilation. Continentally, we seem destined to follow forever the lead of the Americans. Within Canada, our young people lack a sense of purpose, of mission, and seem consigned either to a life of unemployment or of thoughtless, self-centred consumerism. Our industries have trouble competing in world markets. Most important, as a country we seem to have lost our way, our sense of what we are to do and be internationally, of our historic purpose.

Thirty years ago another prime minister of Canada, Lester Pearson, proposed the creation of the first United Nations Emergency Force for peacekeeping. Today, I am proposing the creation of the first United Nations Development Corps to deal with future disaster relief operations in Africa and other developing areas of the world. Canada will offer to contribute to and to co-ordinate the deployment of non-combatant military units specializing in engineering, transportation by air, sea, and land, communications, medical and health support, and logistics. Such a multinational corps, wearing the blue berets of the United Nations, would be sent on the specific request of a developing nation and would be part of a United Nations team.

Canada is today challenging other nations in the developed world to follow our lead in creating the United Nations Development Corps. Not only would deployment in a difficult "real life" situation far from our shores provide valuable training for our own armed forces personnel; it would also represent a real, if modest, transfer of resources from military to humanitarian purposes. The extraordinary sight of Russian, British, Libyan, Canadian, and East German aircraft gathered at Addis Ababa airport in December 1984 to work for a common purpose—saving lives—gave us a glimpse of a future in which the people of the world might concentrate their resources on protecting each other rather than investing in ever more sophisticated and unstable systems of destroying ourselves.

My second major proposal relates to the Maritime provinces and has two aspects: the creation of an organization to be known as Emergency Measures International, to be located in Halifax, and the simultaneous unveiling of a new industrial strategy for the Maritimes to provide the research, training, and appropriate scale technologies required by developing countries. Again, these policies have been inspired by our experience in Africa, but the future benefits are not limited to that continent alone.

Emergency Measures International (EMI) will consist of a worldwide communications centre to be located in the World Trade Centre in Halifax. It will function as a combination volunteer fire department and commercial expediting operation. In international emergencies, such as those caused by the African famine or the Mexican earthquake, the centre would co-ordinate Canadian relief efforts in close co-operation with the appropriate authorities in Ottawa. The use of ships and civilian and military aircraft, the assembling of emergency medical shipments, and the formation of appropriate teams of personnel for immediate dispatch overseas would be co-ordinated by the EMI centre, drawing on lists of personnel and supplies prepared beforehand. With their concentration of ports, airports, military resources, and medical facilities, the Maritime provinces are ideally located and equipped to undertake such operations.

Since emergencies are infrequent and unpredictable, during quiet periods the centre would apply its expertise to worldwide commercial express expediting—airlifting drilling parts for oil rigs in West Africa, for example, or assisting Canadian industries in global rush-freighting. Once the EMI centre became known as the "Red Adair of international expediting," not only would the exports of Maritime industries benefit, but the region would begin to develop a different reputation in Canada, and a different perception of itself. The humanitarian program would be, as it were, the "loss leader" of an international transportation and trading network which would take its lead in this field from the success of countries such as the Netherlands and Singapore.

The new industrial strategy for the Maritimes will be directed to assisting Africa and the rest of the developing world. Rather than jumping on the Silicon Valley bandwagon, the Maritimes will concentrate on refining and developing technologies that are appropriate in assisting developing countries in agriculture, at the village level, and in the area of ocean resources. What Africa needs is not the microchip but a good, reliable water pump. What Bangladesh needs is a small indestructible tractor for rice farmers, not STOL aircraft.

Maritime industries have already developed certain export markets in Africa and the developing world: they now export ambulances, for example, as well as fishing gear. They will be further encouraged to make this export market their special niche, taking advantage of Canada's excellent reputation in Africa and the Third World.

Maritime universities will be called upon to support this initiative by training a new generation of young Canadians to work in Africa and elsewhere. A new species of engineering studies will be created— development engineering—whose graduates will produce not high-tech solutions but enduring low-tech projects that are consistent with the specific culture of the people involved. The federal government will support training in tropical medicine, outpost nursing, development studies, language, and all other forms of education that will make the Maritimes Canada's voice for international development abroad. African students will be given special assistance to attend Maritime universities.

The third proposal in our new African strategy is to give new support and direction to Canadian non-governmental development agencies. Every new crisis produces new responses and solutions. From the African crisis we learned about the strengths and weaknesses of traditional Canadian involvement in Africa. We discovered, for example, that many of the international non-governmental organizations to which Canadians give so generously are simply word-processing centres in Toronto which pass the money along to their headquarters in New York or London, and that when the money is finally spent in Africa, no credit or recognition is given to Canadians for their contributions.

It is important that Canadian-based development organizations with Canadian personnel in the field in Africa be strengthened, and that international organizations be strongly encouraged to develop distinctive Canadian programs abroad. Frequently, these organizations receive extensive funding from the Canadian government, as well as from the Canadian public. It is vital that Canada and Canadians receive appropriate credit in Africa. It is important, too, that when these organizations purchase equipment such as trucks for use in Africa, Canadian manufacturers be given a fair chance to bid. There is no dishonour in helping both Africans and ourselves.

Finally, we intend to involve the people of Canada directly in the African recovery process. How can the average Canadian play any meaningful role in Africa? A new idea has been emerging in the Maritimes and Ontario called Adopt-a-Village or village twinning. This scheme takes its inspiration from the Foster Parents Plan and from the experience of Canadian families and communities a few years ago in adopting "boat people." Rather than being overwhelmed by the vastness of the crisis in Africa and therefore doing nothing, Adopt-a-Village arranges for individual Canadian communities to "adopt" a single African village, to learn more about its problems, to follow its story through bad times and good, to put people here in touch with people there, and to provide whatever assistance is required to help the village become self-sufficient. The idea is to move beyond the quick fix to a long-term relationship between Africans and Canadians.

The Maritime provinces led the way by adopting the village of Degahbur in Ethiopia and raising over $500,000 to buy a truck and mobile medical clinic, to drill wells, to inoculate children, to build a school, and to establish health centres. The key to success in such a project is communications—the role of television proved to be critical. The local ATV supper-hour host, Dave Wright, went twice to Degahbur and produced two specials on the village, giving Maritimers a first-hand account of how their money was being spent.

The idea has since spread to a dozen communities in Ontario (such as Toronto, Scarborough, Ottawa, the Ottawa Valley, Thunder Bay, and Durham County) as well as to Montreal, Britain and the United States. We believe that the Adopt-a-Village concept has earned its place as a unique Canadian contribution to international development and that it should be encouraged to spread throughout Canada and, indeed, throughout the rest of the world. I am therefore announcing today the establishment of the Canada-Africa Village Twinning Program.

The Government of Canada will work closely with Canadian communities and other groups, such as trade unions, co-operative organizations, and churches, in the development of the program. A small office will be established in Ottawa to serve as a clearing house, information centre, and monitor for the program. It will function essentially as a "dating service" to introduce Canadian communities and other constituencies to African villages. The centre will collaborate with Canadian-based non-governmental organizations (NGOs) working at the village level in Africa to create a list of potential villages to be adopted or twinned. The centre will also receive and investigate requests coming directly from villages and organizations in Africa. It will then attempt to match up appropriate villages with appropriate Canadian communities (for example, villages in francophone Africa with towns in Quebec).

Thus, a Canadian community will be twinned with an African village, through the intermediary of a Canadian or African NGO which will implement the program in the field. The NGO will report back directly to the Canadian community or constituency about the progress of the village and will propose new projects. An important component will be a school program linking schools in the Canadian community with the village school in Africa. To assist the twinning process, the government will match dollar for dollar the money raised in Canadian communities. The government will also arrange for a yearly visit by community representatives and journalists (especially from local television stations) to every village adopted by Canadians. The Department of External Affairs and the Canadian International Development Agency will provide every assistance for the program both in Canada and through Canadian personnel in Africa.

As with the United Nations Development Corps, the Canadian government intends to challenge other communities in the developed world to follow our lead. We have decided to collaborate with the Nairobi-based United Nations Environment Program (UNEP) to create an initial target of a hundred and fifty adopted villages in drought-affected countries in Africa. To get the ball rolling, it is our aim that Canada will adopt twenty of these villages. Canada will undertake a pilot project, a prototype, to launch the first few villages with UNEP so that we can establish a framework and objectives, and prove the feasibility of the concept. Our own International Development Research Centre in Ottawa will co-ordinate the requisite research support. Through various international municipal twinning associations, trade unions, and service organizations, as well as through our own diplomats, we shall then issue our challenge to the world to match our Adopt-a-Village program. Enlisting the support of world television and local community television stations will be a critical factor for success. To revive interest in Africa, we need to launch a major, dramatic program. The global village may yet become a Canadian-inspired reality for the people of Africa.

This, then, is our new policy on Africa. It builds on our previous experience and good reputation in Africa. It concentrates our resources on the resolution of a major world problem. It gives back to Canada a sense of world mission. It offers young Canadians a challenge to live worthwhile lives in the service of humanity. It offers our manufacturers, engineers, and educators a blueprint for a new international strategy. It strengthens the role of the United Nations and contributes both to peace and to the preservation of the world environment. Most important, it will save future lives in Africa.

Canada alone can never solve the world's problems. Nor can we lecture and preach at the world to reform itself. What we can do is offer the world examples, successful models for solving difficult problems, and urge others to join with us in a common cause. We need to rediscover in ourselves some ethic of fraternity that will bring us together not only as Canadians but as citizens of the planet.

J. L. GRANATSTEIN

I am a Canadian historian by trade, and if I were prime minister I would certainly try to conduct myself in keeping with my understanding of the way our prime ministers have acted in the past. On a policy level, that would mean paying careful attention to the tariff (remember the National Policy) and worrying about the possibility of war (conscription is so divisive).

But such matters, while important, would initially have to take second place to the real and important benefits that accrue to those in power. Every prime minister, from John A. Macdonald to Brian Mulroney, has used his time in office to make himself comfortable and to take care of his friends and supporters. So I, my fellow Canadians, promise to do the same.

The first step is clear and hallowed by tradition: I shall redecorate the prime minister's residence on Sussex Drive. The pool that Pierre Trudeau's friends had installed for him is getting ratty at the edges and needs replacement. I want a hot tub, too, and a sauna. The taste of my predecessors was execrable (Mila's washroom!), and new wallpaper and rugs (in earth tones, I think) are essential. The kitchen, while large and airy, lacks the homey touch for conversations with my kitchen cabinet so must be redone to get rid of the arborite. And I think a few new cedar decks on the river side of the house would be a nice touch (and we must be sure to use B.C. shakes and shingles somewhere). I expect these items will come in at about $3 million, a mere pittance.

We shall also need a new chef (my predecessor's cook couldn't boil water properly, and I think the real reason I won the election was that his cabinet never recovered from its collective indigestion). As well, we'll need one or two more household staff and (I know I said during the campaign that I wouldn't do this, but it is essential) a nanny to interface with the kids. Why shouldn't the state pay for all these things? After all, the people expect their prime minister to live like an emperor. In keeping with this, the nation will pay for all the food we eat. We do entertain on official business a great deal, and it is so hard to figure out if tomorrow's eggs are for my breakfast or for the working lunch with the media.

Now, no one has ever said I am a fool. The leader of the opposition, I am certain, will feel exactly the same about her government-provided residence as I do about the Sussex Drive house. So whatever she wants in renovations is hers for the asking. This will guarantee that there is no criticism from across the floor of the House about the alterations I'm making; and if I ever lose power (perish the thought), it will mean that I can redecorate the opposition leader's house to my taste.

Fortunately, there will also have to be renovations to my offices in the Parliament Buildings and the Langevin Block. My predecessor had this unhappy fascination with old Canadian pine furniture (did you see the size of his liquor cabinet?), and I prefer Danish rosewood. I'd like a desk the size of an aircraft carrier, new rugs, of course, in the party colours, a completely redone bathroom (make sure they remember the sauna), and completely new furniture. And if I do this, I can scarcely deny the same things to my cabinet colleagues—every single member of the previous lot had the taste of a lumberjack.

By the way, we shall have to increase the size of the ministry. I know that Mulroney was criticized for having forty in his cabinet, but I think fifty is now essential, given the complexity of modern government—and the need to take care of my friends and to neutralize my enemies within the party. That little rat who turned against me at the leadership convention will just love being minister of science and technology.

Well, this takes care of the immediate physical comforts and problems. Now to the important matter of jobs for the boys (and girls). All members of my office when we were in opposition are now employed in the Prime Minister's Office—at a higher grade and salary. Although we denounced the previous PM for increasing the size of the PMO, we will, naturally, make ours even bigger. I expect to counter the complaints of the opposition at this gutting of a campaign promise by attacking the public service and ramming through all the cuts there that I can, particularly of those senior officials named by the *ancien régime*. They were all party hacks, every one of them, and I have some first-rate men and women from the private sector (and our party ranks) to put into those slots. I'm sure this will make a major difference to the efficiency of the civil service, as well as repaying hundreds of debts to those who helped us in the dark days of opposition.

Then there is patronage, the "business side of politics," as Senator Norman Lambert who ran Mackenzie King's election machine called it. Lambert used a tollgate system that extracted 10 per cent of the cost of government contracts as a contribution to the party, and he even charged lieutenant-governors a price for their posts. I wholly support this tradition and will see that it is implemented. The party fee for a lieutenant-governorship will be a minimum of $100,000—a bargain price for one who will be hailed ever after by the common folk as "Your Honour." A senatorship has less honour but lasts longer. So let's say $150,000. Ambassadorships will vary; London or Paris or Rome must go for $200,000, but Ougadougou and Kinshasa will be reserved for the professionals in the Foreign Service—some campaign promises, after all, cannot be broken. Fortunately, I have thousands of posts on commissions and boards, and I trust my staff to work out an appropriate sliding scale for these. But remember that it's only our supporters who get a chance to bid for these posts. I won't appoint a member of any other party to anything until everyone on our side has had his reward.

Then there are the advertising contracts. The government is Canada's largest contractor for advertising, and the old bunch used Bloor Street hacks with the creative instincts of newts. I prefer the admen who dreamed up the campaign that won us the election (picturing me mounted on a white horse was pure inspiration), and they deserve their reward. Also, I think it really is necessary that all government ads in the future should use our party's colours.

Lawyers, too, will have to be switched. I have to ensure that all the drug prosecutions in Vancouver, for example, are handled by our friends there. And I want each MP to draw up a list of party supporters who can provide services—from apples to embalming to uniforms—so that all government procurement is routed to our people.

Then there are policies—I guess we shall have to have some. I know we campaigned on a promise to give out more goodies to each and every region. I know we pledged to increase the armed forces and spend more on defence. I know we didn't say anything about free trade or selling crown corporations to the private sector. I know. I know.

But it is one thing to win an election and quite another thing to govern this fractious and divided nation. The simple truth is that bankers, newspaper publishers, and corporation presidents don't count for much in an election where the rich man's vote is worth no more than the welfare mother's; but they certainly matter after the votes are counted. They want cutbacks, and they'll get them. The bankers say they can do without the baby bonus and that the poor get too much for nothing. So all the universal social programs will get slashed and de-indexed.

I think I can find buyers for some crown corporations, especially the profitable ones, and those that lose money can probably be handed over scot-free to some American aircraft company. My friends on Bay Street and St. James Street (whoops, rue Saint-Jacques) tell me that things would go easier for business if there were a closer relationship with Washington, and I like that. So much nicer to have the president slap my back and call me by my first name than to have that mean SOB glowering at me and flexing his ICBMs. Unfortunately, the president won't be happy at our defence policy, but I hope the army can make do with obsolete weapons a bit longer. NATO and NORAD don't really need Canadian participation anyway, and we can mollify the retired colonels by returning the forces to the old uniforms. I'd bring back the Lee-Enfield rifle if I thought it would save money. After all, don't we still live in a fire-proof house far from inflammable materials, exactly as Senator Raoul Dandurand told the League of Nations in the 1920s?

Finally, this government is going to keep its secrets to itself. The worst sin in my books is telling the press anything. If it's in the *Globe and Mail* Monday morning, you can be sure that some attention-grabbing opposition MP will be asking about it in question period that day. One of our high-priority items, therefore, has to be to shut off this flow of news. All statements will have to be cleared through the PMO. We'll gag the bureaucrats and put the fear of god into them, and threaten any minister with his walking papers if he says a word he shouldn't. And let's alter the Access to Information Act. We'll tell everyone that we're making access easier, but I think that if we play it right (and stress the ascendancy of the Privacy Act), we can buffalo everyone and close off virtually all access. The best government, I always say, is the government that leaks least.

These are my principles, my friends, and if you don't like them, I can always change. I do want to assure you that every bit of this program is sanctioned by the past. There is nothing here, not one iota, not one jot or tittle, that hasn't been done to you by one or another of your governments. Tradition matters, after all, and I propose to let the past be my guide.

RAY GUY

The hardest and most important job facing any Canadian prime minister is how to straighten out the problem of the Canadian–U.S. border by putting some kinks in it. It's a problem so weighty and so obvious that it has gone largely unnoticed and unaddressed.

To make an analogy, when some Australian Aborigines first gazed on tall, billowing European ships in Botany Bay, their reaction seems odd to us. They simply looked away. They convinced themselves the ships weren't really there. Anthropologists tell us (and if at all encouraged, anthropologists will tell us the damndest things) that because the ships were completely outside any of their points of reference, the Aboriginal brain simply could not register them. So it is with much of the Canadian–U.S. border. It's so ludicrously, improbably, unnaturally straight that the rational mind just can't take it in. There's such a ridiculous excess of it that it's ignored—like dandelions or anthropological theories.

It's one of the longest straight lines in the world. A carpenter might have snapped a chalked line on a map of North America. A youngster might have slapped it down with a ruler and a Crayola. The damage this does to Canada's image among the family of nations is incalculable. Who can take a country seriously that lays down its boundary with such gross indifference? Until it's mussed up a bit all the way from Vancouver to the Lake of the Woods, we'll always be second or third rate.

Even the most "primitive" of peoples treat it as a huge joke. Stoop down and draw a map of Canada in the dust before some mean jungle hut and when you get to the bottom part towards the left, the natives fall about in gales. They pound it off down the jungle telegraph as "Your Morning Smile." Being children of nature themselves, they know instinctively that there is no such thing in nature as a straight line. It's the largest jest since someone suggested an imaginary lion running around the circumference of the earth. Canadians, if not the gods, must be crazy.

In what are sometimes called the more developed countries our 3000-kilometre-long national shame is no less an object of japery and ribaldry. For example, the boundaries of European countries look like so many ravelled sleeves of care. They're as convoluted as a budgerigar's guts and hence the height of sophistication. For tens of centuries, Europeans have harried each other up hill and down dale, pulling up boundary stakes or planting them according to the ebb and flow of altercations. What laughable bumpkins Canadians must seem to old and suave cultures who fiddle their boundaries almost as often as they diddle their mistresses.

What makes it even worse is that part of the fantastically absurd and dead straight line runs through the Rockies. Here is one of the lumpier parts of the earth's surface. Yet so vast was Canadian indifference and naiveté that our boundary perfectly bisects eagles' nests and subdivides mountain goat pastures. We've tolerated this severe handicap for too long. When a Canadian prime minister visits a slum in India and asks, "What is the totality of your acreage?" is it any wonder he's greeted by waves of Hindi yuk-yuks? In the back of his hosts' minds must be the obvious riposte, "And what is the totality of your string-straight, dead-level, crow-flight, jogger-trance, baby-dream boundary?"

Taken in much smaller doses, a straight boundary here and there may escape the world's scorn and censure. For instance, a few states in the Sahara Desert have edges scribed by the yardstick, some even in dotted lines. This makes sense of a kind because the next passing camel train will scuff them out anyway. Saskatchewan describes itself as a rectangle. It's shaped like a refrigerator door, but only the most uncharitable make mock. That province's Latin motto, "Ne quadratum sasqus est," or "No Squares Here," is self-mocking enough to defuse most unkind barbs. Plus, in much of Iberia and all of the Balkan states, Saskatchewan is believed to be a mythical giant kraken.

A curious aspect of this whole fiasco is that while Canada's fortunes in the wider world have been stunted, frustrated, and seriously hampered by its outrageously careless boundary, the United States, which shares it, is seldom made mock of on the same account. Some political scientists contend that this is because the United States can make bigger bangs than most of the countries which would otherwise be inclined to snicker, smack their backsides, and make kissy noises. Others hold that the United States is spared because the rest of the world has long come to grips with its obsession (Germanic, almost) with mathematical order and the ritualistic subversion of nature. As proof, these latter point to the precise number of chips that always come with a Big Mac "quarter-pounder" and to the invention of those curious paper strips across motel toilet bowls which assure: "Sanitized For Your Protection." It might also be noted that while no more than six lonesome cowboys, a large elk herd, and some befuddled cruise missiles occupy the American side of the barmy blah-line, much of Canada's population is strung out like a grotesque string of rosary beads on our side, which attracts the great heft of incredulous world attention.

A few miserable pessimists are bound to claim that it can't be done—that putting some crooks and crannies in our border, thereby recovering some shreds of international respect, is impossible. But a strong-willed, far-seeing, messianic, not-quite-certifiable sort of prime minister such as myself would respond that without a mussed-up boundary, all else is but spaghetti without the sauce; that if the monstrous offhandedness of our forefathers is not corrected, even St. Pierre and Miquelon will write rude words on our children's bottoms; that we will continue to be the sport of mankind and get no more Pizza Hut franchises if border kinks are not forthcoming.

The answer to the problem may be as simple and as simple-minded as the problem itself. What, for instance, are the prospects of taking two volunteer patriots, seating them on a combine harvester at Lake of the Woods with a case of Seagram's VO apiece, and pointing them in the general direction of Vancouver? I know dozens of unemployed and willing duos in Newfoundland alone who would be glad to make the sacrifice. I can't see any danger of interference from either the U.S. or the U.N. By the time they got many kilometres west they'd be turning both Coutts, Alberta, and Sweetgrass, Montana, into valuable stock-piles of shredded breakfast cereal with perfect impartiality.

My first and paramount act as prime minister would therefore be to summon the cabinet and set forth the greatest and most momentous project in Canadian history. Impossible? Don't give me that line!

CÉLINE HERVIEUX-PAYETTE

A LETTER TO MY DAUGHTERS, NATHALIE, DOMINIQUE AND ISABELLE.

My three loved ones:

What a challenge! I think the question should be changed to: "Why would I want to be prime minister?"

There is so little democracy in this world, the word justice has been so much abused, sharing between individuals and countries is coming about so slowly, and there is so much bigotry on the political scene that one might well ask why one would go into politics. I guess the answer is that those who are there must have a great sense of commitment to our country, to our people, and to the rest of the world. In 1982, when we patriated the Canadian constitution, entrenching a Charter of Rights in it, I was tremendously proud of us and I had a feeling that I was part of the history of this country. So few countries of this world have such a comprehensive constitutional Charter of Rights: a law above all others guaranteeing fundamental rights and freedom to every citizen. So, for a newcomer in politics like myself, it was pretty exciting to begin a career by adopting the fundamental rules I have always believed in. The equality clause for women, especially, was a very dear project to me, and I hope that your generation will be the first to benefit to the full extent from the advantages of this clause. Of course, it will be up to you, my three daughters, to make sure it is respected.

I was proud, yes. But at the same time I was a bit ashamed that the provinces would only agree to it if we included a "notwithstanding" clause. This makes it possible for a government to remove the rights of its people for the common interest. Too many abuses have been committed in the past under cover of this excuse. Government could, for instance, limit the right to associate. We know that unions are not the most popular institutions these days, but we have to recognize that if the workers today are an essential and respected ingredient of our economy, it is because of those who fought for their rights at the beginning of this century.

So I think there is some work left for anyone who asks herself why she would like to be prime minister of this country and for the individual Canadians who make up this nation. To consider governing a country like Canada and growing with it is certainly a big challenge, and it is not the task of only one person but of a team. I suppose the team has to have a leader who will inspire its members and act as a guide for them and for the country.

A government must, after all, lead from the front. For instance, let's take a very controversial subject: the death penalty. It is being discussed right now, as I write to you, purely on political grounds. It's not a question of whether it is appropriate now or of whether the Canadian people wish to have it restored at this time. What any politically aware Canadian should question is the motivation and wisdom of a leader who would bring such a question, with all the negative passions it arouses, onto the agenda of the House of Commons. If I were prime minister today, I would have resisted caucus and explained why I would not introduce such a divisive issue. A country like Canada would certainly not win prestige by restoring the death penalty. It is not just a question of morality. I feel that when we agree in our constitution that everyone in this country has a right to live and, as we say in the Charter, not to be submitted to any cruel and unusual treatment, it would be difficult to conclude that parliament should pass a bill that would allow us deliberately to kill those guilty of certain murders.

There are other questions being discussed today which I would certainly not discuss in the same way if I were prime minister. One is free trade, which was studied in depth by the Macdonald Commission. So if I were a Liberal prime minister, how would I tackle that issue? Certainly, it is high on the political agenda of the Liberals to encourage trade between Canada and the United States. But at the same time, one can see why we have all the reasons in the world, as a medium-sized country, not to abandon the rest of the club of medium-sized countries and stop playing the game with them. That is where our interest lies. We have a giant at our door and there are other agreements with medium-sized countries through an organization called GATT. These agreements on the liberalization of trade are multilateral, and the argument from strength is certainly more balanced when you are part of that group than when you are negotiating alone. So far, since we started the discussion, the Conservative government has been giving away most of our trump cards—FIRA, the National Energy Program, and so on—and gaining nothing from it. We are backtracking day after day, yet not getting to the point of making it easier for Canadians to do business on both sides of the border.

Yes, there will be an agreement. It will not be a free-trade agreement. It will probably be an agreement that will settle some disputes, and I think that we should examine it carefully. Still, I trust that the ten premiers of this country will check and see if it is in the Canadian people's interest and that the overall agenda will make sure that Canada is a place that will continue to grow, that its economy will be restored, and that we will break down most of the barriers that have been damaging to our economy.

This exercise should take place within Canada too. We have a lot of barriers between the provinces. There is much unfair competition in practice, and there is distrust of each other and of the present leadership: the prime minister, who was supposed to reconcile each premier, is not showing very strong leadership. So I am obliged to say that if I were prime minister right now, I would stop begging my neighbour to stand on my foot and I would call for fair play with the American people.

I am not against the American people. I share many of their values. But I stress that our Canadian heritage is too precious to be diminished. We have a system, the federation of ten provincial governments and a national government, inherited from British ancestors, which I consider the best in the world, considering our reality (i.e., our geography, our demography, and our economy). With the autonomy of both levels of government in different fields (for instance, foreign affairs and defence at the national level, and education and social affairs at the provincial level), this allows Canada to carve a place in the world as a country, and it allows the provinces, like us in Quebec, to develop our culture according to our own priorities.

At this point, I feel that if I were prime minister, I would ensure that we gave ourselves the tools to face the post-industrial revolution based on science, research and development, and finally on human resources, rather than on our conventional base for economic development, our natural resources.

We have a tremendous potential. My daughters, your generation is the best educated in our history. But we have serious problems in synchronizing our efforts. A federal leader should, at this point in our history, play a major role in stimulating both the private sector and the provincial governments to face that challenge.

Our education system is suffering from serious gaps. We refuse to promote excellence, possibly because we are looking at the experience of Japan—where the success of a student is obtained at all costs, even emotional and psychological development—or possibly because of our own modern education system, which doesn't accept any form of measurement of progress because it might give students trauma.

Let us be realistic; there must be a kind of balance between the competition in applied sciences and the laisser-faire of the social sciences. When I want us to have, as a nation, the best-prepared people to face the challenge of the twenty-first century, I don't eliminate the arts from the curriculum. I stress that we should come back to basics, such as the recognition of success. But I must emphasize that unless there is a national, cohesive effort in this respect, our economic growth will remain vulnerable. In the applied sciences, we already have a strong base. We should continue our research in our basic industries of agriculture, forestry, and fisheries. In mining, we should experiment with new alloys for new applications in many industries, present and future, such as aerospace or developing the oceans, or the automotive, petroleum, and chemical industries.

But the most important ingredient for our future is the Canadian people. We are seen by the rest of the world as a country of opportunities. Here again, I think that tradition is the essence for the growth of our country. We are faced with a twofold problem. One you are familiar with, the growing racism towards immigrants. The other one, which you are aware of because I was very concerned with the issue when I was elected, is the problem of aboriginal Canadians. I had to concentrate my efforts on the restoration and protection of the status of Indian women, which they lost when they married a non-Indian, while Indian men not only kept their status but could grant it to their wives. It was a blatant discrimination clause which had existed for nearly a century and with which male Indians were not too preoccupied.

Under the leadership of various Liberal prime ministers, the status of Indians started to evolve to give them a proper place in *their* country. For more than the first half of this century, they were still being treated as second-class citizens, just as we women were. With them, we were under the white tutorship of the dominant male ruling class. We were rarely educated; we had no access to the real power, which is economic autonomy. The aboriginal people had a folklore role; we had a socio-organic role. We, like them, were informally consulted, affected by the decision but not involved in the formal process. You may begin, my darlings, to understand why it is so important for a mother of three daughters to recognize this equality clause in the Canadian Charter of Rights of 1982. Because, finally, in the first law of the land, we are recognized as equal to men. Even our American neighbour has not had the courage to entrench this ERA clause in its Bill of Rights.

These are not futile battles just for the sake of haunting the tribunals; they are the base of the social contract established in our country. In the years to come you will experience the positive and dynamic impact of these clauses. In a society, any unfair treatment or negation of a right deriving from a racial, linguistic, sexual, or other background creates a climate for dissension and division. If a country is to grow, each individual should expect full recognition as a human being, with all his or her cultural heritage. It is the combination of all these differences that makes Canada unique in the world, and it is respect for these differences that will give us the strength to influence our own future and the future of the rest of the world.

If I were prime minister, I would build on this feature and make sure that I assumed the kind of leadership necessary to lay the ghosts of discrimination that come back regularly to haunt us.

Take, for example, the refugee crisis that we had recently over Tamil, Chilean and Turkish people. As prime minister, I would not have panicked but would have admitted that we needed to review our legislation on immigration and refugees; I would have inspired myself with the precedent of the Vietnamese "boat people," and in consultation with the United Nations High Commissioner for Refugees and U.S. Immigration, I would have faced the crisis with flexibility, rather than victimizing those who were seeking asylum in our country. Instead of stimulating bigotry and racism in the Canadian people, I would have appealed to their generosity, which has never failed, as we witnessed in the case of Ethiopia.

If the strength of a country is first its people, as prime minister I would be concerned by the stabilization or decline of our population. We are going to live longer, and this will create a burden for the work force—for you, my daughters, and your children—if we don't plan today for a demographic policy that will assure enough people in the productive sector. Even though the manufacturing industry is reducing the number of jobs by robotics and automation, the major change that we can foresee now in the economy is in the world of leisure. Since the beginning of this century we have reduced the working week by almost half and we have switched the rural population from the majority to less than 5 per cent; so we can adapt ourselves to major changes. But to maintain our standard of living, one of the best in the world, we must devote a lot of attention to balancing our population. A prime minister of a country is a bit like a parent. Both must make decisions for the future that will not necessarily bring them much credit. But with or without a poll, I think that Canada should have a generous immigration policy. We are blessed with peace and prosperity, and we should not be afraid to share.

Another way of controlling our demography is, of course, through a family policy. This is a serious matter, in which you are involved. You know how eager I am to be a grandmother. But I recognize that today it is not very encouraging to have babies and plan a career. Our society—and, I must confess, some schools of thought in the feminist movement—seem to discriminate against women who choose to be housewives and mothers. Anyhow, it has not been a major preoccupation among our male politicians to have a special place in government priorities for maternity. Yet it is an immense responsibility to have children, and it should be shared. Society has tolerated violence to mother and child too long, and we are just beginning to realize that it is a very important problem.

In the past, the notion of family was different from that of today. Policy planners at all government levels never took a global approach when tackling the growing social problems arising from major shifts in the population. Even today, when we talk about providing child-care programs, the solutions are short term and costly. It is not necessarily a universal day-care system we need. It is a system that will make the family the cornerstone of our future as a society, one that will stop penalizing parents who dare to have children. It will even encourage the restoration of a link with grandparents. We isolate individuals who have problems. Day-care is necessary when a parent is working outside the home, but why should it be institutionalized? A grandparent or a neighbour could do the same thing. Are we ready to use our imagination to consider other options, sometimes more flexible, that we can afford?

Another growing problem is our older people. Are we going to continue to isolate them in institutions? Again, there is a great lack of innovation in their care. We have opted, again, to discharge our responsibility on the collectivity. But is it a success? Unless older people need to be hospitalized, how can we tolerate continuing to park them in senior citizens' homes, apart from the rest of society? They have talents and experience; they are a resource that we tend to ignore. It is as if they became obsolete the day they retired. If we all live longer, as can be expected, it is about time we devoted our energy to giving a proper place in our society to the preceding generation. They can still contribute, but we have decided that as long as they are fed, housed, and receive medical attention, they should be happy. If I were prime minister, I would be inclined to ask them what they want today. They are considered only once every four years by the politicians. We should be ready to listen to their dreams and to care for them every day.

To complete my tour of our society, I would not like to forget those we tend to ignore because they have no place in the system, namely welfare recipients—those we accuse of laziness, of lack of courage, and so on. You remember our neighbours who were on welfare. You saw a very disturbed cell of our society. Even in your teens, you tried to help them. It was far beyond our competence. A drunken father, a disturbed mother, juvenile-delinquent children, battered wife and children, a totally disorganized family. Poor nutrition, no discipline, no hope. I must confess that if I were prime minister, I would be very much concerned by this phenomenon. I would make the fight against poverty a priority. Each year, a Decima poll tells us that Canadians want to share and are ready to help.

If I were prime minister, I would like to find the answer to why the aboriginal peoples are dying younger, why their children do not enjoy the same opportunity as ours, why they are poorer and less healthy. Those who are mentally or physically handicapped should be our main concern.

Why can we launch satellites in space and send astronauts to the moon and yet are not able to manage our planet? Why do we tolerate the increased rate of cancer and not question the way we treat our environment? Now that we know more about applied sciences, why don't we use that knowledge to improve our quality of life?

If I were prime minister I would work to find a solution to the declining demand for Canadian grain and would make the necessary shift to diversify the economy of the West, to restore the forests of our land, and to preserve the quality of our water.

The agenda is very long and should not ignore the role Canada can play in the rest of the world to improve the aid we give to Third World countries or to find a greater role for Canada as a broker between developed and developing countries. In this capacity, we would restore our reputation as a country that enjoys a special status before the United Nations, instead of being considered a valet of our big neighbour.

If I were prime minister, I would ask each and every Canadian (Canadians being great travellers) to be true ambassadors of our country around the world. We should use our dynamism and confidence to launch our country in the twenty-first century as a champion of freedom and peace.

If I were prime minister, I would invite all Canadians to earn the respect of their neighbours—whether they were one kilometre away or a thousand kilometres away—by giving their neighbours as much as they themselves have received from this country.

My darlings, you may ask yourselves why I am not talking about our institutions. It is mainly because I think it is easier to talk about structure and means than to determine our goals and objectives. If I were prime minister, as you can see from this letter, I would challenge the people of my country to trust themselves. To enjoy our freedom, each of us must have our basic needs fulfilled. So I would make this a prerequisite. This would be a global commitment that I would share with you, with my friends, and with all Canadians. And I think we could succeed in this attempt.

Would you help me?

Your Mom,
Céline.

HUGH HORNER

The first approach must be to the structure of the federal government. The present system will shatter if left unchanged. A "triple-E" Senate is essential—equal, elected, and effective. I suggest four senators elected from each province and four from the northern territories. They must have some power over the powerful forces of the Commons—which, essentially, is elected by central Canada.

The provinces would have to give up provincial preference and make trade and commerce truly free within Canada (with no behind-the-scenes manoeuvring, such as weight limits on transprovincial connecting highways or rigged bidding for construction and services). They would have to agree to a minimum standard of education, health, and social services. In return, they would get equal representation in an effective Senate that could veto (at least for a time) and could investigate and report.

The second approach to government structure must be to streamline and consolidate the federal government. The country is now run by bureaucrats from central Canada without regard to what is happening in the rest of the country. A good start would be to abolish the Treasury Board. It was not many years ago that this was a cabinet committee chaired by a senior member of cabinet. It has now grown into a second government with "specialists" in all areas. I cannot think of one positive thing this department has accomplished in the last ten years. But I do know that it has delayed decisions, procrastinated, and thrust for its own empire.

There needs to be a great reduction in the size of the civil service, especially in Ottawa. Consolidation of departments is a "must"—agriculture, forestry, and mines and energy for starters. We should make the role of parliamentary secretary to the ministers more meaningful so as to involve more of the government caucus. Indeed, the parliamentary secretary should be the liaison between the minister and the caucus, and should be able to answer in the House when the minister is absent.

The next step to streamlining government would be to pass a bill rescinding all orders-in-council that are more than fifteen years old. Give the departments six months to show that the orders-in-council are needed. This should be a rolling procedure so that each year new ones would come up for review (in effect, a working sunset clause).

Constitutionally, our native people need to be accommodated into our constitution by guaranteeing their treaty rights and granting them self-government rights to run their own affairs. An ongoing royal commission to settle outstanding land claims and to deal as an arbitration board for native people's concerns would allow for the dissolution of the Department of Indian Affairs and Northern Development.

Our policy on external affairs should follow the path that the Rt. Hon. Joe Clark is taking—a fair but firm stance with all, including the United States.

We need a new National Energy Policy that will ensure fair prices and self-sufficiency in the years ahead. A small tax per litre at the pumps across Canada would enable exploration and development to continue in Hibernia, Sable Island, and the Beaufort Sea, as well as in western Canada. At the very least, the Syncrude expansion and the Husky upgrader should take place. Sulphur-free western coal should be encouraged as an alternative to the high-sulphur coals now being imported from the United States. Whenever possible, the expanded use of the renewable hydropower should be encouraged, and this would include research into the feasibility of the so-called low-head hydro.

The next most important sector for a strong, united Canada is transportation. A coherent and national policy that relates to rail, road, air, and sea (including seaports) is required. Transportation must be declared an essential service, and strikes must be outlawed— though with a fair system of arbitration installed. We need to get on with the measures that the Mulroney government now has before parliament in regard to rail and air. We must have national standards for interconnecting highways between provinces. Never again must issues such as the one plaguing Vancouver (container clauses) be allowed to hurt so many innocent third parties.

Food production for ourselves, as well as for worldwide trade, must be carefully looked at. The structure and rules of the Canadian Wheat Board need bringing up to date. Wherever possible, we should be upgrading our grains and meats before shipping. Not only would this save on transportation costs but it would provide large numbers of jobs in this area across the country. We have various types of marketing boards and restrictions of one kind or another that block this important diversification and upgrading. If a marketing board is going to issue quotas, then, as a monopoly, it must be placed under a public utility board to ensure fair prices to the consumers. Those marketing boards which, in effect, are single-desk sellers and promoters of a product are of a different character and need no supervision as to price.

For wheat, our two-priced system is self-destructive. It causes consumers to pay more than they should for bakery products, and we are undercut by a flood of bakery products from other countries, particularly the United States. Far better to have a bakery products tax so that we could compensate farmers more fully. Such a tax would also apply to all imported cereal and bakery products. Our livestock producers generally favour free trade, but they cannot stand the dumping in Canada of red meats that are heavily subsidized in the home country (i.e., Irish beef and EEC pork products).

As an agriculturally based country, research and development are essential. There must be review and expansion in the key high-tech areas (biotechnology). And we should aim for a broadly based family-oriented agriculture with a real desire to ensure a healthy rural environment by upgrading, to the greatest degree possible, the products produced in those areas. The principle of natural advantage should apply.

Canada is also blessed with an abundance of other hard resources, both renewable (forestry and water) and non-renewable (coal and minerals). Good husbandry of these resources is really the legacy we leave to our children and grandchildren. This good husbandry means that we must take care not to pollute the environment, that we ensure an abundant supply of fresh water for Canadians, and that we again upgrade these resources here at home. Among other things, we need reforestation, fisheries renewal, resource identification, and land type evaluation.

To do all these things, it is important that all Canadian young people should have an opportunity to get the education and training that will enable us to develop the technology and processes required. It should be a federal responsibility to ensure a minimum standard of elementary education and opportunities for all at a higher level. Our higher centres of learning, such as the universities, have a need to strive for excellence in all ways, but in the sciences and technology in particular. This means a commitment by the federal government, which must co-ordinate research and development across the country. This must be done with fairness and with some regard to natural advantage (for instance, coal research where the coal is, and fisheries research on our two oceans). Everyone wants to jump on the high-tech bandwagon, so care and fairness should be the rule in this research.

In a large country such as Canada, which has huge resources and tremendous potential but a small population, trade is essential to our well-being, to our way of life, and to our very standard of living. It follows that the federal government should do all in its power to enhance worldwide trade through GATT and through bilateral agreements with other countries. Once we have concluded an agreement for fairer trade with the United States, we must turn our attention to Japan, Korea, and other Pacific Rim countries. The impediments to trade created by tariff and non-tariff barriers are just as evident in the Pacific Rim as they are in the United States. In this area of world trade, we need to upgrade the skills of our traders, our banks, our processors, and our manufacturing sectors. We need to become smarter, more knowledgeable about our trading partners, and tougher and more skilled in our approach.

Next, let me move to the social side of things. Let no one think that we can continue to have the social net we have without a sound, prosperous economic base. Unemployment insurance has been an important part of this social net; but there are improvements that can be made and alternatives that should be considered. One such consideration should be a voluntary two-year stint in the militia of our armed forces. What better way to train, enlighten, and broaden our young people in today's world? Not only would it increase national pride but it would be a real way to introduce young people to all parts of Canada. It would provide training, a chance at maturity, and would give these young people a wider range of options when choosing a career. It would also provide us with a trained group to deal with disaster of nature or man, and would at least give the impression that we are willing and able to defend ourselves from aggression. How much better and, indeed, more economical this would be than paying UIC!

There are many other measures I would like to see taken. These include joint federal-provincial programs to increase tourism and to train our young people in tourist services; a more pragmatic approach by labour, which should be working with business and government to adapt to technological change, while ensuring that jobs lost through change are replaced in other areas; a new criminal code more appropriate to the Canada of the 1980s and 1990s; simplification of the income tax laws, with a minimum tax being paid at all levels of income (this alone would greatly reduce the number of civil servants in financial departments), and consideration of the negative income tax plan put forward by Bob Stanfield and others. I would also like to see changes to the Canadian Broadcasting Corporation. The CBC could continue to be an important cultural and artistic component, but a national communications system owned by government should surely not be in the news and commentary business. Finally, I have not mentioned women as such, because I believe them to be equal. Steps necessary to ensure this can quickly be taken.

To conclude, let me say that I consider the bloated bureaucracy in Ottawa to be the greatest stumbling block to Canada achieving its potential status and its potential level of prosperity. The reduction and simplification of government, along with equality for all regions, could make this country truly great.

STEPHEN HUME

Nations are spiritual entities, whatever their trials in the material world. History teaches us that decisions rooted in concerns of the spirit endure where those based on expedient political pragmatism wither with their masters.

Thus, while I acknowledge the need for sound fiscal policy, including control of deficits, these are merely housekeeping items in the broader sweep of national progress. As the country's chief executive officers, prime ministers have the role of setting broad policy, not troubling themselves with the details that are the responsibility of competent deputies. The leading item on my agenda has more to do with the soul of Canada than with its immediate economic problems, since I am convinced that the placing of material matters before spiritual ones is to chart a course towards mediocrity and the ultimate decay of national purpose.

First priority goes to the place of aboriginal peoples within Confederation. This issue demands precedence because the ethical and moral principles evoked strike to the heart of our ideas about democracy and self-determination. In fact, if we cannot bring ourselves to assure the cultural sovereignty of those aboriginal minorities submerged in our own plans for nationhood, how can we expect to find the spiritual strength required to sustain Canada's national identity within the continental context?

The future of our own national desires for cultural sovereignty, indeed, the whole issue of what kind of nation we wish to construct for ourselves, hinges upon the way we interpret and meet our powerful obligations towards the powerless minority whose country our ancestors took and which we occupy by circumstance of history. This matter forces our examination of the nature and purpose of democratic governance itself.

On the one hand, we may fulfil the expectations of past experience. We may deceive and deny and dispossess. We may invoke all the pettifogging, legalistic authorities necessary to ensure that we yield to native peoples the bare minimum with which we feel comfortable. Or we may be open and generous and accept the primary nature of our obligation. The direction chosen will have profound and lasting effects upon the kind of society we build for the generations that will follow us.

The record of our dealings with aboriginal peoples to date is a litany of dismal failure and horrifying consequence. Many of the worst excesses lie within the living memory of Canadians of native ancestry. They include suppression of religion and culture by act of parliament; denial of voting rights; discriminatory limitations upon individual freedoms; suppression of mother tongues by "silent" policy in federal classrooms; removal of children from native communities, ostensibly to improve cost efficiency in education but in practice to ease the effective propagandizing of youth as to the superior values of the dominant culture—regardless of the subsequent erosion of self-esteem.

The legacy of these destructive influences is the spectre at Canada's banquet today. Despite the expenditure of billions of dollars over more than a century, most aboriginal peoples remain squeezed into regions of marginal economic potential and represent the nation's most severely depressed community; collectively, they benefit least from educational programs and suffer the most grievous consequences in terms of unemployment. A comparison of native mortality rates against mainstream populations is a powerful indictment of Canadian nationhood and the myth of the caring society.

Today, in Canada—a nation which takes pride in one of the highest living standards in the world—aboriginal citizens are four times as likely to die before reaching the life expectancy the rest of us take for granted; they are three times as likely to die by violence; three times as likely to commit suicide; twice as likely to suffer hospitalizing illness or injury; ten times as likely to be diagnosed as alcoholics. A scant 2 per cent of the Canadian population, native people provide 10 per cent of its prison inmates—most of their offences being associated with alcohol abuse. These statistics say as much about the dominant society as they do about the suffering that many native people continue to endure. Cheated of their promised patrimony—cheated, indeed, of an equal chance at life itself—these first Canadians remain deeply estranged from the political process that claims to represent their interests. Their sufferings stain the aspirations of Canada as a nation. Whatever those aspirations will be, they are destined to ring hollow until we grapple with our collective responsibility to make native people full participants in Canadian society.

As we found the will to do with Quebec during the 1970s, we must place at the top of our agenda for the remainder of this century the creation of a vigorous national policy aimed at defining and securing the place of aboriginal peoples within Confederation. This cannot be achieved without developing mechanisms for transferring real power from federal bureaucracies to native people—and these minorities must not only have power; they must perceive that the power belongs to them. Only the visible wielding of such power offers the possibility to create an environment that can foster cultural sovereignty and the autonomous political responsibility our dominant social order takes for granted. It seems logical to begin with a massive reorganization of the federal Department of Indian Affairs. Why, after so many decades, do so few native people hold positions of public profile and authority in the very bureaucracy charged with representing their interests?

Leave aside the specifics of proposal and counter-proposal. Those are matters to be negotiated. Begin instead with the acknowledgement that many native people do not believe their interests are adequately served by existing institutions. When the governed lose faith in the ability of government to serve their needs—when government is by imposition, however benevolent and paternal, rather than by consent—then we have a fundamental obligation to modify the existing order. Democratic government is based on rule by the majority, but that does not infer the legitimacy of tyranny over its minorities.

It is evident that new structures and forms of native government may have to be invented. This must be done in collaboration with those who are to be governed. Those who shy from the prospect of unorthodox forms should remember two things. First, it is a fundamental precept of democracy that consent by the citizens to be governed includes the right to determine the structure of their government. Second, change is life for democratic institutions. Like language, they are functionally dead when they cease to evolve.

Effective political power demands transfer of the economic power required to nurture cultural sovereignty. Such strategies must be designed to provide an avenue for native peoples to share in the national wealth that is their cultural birthright. Why not, for example, launch a program for evolving ownership and management of West Coast salmon fisheries by native peoples? Why not have similar objectives regarding management of game and wildlife resources in general (since aboriginal claims on such resources predate our own by thousands of years)?

These are not ends in themselves, merely points of argument from which policy might evolve in discussion with native people. The end, indeed, is less tangible and more profound. It is not only to find justice for aboriginal peoples; it is to embrace their rights as no less than our own and to find the voluntary capacity for justice in ourselves. It is to find the generosity of spirit sufficient to seize an opportunity to build ourselves a fair, flexible and moral society—not simply because it is right, but also to serve the broader obligation to provide a model of good nationhood for a world facing an increasingly cynical and precarious future.

With a weather eye to precisely the cynicism of global geopolitics in the next century, I leap to the second priority on my national agenda: to extend and entrench Canadian sovereignty over its northern territories and waters. Our generation is the unfortunate witness to a growing challenge to our assertions of sovereignty in the Arctic. I believe the threat posed by this challenge is grave. Concerns over northern sovereignty that characterized the early years of the Trudeau era appear to have been abandoned. But if Canadian sovereignty has been assumed secure by recent federal governments, it is clearly not a view shared by everyone—particularly not by our continental neighbour north of the 60th parallel, the United States. Armed American vessels sail uninvited and unhindered through waters claimed by Canada; the nuclear submarines of the two Arctic superpowers play hide-and-seek among the ice floes; American commercial interests threaten unilateral industrial developments in the rich Beaufort Sea. To meet these challenges even symbolically demands a vigorous and well-planned expansion of Canada's military presence in the Far North, particularly a maritime presence.

For Canadian claims of sovereignty to have meaning, our naval and coast guard units must have year-round operational and surveillance capability in Arctic waters that remain ice-bound for eight months. Canada's northern coastline extends almost 50,000 kilometres and is clearly of the greatest strategic importance in controlling resource development and commanding the sea lanes that will make this possible. This means that Canada requires not one but a fleet of heavy polar-class icebreakers. Permanent all-weather coast guard bases should be established in the Beaufort Sea and the Eastern Arctic. In addition to patrolling Canadian waters, these ships could assist scientific research and settlement resupply, and would spin off additional civilian employment in communities that need it. The port of Churchill might be kept open for western Canadian grain shipments—indeed, access to an all-weather port on Hudson Bay will undoubtedly prove a critical component in the future development of what might be called the mid-Canada corridor from the Peace River block in Alberta across Saskatchewan to northern Manitoba's mineral belt.

Furthermore, since the likelihood of conventional military campaigns within Canada is remote, and since NATO commitments call for deployment of troops to arctic Norway, establishment of a specialized permanent deep-cold training facility in the Far North seems eminently logical. We are northerners; we have frost in our blood. If frigid conditions are the implacable reality of Canadian life, let winter be our ally rather than our enemy when it comes to establishing our sovereignty; let our climate and geography become formidable instruments in our arsenal of defence. These are all-important symbols of the state's manifest authority. The other bulwark of sovereignty lies in the civil realm. It is the people who dwell in the region and offer allegiance to the central power. The strengthening of northern governments and a serious commitment to their evolution towards greater autonomy and, ultimately, provincial status—these are key components in any strategic plan for securing the Arctic. What is required is not merely a resurrection of the northern vision of John Diefenbaker but the political courage to make its realization an act of national will.

Programs must be paid for. So item three on my agenda calls for the development of a coherent national industrial and economic strategy. We haven't had one of substance since the federal effort produced in the aftermath of World War II. Recent attempts by both Liberal and Conservative governments to devise national policy have proved either ill-conceived attempts to exploit regional differences for short-term political gain, as with the Liberals' disastrous National Energy Program; or as off-the-cuff public relations, as with the Conservatives' free-trade policy—apparently created in the absence of any preliminary intelligence regarding the mood of American politicians and powerful anti-Canadian lobby groups.

The kind of strategy we need is not the desperate "foot in the door before it slams shut" approach that characterized federal policies on free trade. It must take the long view and be aimed at positioning Canada in the international market place of the next century. To do this requires careful, reasoned reflection upon what that market place will be and what forces will drive it. Surely the future of an economy based on the sale of raw materials at bargain basement prices is limited at best. We need to develop intelligent alternatives to the traditional revenue base in resource exports. The Scandinavians offer a lesson. While Canadians export unfinished logs to China, the Swedes export high-fashion furniture design to Canada. Or, more immediately, while Canadians export electricity to Los Angeles, Los Angeles exports advanced computer software to Canada.

Any comprehensive industrial strategy for the twenty-first century will have one essential cornerstone: secure and stable supplies of domestic energy. An important sub-agenda in a national industrial policy must be a plan to evolve an acceptable umbrella strategy for development of hydroelectric and nuclear power, coal, natural gas, crude oil, synthetic crude, and alternative energy sources. In addition, the wedding of advanced technologies to Canada's traditional strengths in agriculture, energy, mineral and timber production will require a greater commitment to research and development—and concurrent commitment to broad public access to high-quality advanced education. Finally, no comprehensive industrial strategy will be possible without greater harmony among Canada's economic regions. We must find a mechanism for reducing regional tensions and providing a forum where grievances may be aired in an atmosphere of non-partisan equality.

The cheapest and least painful way of achieving such a mechanism is to reform the Senate. Elect its members. Make their term equal to the terms of two governments—say, nine years—but limit senators to a single term in office. This would encourage the wise and the judicious to seek culmination of their careers with a period of national service, and it would discourage the merely ambitious. Weight the number of seats according to a regional formula that provides for equal representation. Make the Upper Chamber a forum for discussion of the moral and spiritual dimension of national policy rather than a tawdry Valhalla for burnt-out politicians and party hacks in their nattering decrepitude.

JOHN HUTCHESON

Canada, as Robertson Davies writes in the January 1987 issue of *Saturday Night*, is a psychologically introverted nation. One consequence of this is that not only is it difficult to list any admirable reasons to explain why anyone would want to be prime minister of Canada, but it is even difficult to articulate the reasons why anyone would even want to be a Canadian.

Of course, most Canadians do want to be Canadians. The elusiveness of the Canadian identity does not result from the fact that Canadians do not know who they are or where they are. But the identity is private and inward, and seldom expressed in public.

There is, however, always one theme that any Canadian can, and always does, resort to when trying to explain what it is to be a Canadian. Try imagining yourself in a dialogue with someone from another country and see how long it is before your explanation of Canada involves a comparison with the United States. Robertson Davies' point about Canada's introversion owes part of its explanatory power to his prior observation that the United States is an extroverted nation.

There is no question that what happens in the United States is of immense importance for Canada. No aspect of Canadian life is entirely free of the shadow of the United States, and no Canadian government can afford to be ignorant of the political climate in Washington. But the question of whether Canada has any degrees of freedom in its policy-making is ultimately a question of whether Canadians can articulate the fact that Canada is a distinct and unique society, with its own history, its own values, its own way of existing in the world.

Questions of Canada's past and values might seem abstract, even academic and of interest only to historians, but in fact the present political climate in Ottawa makes them not only relevant but urgent and pressing. The decision of Mr. Mulroney to enter negotiations for a comprehensive free-trade arrangement between Canada and the United States has made the identity of Canada a central issue in the politics of this country today.

"Managing" the U.S. relationship while maintaining Canadian sovereignty is obviously one of the major challenges faced by every

Canadian prime minister. A prime minister who has decided to pursue a bilateral free-trade agreement with the United States has picked up this challenge with both hands, and not only his future but the future of the entire country depends on how he fares in the contest.

In the past few years a fierce debate has been carried on in this country. On one side have been the opponents of the free-trade strategy who, alarmed by the prospects of a dramatic shift in Canadian policy, have warned that economic stability, cultural identity, and ultimately Canadian sovereign existence are all at risk. Among those who are supporters of a free-trade deal are some who argue that we no longer have any choice, that we have in effect lost our independence, whatever independence we might have had in the past. There are also those who do not care for what remaining independence we have, because they do not like the different ways of doing things—different from the United States, that is—which are a consequence of that independence. There are, of course, some supporters of free trade who argue that a free-trade deal has nothing whatsoever to do with Canadian survival, that the pursuit of such an agreement is a narrow economic issue—a matter of Canada making the best possible arrangement in difficult international circumstances, without measurable prejudice to Canadian sovereignty or culture.

But strangely absent from this debate has been the man responsible for the policy that has occasioned it. Yet it would seem that a government that is undertaking a major policy initiative owes the electorate some clear explanation of its motives and some informed analysis of the consequences.

There is certainly room for debate about the politics of Pierre Elliott Trudeau, but when Trudeau went to Ottawa with a mission to change this country, he left no doubt about his vision of the country and his commitment to the task of fulfilling it. Trudeau's image of the "just society" of harmony between the two great linguistic communities of Canada was not every Canadian's idea of the future, but you certainly knew that Trudeau knew where he was going and that he wasn't afraid to tell you why. Perhaps Trudeau's confrontational style was too much for an introverted nation. Perhaps we yearned for the devious style of Mackenzie King. King's success resulted from his consummate mastery of the political realities of the country, and he was wise enough to know that his style worked because he reacted to circumstances rather than embarking on any foolish initiatives. He certainly knew enough to stay away from free trade with the United States.

Diefenbaker did have a vision, but it was not matched by any grasp of the circumstances, and his government gradually fell apart as a result. George Grant saw very clearly the personal flaws which contributed to Diefenbaker's decline, but Diefenbaker's vision of the country at least was on a grand enough scale for Grant to be able to lament his failure as a national tragedy. It is unlikely that anyone will be able to do as much for Mr. Mulroney.

Just as it has not been easy to articulate the meaning of Canada, it has never been easy to find the policies that would promote the interests of Canada. But just now, perhaps more than ever, we need a prime minister who can remind us of why we do want to be Canadians and, furthermore, a prime minister who can match his understanding of the country with a program for survival.

GEORGE IGNATIEFF

The duty of a prime minister is to serve the vital interests of the Canadian people. In an age dominated by revolutionary changes wrought by science and technology, including the threat to survival by the risks of nuclear war, top priority must be given to trying to ensure survival.

The dangers of nuclear war must be kept in check by active Canadian participation in negotiations for drastic arms limitation and increased international understanding. Only so can a prime minister serve the imperative human requirement of preventing nuclear war, which—because of our geographic location between the two nuclear superpowers—could bring about the devastation of Canada.

Those who argue that nuclear war can best be prevented by the fear created by the accumulation of increasingly lethal nuclear arsenals, and by dependence upon American military might, dodge the question of the personal responsibility, which inevitably falls upon political leadership, of being accountable for making the right judgements concerning the protection of the Canadian people. For such protection, Canada must actively participate in a collective security system like the North Atlantic Treaty Organization; the North Atlantic Council and its various committees provide the necessary political fora for consultations and control over military planning by politically responsible ministers.

In an age when the civilian population would be the main victims of war, authority to declare alerts, or to make decisions on war and peace, cannot be left to militarily integrated command structures like NORAD or to computerized systems of automatic control. (However foolproof, every technological device is apt to be handled by some fool.) Moreover, this delegation is a carry-over from an earlier age when military fought military on the battlefield, in the air, or at sea. Now it is a whole population that is at risk. In any decision-making where their vital interests are concerned, the people must be represented by their elected political leaders, starting with the prime minister. This is what I mean when I say that there must be "no incineration without representation."

Following this logic, I would insist that all military commands of the alliance should be under the direct control of a political central body such as the Atlantic Council. This must include NORAD. As an integrated command structure for North American aerospace defence, NORAD currently comes under the control of the American hierarchical structure, rather than under the joint control of the Canadian prime minister and the American president. No military alert should be applied to Canada without prior consultation with and consent from the Canadian political leadership. Such alerts open the way to deployments of American nuclear weapons and to flights into and over Canada, as well as the use of Canadian waters by American submarines. Under a collective security system, which NATO is, decision-making must be collective, after proper consultation, and defence measures must be fully shared. The present fragmentation neither provides security nor defines responsibility.

The scientific and technological revolution has changed the whole problem of survival in the age of nuclear weapons and missiles of all kinds. This requires new thinking as well as new measures of promoting international understanding. Canada should no longer drift between two strategies—accommodating to the United States bilaterally, while using the multilateral fora of NATO and the United Nations to pursue a policy of collective security in an increasingly interdependent world. The latter approach should prevail.

Canada, as the country with the largest space in relation to population, has a major stake in world co-operation and stability. I would give priority to the pursuit of international co-operation and global relationships, and would expand trade relations with all countries—including the Soviet Union, China, Japan, and the developing countries of Asia, Africa, and Latin America—rather than concentrating on a bilateral agreement about access to a continental market. I would also give priority to fighting American protectionism, which is inconsistent with the spread, throughout the world, of revolutionary changes in finance and technology.

Parochialism or regionalism is appropriate to the local community level, rather than the national. Indeed, the growing importance of the city-state within a global structure of co-operation tends to supersede the nation-state, as well as serving to preserve local cultural traditions. Canada's traditions of multiculturalism enable us to set an example for peaceful coexistence throughout the global village. This gives us an enviable influence in world affairs. Moreover, Canada's contribution to United Nations peacekeeping and peacemaking (which should be indivisible) gives us a unique destiny. We should be approaching the new millennium with confidence, knowing that we can look after our vital interests of security in an interdependent world society, rather than leaning towards dependence on the superpower-oriented world view of the United States. In any case, American hegemony is being increasingly challenged by the emergence of new economic powers (such as Japan and China) which have competitive advantages of technology or population, as well as by the spread of industrialization and by new technologies in the processing of raw materials.

Individual security and support services are the other priorities to which I, as prime minister, would give my attention. We are moving away from the neoconservative reaction, when it was thought that free-market forces would somehow ensure full employment and competitive advantages in world markets. In fact, profits do not necessarily mean prosperity for the majority. The ideology of the "mean and lean" has produced a further gap between the government and the people. My concern would be how to cope with the problem of information—the crucial indicator of power in the information age. The executive, even in such a democratic and traditionally egalitarian society as Canada, seems to be obtaining an unbreakable monopoly on information, despite remedial legislation. Is there much benefit, for instance, in having access to information about the expense account of the prime minister, or his journeying—including such trivia as to whether he was accompanied by a valet and a maid—when our elected representatives are denied essential information about the issue of survival, flowing from Canada's nuclear commitments under NORAD?

Education offers part of the answer. Education and research would not only contribute to help train the younger generation for the many new services opening up in the information age, but they would also provide the necessary background knowledge so that Canadians could ask the right questions when seeking to become better-informed citizens. In an information society, education and training must have better public funding. We badly need trained minds to cope with the problems of the twenty-first century, especially in using science and technology for the enlargement of human knowledge, for the development of social controls, and for improved standards of living.

Canada's priorities should be related to the values most Canadians accept—values that include a sense of responsibility for oneself, as well as for one's neighbour. Unemployment in our society is primarily related to the question of human dignity and the individual's freedom of choice. When seeking solutions, it is not enough to place our faith mainly on the value of the market place. Solutions require changes in policy, in responsibility at all levels—federal, provincial, municipal, and community. But this necessary move towards equity and justice is hindered by numerous difficulties: the problem of adjusting the thinking of a large government bureaucracy; the seeming lack of genuine leadership and initiative at the political level; the remaining discrimination against women; disputes between large businesses and small ones; the dislocation of employment by technological changes; disagreements among economic experts; feelings of frustration among the young and the handicapped, and the lack of educational opportunities in an informational society.

In coping with these inequities, priority should be given to unemployment rather than to fighting deficits or inflation. Women must be given equal pay for equal work, and any woman should have the right to six months' maternity leave. Day-care centres, with properly trained personnel to care for the children, should become part of medicare, as should compulsory medical examination through grade and secondary schools.

A fund should be created to finance public works at the municipal level, with emphasis on low-cost housing. An industrial strategy needs to be worked out to create permanent jobs for people in local communities, especially with regard to better social services, care, and pensions for the increasing proportion of aged in the Canadian population.

In co-operation with labour unions, workers should be invited to play a more decisive and responsible role in developing strategies for employment (such as a shorter work week, staggered holidays, and subsidized travel on railroads and other public transport). There should be a more balanced and equitable program of tax reform, including increases in taxes to keep the deficit under control (the principle being that governments should set an example to society by paying their bills). Various tax deductions allowed to businesses should be reviewed, eliminating "tax expenditures" by corporations. Every effort should be made to improve medicare and social security benefits, and there must be pension reform, especially for those most handicapped by technological displacement. Finally, the farmers must be given greater protection from interest-rate hikes and debts, as well as being provided with co-operative insurance schemes and credit guarantees to give them protection against crop destruction.

Modernizing the economy should be accompanied by a process of gradual conversion from defence-oriented industries (dominated by the defence-sharing agreement with the United States and the various subsidiaries of American defence production) to providing tax incentives to encourage the production for Canada's civilian needs, as well as for export. For too long, high technology has been allowed to flourish in the production of lethal or unusable weaponry, while research and development in the civil sector have suffered from chronic underfunding. If the arms race is allowed to continue uncontrolled, we shall only sacrifice our security further, by trying to cope with twenty-first-century weapons with twentieth-century mindsets.

Finally, the unity of Canada under a federal system needs more than the patriation of our constitution and legislation on human rights. Canada needs a functioning common market. Instead of having a federal minister responsible for regional development and the cabinet operating a regional "pork barrel" according to its transitory party interests, I would set up in Ottawa a council of ministers, appointed by each provincial government, that would be responsible for making a common market work for Canada. This council would report quarterly to the meeting of premiers and would be staffed by a group of permanent officials, appointed by each province, with the task of promoting on-going federal-provincial economic and social co-operation. As prime minister of Canada, I would then feel more qualified to speak for Canada with a single voice when dealing competitively with the other members of the international community in protecting Canada's vital interests in the common interest.

However, if a woman with similar views should care for the job, I would gladly yield to her.

JANIS JOHNSON

It is fundamental to governments that they accept the responsibility to act in accordance with what would be perceived to be in the best interests of the society they serve. To imagine oneself as prime minister and address the question "What would one do as prime minister?" requires some stage setting. One's view of what to do depends on one's outlook for the Canada of the future and an assumption of what challenges our country is likely to face.

For me, the stage would have a double set of regional backdrops because I look at our government from two geographic perspectives—that of a Manitoban and that of a Newfoundlander. I know intimately and personally the two parts of Canada that more people are said to leave than all the other provinces put together. The reason is not that we seek the greener pastures of other provinces but that we want to help the rest of Canada solve its problems.

Perhaps because I have this dual set of roots in Canada, I think that I would be lonely if I were prime minister. I would be lonely precisely because prime ministers are obliged to live in Ottawa. One of the greatest weaknesses of our system of government is that our national government and its leadership live in a city that is fundamentally disconnected and insulated from the realities that Canadians live with day by day.

As prime minister, I'd be surrounded by the objective view, the view that people who have traded their roots for public-service tenure (or private-sector privileged access to contracts) propound as representing what they call with such ease the national interest. The objective or Ottawa view assumes that there is somehow a real Canadian view which only those who are comfortable in the nation's capital can see and which all those others with their narrow sectional interests cannot. This is a view that reduces to rage those whose roots are still deep in Manitoba and Newfoundland. And it's a view that increasingly has infected and undermined the legitimacy of the central government in Canada.

This is where my labours to reform government in Canada would begin: with a resolute and unbending effort to get our government free from the Ottawa complex, with its lack of links to Canada and its strange assumptions. Such assumptions are that Pierre Berton speaks for the Territories and Farley Mowat for the East Coast, that Claire Hoy's murderous rudeness in his *Toronto Sun* column is really just journalistic high spirits, and that a $200 annual tax credit is a significant response to the need for child care in Canada. We have to escape from Ottawa's incestuous, public-service, private-sector, opportunist, self-important, journalistic substitute for living in this country.

The rescue mission would start with the men and women whom real Canadians in all parts of the country elect to help govern them—our members of parliament. If I were prime minister, I'd be grateful there'd been a Mulroney before me. The reforms that Mulroney made in the roles available to members of parliament (at the recommendations of my fellow Newfoundlander, Jim McGrath) mean that people elected to govern can begin to reflect and express their roots in the decisions of government in a way that was never possible before. The vastly broadened scope given parliamentary committees provides each member of parliament with a broader ability to initiate actions than anyone but cabinet ministers have had in the past. Time and again, parliamentary committees have found solutions to issues that have eluded cabinet ministers. The recent suggestion that parliamentarians be more involved in discussions on constitutional amendments is a sound one.

Properly nurtured, the new scope that exists for individual MPs can result in a fundamental shift of power away from the prime minister and cabinet in the government party (and from the party hierarchies in the opposition parties) to the individual MP and those who elect him or her. The newly independent and potent committees of the House of Commons represent a broad new avenue which those who wish to influence or reason with government may travel.

When this avenue becomes well travelled, life may become very uncomfortable for all those who have traditionally been most potent in the Ottawa version of Canada. The public-service monopoly on the provision of information to government will be broken. A backbench MP from Manitoba will be far more receptive to views provided by the farmers or native people or business people of Manitoba than he or she will be to the comfortable briefings of the public service. And it will mean that ministers will have to watch the goings-on at committees very carefully indeed. There will be a temptation, in the first instance, for the government and the opposition to try to manage the committees for partisan purposes. There will be efforts to dictate agendas and to prejudge findings along party lines.

But the MPs from both of my provinces, regardless of their party affiliation, have a natural tendency towards independence and an unwavering streak of perversity that emerges when people try to tell them what to do. So I'm confident that sooner or later the committees and their MP members will declare their independence of the government and of the fixers and managers in the opposition parties. And they'll get down to the serious business of finding better ways to govern Canada, based on their own best judgement, fortified by their own broad access to information, and shaped by the direct sense of accountability to and membership in their home regions.

It will be chaotic. All the comfortable public-service incrementalism that has been the mainstream of government in Canada for so long will be in jeopardy as the newly empowered MPS inject more energy into the system than it has seen in our lifetime.

As prime minister, I'd do all I could to nudge that process along, to speed it up. I'd start by making it clear to my ministers that I expected them to appear before the various committees of the House whenever they were asked to do so and that I expected them to meet informally with the committees as often as possible.

The fundamental reform I am talking about is not, in the first instance, a matter of issues. It's a matter of giving government a chance to grow some roots again, to have the strength to reflect the people at home, the people who elected it, rather than spending so much time explaining that there is more to democracy than simply playing back the views of the good old constituents in their local parishes. Canadians and government have to learn to stretch their minds from coast to coast.

Of course, there would still be more members from Ontario and Quebec (from central Canada or the Mainland as we call it in my two homes) than from the other regions. But I do not believe for a moment that if individual members had more power the result would be increased abuse of the smaller regions by the more populous ones. I think quite the opposite would occur, for two reasons.

The first reason is that as the process of balancing regional interests gradually came to involve individual MPS in a more decisive role, it would be a less cynical process than the one that applies now in Ottawa as rootless Ottawans set out to manage and manipulate the various parts of Canada. The fatal flaw in the current process is that it always assumes that the regions are fired only by narrow self-interest, that none will agree to sacrifice in order to serve broader national goals. But Manitobans and Newfoundlanders know that over the years they have collected equalization payments given freely by more fortunate regions. They know that they have agreed to levels of taxation and other government impositions that grow at least in part from the need to keep central Canada strong. Accommodations among the regions would be fairer and would be seen to be fairer and more acceptable to all parts of the country as individual MPS played a larger part (and cynical manipulators a smaller one) in the hard choices and decisions that have to be made in a diverse nation like ours.

The second reason is that MPS would be encouraged to adopt views that are not narrow or parochial. As committee members, they would travel. They would speak to Canadians from coast to coast, sampling the diversity of viewpoints in our nation. They would begin to see Canada's problems not only on a geographic map but also on an issues map.

Most MPS I have known are, by instinct, reformers. They differ in their views relating to the efficacy of government intervention as a mechanism to achieve reform; they differ in their levels of sensitivity to the costs, economic, social and spiritual, of government regulation and control. But I have never met one who has accepted all the sacrifices of running for public office just to preserve the status quo. People elected to public office want to make things better. And as the committees become focuses through which they can do exactly that, we shall see a new sense of shared purpose and accommodation that will transcend both regional and partisan considerations. We shall see MPS striving to persuade their parties to support basic directions hammered out in parliamentary committees, rather than MPS manipulating the committees to gain partisan advantage. We shall see MPS working to persuade their regions of the importance of the concerns of other parts of Canada, rather than horse-trading regional interests.

As prime minister, I'd adopt a very narrow view of what constitutes a non-confidence vote, because I'd adopt a very broad view of the scope and freedom MPS ought to have to make their own decisions. And I'd put more of my energy into trying to help set the agenda and less into trying to do what governments normally do, which is to exert total control of the outcomes.

I would try to achieve some fundamental changes in the nation's perceptions. I'd try to focus the attention of parliament on the development of a more realistic understanding of the nature of the family today in Canada. Today only 16 per cent of Canadian families fit the traditional mold—two parents with only the male working outside the home. The rest are families with two working parents or, increasingly in these troubled times, single-parent families.

Our perceptions, and the public policies and programs that grow out of them, have not yet really caught up with these realities. And so when one parent leaves, we talk about "family break-up," as though the remaining parent and children were not a family at all but simply a small social wreck. We have to change these perceptions before we can hope to make the right changes in the public policies and programs that affect families. If I were prime minister, I would make changing these perceptions an important part of my job, on this issue and others. I would want to appeal to the determination to reform and improve which brings people into politics. I wouldn't be satisfied with the Ottawa viewpoint alone, because I know my country too well.

We used to say in Newfoundland that federal fisheries policy was based on the yield of the Upper Ottawa River. In Manitoba, I grew up hearing about how Ottawa didn't care about the farmers or the West so long as the grain went East. Thus, the current debate on these issues is not new. It is as old as the country itself. Only a strong commitment to changing the system will bring some resolution to the problems and the feelings of regional alienation that are affecting yet another generation of Canadians.

My own generation grew up in the sixties in an era of radical change in our society at all levels. The events of those years made us politically aware, and we learned that we could have an impact on the political system. We took action, we marched, we protested. We were idealistic, but we cared about ending the war in Vietnam, about pollution, women's rights, equality and peace in the world. I think we still do. I do.

As prime minister I would place a high priority on arms control, the environment, economic equality for women, minority rights and, as I said, the family. I would want to restore people's confidence that politics is an honourable profession and not one to avoid, as recent polls have shown. It would be very important to me to give the younger generation a positive image of the political system and to encourage them to participate.

Alienation grows when people don't feel they can have any effect on the system and the decision-making process. Government looks—and is—so big and overpowering that people lose faith in the institution itself. But our parliamentary system has served our vast country reasonably well, and so long as it remains flexible and open to change it will continue to serve us well into the twenty-first century. As prime minister I would encourage reform and would not shy away from exerting strong leadership to ensure that the process continued, both in the House and in the Senate.

For this, I would have to travel out of Ottawa. I'd miss parliament sometimes and I'd encourage every other member to do so too. I would want to visit provincial legislatures and city councils in all parts of the country to talk informally about the kinds of reform we had to make together. I'd be inclined not to take a lot of members of the Ottawa press gallery with me. As prime minister, I think I'd probably have enough trouble dealing with my own sense of self-importance without exposing myself overmuch to theirs. I'd be inclined to avoid partisan fights. I'd be inclined not to answer questions from the media which I thought were rude or stupid. I'd be content not to be news a lot of the time, or at least not to let anyone else's definitions of what is news dictate my actions.

If I were prime minister, I'd want to commute to work, from Manitoba or Newfoundland. It would cost a little more I suppose, but I'd happily defend the cost by saying it made it possible for me to avoid being taken over by Ottawa.

STEVEN LANGDON

There's an old story that says, "If I were elected prime minister...the first thing I'd do is demand a recount!"

As a federal member of parliament, I've seen one prime minister, Brian Mulroney, chewed to pieces by scandal and incompetence. Earlier, as a member of the parliamentary press corps, I saw another, Pierre Trudeau, turn from creative starts to frustrating disappointments in his impact. And his predecessor, Mike Pearson, sat in my living room after he'd resigned and talked about how hard it had been to do anything exciting and innovative in the job.

But there is a crying need for fresh, dramatic changes in important parts of Canadian life. Left to present trends, Canada will sink slowly and quietly into a pale copy of the United States; we'll wearily accept joblessness for far too many young Canadians; we'll put up with decisions that affect us being made by small groups in Toronto, Ottawa, Washington, and Los Angeles; and we'll gradually let our environment deteriorate to where it poisons more and more of us.

So Canada desperately needs a new direction. Not a direction that comes from our powerful and secure Ottawa bureaucracy; nor from our large corporations and banks, so caught up in foreign ownership or ambitions. We need a direction that comes from people all across this country, a new direction we can all give in our own communities, and new priorities that "people power" will give Canada.

There's Gloria Seal in a low-income housing project in Windsor, for instance. Left on her own with two children, she's fought for recreation programs for the project and tried to organize people left in very difficult personal situations—to obtain day care, for instance, which would allow them to train effectively for jobs.

Or there's the head of the Juniper Lumber enterprise in New Brunswick. His is one of the ninety-four small lumber mills in Atlantic Canada that were badly damaged by the softwood lumber surrender to the U.S. interests—and yet he has had the driving energy to try to save his small business, and others like it, by pushing hard on Ottawa to make changes that would give small firms a fair chance.

There are the forty-five francophone and immigrant women in the clothing industry in Montreal who flooded into our hearings there, during our cross-country NDP Action Group on Jobs, telling us how the federal program that was supposed to help them as older workers in declining industries was instead a disaster, and pushing for much more organized industrial efforts in our country.

There's also Doug Hallett, who felt he had to quit Environment Canada and work outside the bureaucracy to start getting Canadians to take seriously the threat of toxic wastes in the Great Lakes basin where many of us live. The recent reports of the International Joint Commission and of Great Lakes United show that the St. Clair "blob," which I helped to reveal in 1985, was just one danger sign of what's happening in our environment.

Then there are farming friends, like Carolyn and Rick Fuerth, young people who are struggling to keep a new generation of family farms going in the face of high farm interest levels and low commodity prices. Yet they're super-active in their farm organization, pushing hard for policy changes from Ottawa and helping me with a national survey of farm women to try and improve such women's lives.

Finally, there's Coro Strandberg, who works in Vancouver. She's done a detailed look at dozens of community economic development efforts that have sprung up all over B.C.—a trend towards local community economic initiatives that our Action Group found all across Canada. Coro especially, though, speaks of them with a passion and knowledge, and is one of many Canadians pushing for real commitment to this approach in Canada.

If I were prime minister, then, it's to these people and these concerns that I would want to shift attention in Canada. Because our country does so badly need a new direction.

How could this new direction be best summarized? Perhaps through six themes—all adding up to a much more participatory, environmentally safe, made-in-Canada society:

– Canada should put a dramatic new stress on community economic development. Laws should be changed to help co-operatives, credit unions, and local development corporations, so that organizations like VanCity, the billion-dollar credit union in B.C., can more easily draw in deposits and channel them to help hundreds of small businesses and co-ops create long-lasting jobs. And much more taxpayer money should be left by Ottawa in the local community, under the control of democratic community councils that are able to plan and start up local services, businesses, and training efforts.

– Small businesses will also need much more support than they presently receive in Canada if they are to expand jobs for younger Canadians at the community level. The Federal Business Development Bank and the Export Development Corporation will have to be much more responsive to small firms; and new laws will be needed to push the banks to help small firms more.

- We need widespread use of Canadian content commitments throughout our industrial sector, just as we have from the "big three" auto companies under the Auto Pact. This means working out economic plans with large companies and their unions to set such goals for different parts of the economy. An effective industrial thrust for Canada would also require much more stress on research and development, trade expansion efforts for small and medium firms, well-planned industrial adjustment assistance, and serious long-run training moves tied more to workplace experience.

- Canada also needs to build on its own resources much more, by giving more support to our farming, fishing, and forestry sectors, by seeing to it that we process and manufacture much more from what we extract here (we should export more of our nickel as specialized alloys, for example), and by producing much more of our resource machinery in Canada (it's mostly imported now). Thousands of jobs would result.

- We should also make Canada an environmental leader in the world. This requires a massive clean-up of the Great Lakes and much more action here on acid rain; it means much more money for environmental research, too. New findings will help clean up Canada and will also spur products we can export abroad. Again, job growth would come from all this new effort—and so would safer, fuller lives for all Canadians.

- In a new Canada, male and female equality will be crucial in the workplace and elsewhere. But that won't just happen. Pay equity laws and affirmative action enforcement will be needed. So will a serious day-care program for children. And so will equality built into the training system for jobs. This priority will have to be matched by fairness and action towards aboriginal Canadians, visible minorities, and the disabled.

All of this would represent a new direction in Canada. But there are many people who would wonder: Could we take this path? Would there not be financial blocks to such moves, given the large federal budget deficit? And would there not be other barriers, especially with our relationship with the United States?

The most recent yearly budget deficit for Canada (1986-87) was over $32 billion, and the Mulroney government has seen this as a major constraint on new initiatives. Instead, tax increases of over $1300 per family have hit the average family, and government cutbacks have reduced public services, scientific research, and regional development concerns.

However, a new philosophy should be applied to these budget concerns. First, there clearly are sources of revenue from the corporate sector that are being given a free ride. Tax loopholes for large companies mean that each year only half of the profitable companies in Canada usually pay corporate tax; capital cost allowances, for instance, cost the government well over $2 billion in 1980, without (most studies suggest) actually encouraging new investment; corporations borrowing to take over other firms, too, can subtract the interest from their tax bill (which not only costs the government revenue but also increases concentration and monopoly power in the economy). The overall result is that the corporate share of tax has fallen from 50 per cent to less than 25 per cent between 1950 and 1987, while the share paid by personal tax has shot up. Obviously, a fairer level of tax on large corporations could very much increase government revenues and reduce the deficit as a constraint.

Most important, though, the deficit can only be seriously reduced by reviving the Canadian economy. Economic growth is falling year by year in Canada (a result, the Conference Board said recently, of the Mulroney government's heavy personal tax increases). The new direction suggested above would spur new economic expansion, get most Canadians off unemployment insurance, get many off welfare, increase consumer spending (and then, in turn, business investment), and would thus over time reduce the deficit. Getting Canada back this way to full employment (only 3 to 5 per cent unemployed as they shift jobs, instead of the almost 10 per cent out of work now) by new initiatives and by personal tax cuts for average families is the real answer to the deficit.

Our relationship with the United States is a more important barrier, not because the U.S. would deliberately try to block a new direction in Canada, but because the free-trade plan of the Mulroney government would end up by blocking many of these new initiatives in Canada.

The greatest danger of free trade with the United States is that the American government will insist on what it calls "a level playing field" in economic affairs; that is, the U.S. will require that we do not help particular regions, sectors, or firms in our economy—because that would be seen as unfair to U.S. companies competing in the same open continental market. The cost to Canada would be immense. We would have lost our political freedom to take on a whole set of new economic steps, including most of those suggested above. Community development initiatives, help to small businesses in various regions, a new industrial thrust with Canadian content commitments, building on Canadian resources by more processing here—all this would be prevented by a comprehensive free-trade accord with the United States. In effect, we would surrender our economic independence and would leave it to the continental market place to decide what happens to Canadians.

That's why, in the House of Commons, I have been arguing so hard against any comprehensive accord. It makes sense to have a new agenda between the two countries to help work out the trade disputes we run into in our important trade relationship; but it doesn't make sense to give away our choices over Canada's economic future with a full-scale free-trade pact.

However, the fight against free trade has not just been in parliament, but with people outside the House of Commons. And this takes us back to the beginning: people power. This is what will overcome and defeat the free-trade move—through demonstrations, conferences, local protests, petitions, and arguments.

Just as the people I wrote about at the beginning of this essay are the heart and soul of this country, so they have to retain their power to shape what happens to Canada. That's what I'd try to encourage and support if I were prime minister. Free trade would take away that power, perhaps forever, and that's why, often in an instinctive way, people are coming to reject it and to fight it actively.

But this is all part of a much broader process that Canada should be all about—making our country much more democratic, with people having much more say in their own economy, in their own local communities and at the national level. The elites have had their day in Canada. Now it's time for the Gloria Seals, the Fuerths, and the Coro Strandbergs. They'll have to fight hard, and organize together, to win these changes. But it will be an exciting new direction they'll give this country—a direction that is fairer and more democratic for all of us.

DANIEL LATOUCHE

If I were prime minister, the country would be in real trouble. Can you imagine a Québécois who is both a crypto-federalist and a closet separatist, a known left-winger and a business consultant, being prime minister of a NATO country?

If you can believe this, you'll believe anything.

If I were indeed prime minister, it could only mean one of two things: that Canada had solved all its major problems and could now afford some experimentation; or that Canada was way past any possibility of salvation—so who cares if I'm prime minister? In both instances, my job would be an easy one. Not that the prime minister's job is a difficult one at present. Even the myth that Canada is the most difficult Western country to govern has proven relatively easy to sell to Canadians. They will buy anything, including the idea that they are not sold easily. (If you already have the vague impression that this text sounds like prime-ministerial gibberish, you're right! Maybe I'm cut out for the job after all.)

Can you ask for a more suitable country to govern? San Marino, perhaps. Canadians like to think they are an uneasy lot, a complex society held together because of some formidable skills on the part of their leaders. It makes them feel good. But Canada is not difficult to govern. The proof: nobody has even tried it for twenty years. Canadians don't need to be led. They can drive themselves into any mess all by themselves.

This is not a serious country. How could it be when we haven't had a sex scandal for twenty-five years and most of our young people don't even remember the Munsinger Affair? (Not that they are missing much.) They know that a decent sex scandal would never select the Prime Minister's Office; that would be the day that sex died in Canada.

What we need in Canada is an NSP, a National Sex Policy, and as prime minister I would push in that direction. Frankly, it's a better way to pass the time than by worrying about the survival of the Canadian Football League. I would also send my RCMP agents, on horses since it helps find out who is the agent, to inquire if Kapuskasing really exists. On the radio, they insist on telling us about the daily weather in this Canadian Timbuktu, so now is the time to find out if this city is for real or if it's just a joke of some weatherman anxious for a raise. And then there is the pool. It would have to be rebuilt, maybe in the National Press Club. How can a prime minister hope to survive if he doesn't know how to swim ... the backstroke?

The Rockies! I almost forgot about the Rockies. The last time we had fun in Canada—I mean real fun and not simply listening to the Queen giving, in French, her best wishes for the New Year—it was at the time of the Quebec referendum. You remember. That was when federal politicians repeated ad nauseam that if we kept insisting on having our cake and eating it too (and only in Canada do you have to choose between liberty and prosperity), we would "lose" the Rockies. Can you imagine? The Rockies—gone! Pluff! Disappeared. Obliterated. Moved to Arkansas. As prime minister, I would have the Rockies bolted to the British Columbia soil so that not even Albertans could take them away. How dare they make such a threat! Little Quebec children still have nightmares about bad separatists stealing their mountains.

Sex, Kapuskasing, the pool, the Rockies ... so much to do and so little time. Help! Yes, a royal commission. Why didn't I think of that before? It must be that I'm new to the job. Having noticed—political scientists like myself are good at "noticing"—that royal commissions are the best way to send a problem and its potential solutions into oblivion, I would appoint one on the opposition and one on Ontario.

I can't think of anything else to do. My god!—I've just read the list of all the other people who will be describing their prime ministerial dreams. There's Tom Axworthy. Didn't he work in Trudeau's office? Why would he want to go back? Maybe he forgot something. And there's Keith Davey. Isn't he the one who believed the country had to be saved from all those prime ministers he "gave" us? And Richard Rohmer. I trust he's going to write a novel. And all those women: Shirley Carr, Dian Cohen, Sheila Copps.... They're probably going to say wonderful things about being the first woman prime minister of Canada. And here I am with nothing intelligent to say about the highest office in the land. Readers will think I don't have any respect, because it's the job of *Canadian* prime minister.

Maybe I could force Quebec to separate. That would sell well in Toronto, but the Québécois are a tough lot to convince. Recently, Lévesque and his bunch tried the soft sell by insisting that Quebec sovereignty would be well accepted in English Canada. They failed miserably. Who has ever heard of the Québécois buying something that's "well accepted" in the rest of the country? We do have our pride, and in any case we have already been through seventy-four national unity crises, and they are too dangerous to handle. One never knows, though. Jean Chrétien could come back and save us. But twice in the same century? Surely this time we would not survive.

Whoever gave me this job? Why didn't I read the fine print? Is it the job that is boring or the country? Certainly not the country. How can a country be boring when it has pearls like Trois-Rivières and Moose Jaw? It must be the job then. Travelling from Trois-Rivières to Moose Jaw has a way of killing any job. Maybe a Japanese-style Job Enrichment Program would help, assuming that there is something to enrich.

Sharing the job would certainly be a way to enrich it: one could set up a system by which, each year, a provincial premier would be called upon to chair the First Ministers' Conference and sit as *de facto* prime minister of the country. Of course, nobody would know the name of the prime minister—a definite disadvantage for a job that exists in name only—but in Switzerland the prime minister (or is it a chancellor?) is not a household name. The Swiss are special, though; they like to be different, original, happy, and rich. It would never work with Canadians. All the same, that's what I would do if I were prime minister: I'd work hard to turn my job over to the provincial premiers. One could hardly imagine a more Canadian enterprise: it would be good for the country and its citizens; politicians would hate it; and it would save us from collective boredom. Careful, Latouche! You're getting serious here.

Mr. Spock, where are you now that Canada needs you? What do you mean there are certain jobs that even Vulcans won't take?

RICHARD G. LIPSEY

Before I became prime minister I would have fretted about the function of the opposition. In the United States most measures that become law are supported by *ad hoc* coalitions drawn from both parties, but in British parliamentary systems the government routinely proposes and the opposition routinely opposes. No matter how good or how bad any government proposal may be, the opposition must oppose it. As leader of the opposition, I would have instructed my finance critic to revolutionize this system by judging each government proposal on its merits, supporting some and opposing others. Hopefully, when we did oppose for good reason, rather than as a knee-jerk reaction, we would have been listened to.

Having been elected, I would worry about what I could accomplish and how. Many of the things a Canadian prime minister would like to change are under provincial or municipal jurisdiction. Even when federal control is involved, the prime minister must carry his party, and eventually the electorate, with him. No doubt, however, all of us who are writing in this volume would be able to carry through a really substantial list of policy reforms by making effective use of power—where we had it—and by persuasion, where we lacked legal power.

Leadership versus Followership

That power would not lie easily on my shoulders. I would wake up at 4 A.M. asking myself: What is democracy? Must I follow every twist of public opinion, or can I lead by taking the public where they currently do not want to go but where they will accept as being desirable once they are there? I would seek to be a statesman by pushing people against their short-run choices while accepting that in the long run they must be the judges of all of my policies.

Choosing People on Merit

Brian Mulroney never seems to have understood the enormous symbolic importance of his televised defeat of John Turner on the patronage issue. He behaved as if his was a victory in a high school debate that did not preclude him from going on to greater uses of patronage. Yet the public was moved and the public had a right to expect some changes in the system. Patronage is inevitable, but its incidence can be changed.

I would appoint directors of crown corporations, and other important bodies, on merit. If necessary, I would create useless jobs to employ political hacks, but I would not put them where their decisions mattered. I would also reform the system of appointments of judges, which threatens the integrity of our legal system. For federal appointments I would adopt (and for provincial appointments urge) a system by which the law society would draw up a list of acceptable names and we politicians would dispense patronage to our friends from this list of competent people. To a purist, this much patronage is undesirable; to a realist, it would be a vast improvement on what we now have.

Choosing Policies on Merit

Opinion polls suggest that there is little profit in buying votes by favouring regions. The Conservatives, like the Liberals before them, have been great givers of favours to regions, ignoring what they regard as such politically trivial criteria as cost effectiveness and long-run growth potential. Yet the latest poll shows that the majority of voters in every region feel that the government has discriminated against their own region! The possibilities of acting on this information are stupendous. I would make decisions on objective criteria: give contracts to the lowest bidder; put prisons where they are really needed; bail out firms only if they have a chance of soon standing on their own feet; and so on. Wherever the chips fell, on balance just about as many locally affected interest groups would feel aggrieved as they now do, and just about as many would be pleased. In the process, however, an element of rationality would have been injected into decision-making.

Federal-Provincial Matters

I would worry a great deal about our country's federal-provincial structure. I would fight a heroic but probably losing battle to make Canada one country economically. Today, local beers produced in one Canadian province can be bought throughout the United States but not in other Canadian provinces. Today, workers from one Canadian province find it difficult, sometimes impossible, to get jobs in other Canadian provinces. Ridiculous! We should be one country without interprovincial barriers to the employment of Canadian people and the sale of Canadian goods. When our constitution was repatriated, the principle of the common market should have been written into it—as it is, for example, in Australia. That opportunity was lost; but I would do my best, including calling a constitutional convention, to create a Canadian common market.

I would also try to get more regional representation in Canada. This could be done by making the Senate an elected body with an equal number of representatives from each Canadian province. I would worry about giving P.E.I. the same number of senators as Ontario and Quebec, but the gain in regional representation would probably be worth it.

Foreign Policy

I would make Canada much more vocal in its opposition to many aspects of current American foreign policy. I would support what I perceive as the genuine Russian desire for arms control. I would support the Contadora movement in Central America. Given the feudal systems under which many Central American countries labour, gyrations to the left and to the right will be hard to avoid on the route to their own national destinies; but by seeing every leftward shift engineered by domestic patriots as an international communist conspiracy, the American government is vastly increasing the difficulties faced by less developed societies who are seeking to work out their own destinies.

I would allocate a large sum to pay the fees of foreign students studying in Canadian universities. Citizens often ask why they should pay to educate foreigners. I would answer by making it clear that the funds came from the budget for foreign aid. There are few expenditures on aid more valuable than training the elite of less developed countries in needed skills. Not only is this good humanitarian practice; it is good self-interest. Senior government officials usually look first to the country where they were educated when they want to buy goods or know-how. For this reason, money spent to educate these future leaders pays dividends in later years.

Domestic Policies

If I entered office with the national disgrace of a return to capital punishment, I would do all I could to reverse that decision. I could call a national convention where all arguments would be displayed and subjected to critical appraisal. This would give maximum publicity to the evidence, known for thirty-five years, that not only does capital punishment fail as a deterrent to murder but it actually acts as an encouragement to particular psychotic types. I might well lose in my attempt to restore abolition, but I would have tried.

I would spend a significant amount of money on prisons. First, I would give vent to my sense of outrage over politicians who seek to increase their votes by reducing the welfare of prisoners and their unfortunate families. I would set up a commission to establish and publicize the desirable principles for prison location, making it difficult for future politicians to trade other people's welfare for their own political benefit. Second, I would seek to create job-training facilities within prisons. Prisoners would learn marketable skills by doing jobs much the same as they would do in the outside world—and low-risk offenders could do some jobs outside the prison. The prisoners would earn the same wages as in the outside world (with deductions for room and board). The money would go to their families or would accumulate to help them when they were released.

As for education, although it is not primarily a federal responsibility, there are ways that the tied money I would grant could be made available to the provinces. I worry that ordinary Canadian workers may come out of school in the next decades poorly educated compared to their counterparts in Japan and Europe. If this happens, Canada will in time revert to making the low-valued, low-income-producing goods that less educated people are best at producing. The only way Canada can maintain its position as a high-income country is for our labour force to be high in skill relative to the rest of the world.

I would also put a substantial amount of money into basic research. I would try to create conditions such that Nobel Prize winners would not tell us that if they had to do it again, they would not do their research in Canada's hostile climate. A billion dollars—an amount that is given hardly without thinking to all kinds of industrial bailouts—could work wonders here. Research and development by firms should also be encouraged, but governments too often channel all their available funds into R & D, forgetting that basic research in universities and research organizations is the food that feeds applied R & D.

Funds would also be allocated to the construction of ships. I would build as many fisheries patrol vessels as were needed to preserve our control of Canadian fishing grounds against encroachment by American and French fishermen. I would also consider the call to build a fleet of atomic submarines to protect our sovereignty over the Arctic against American and Russian encroachment. Before giving in to the nuclear demand, I would call a conference of all the sovereignty experts and ask them if we could find ways of protecting our Arctic sovereignty that are less costly than a fleet of atomic submarines.

On a totally different front, I would seek to change the criminal law with respect to prostitution, allowing willing adult buyers and sellers to get on with what they want to do, uninhibited by the state. If their behaviour on the streets caused trouble, I would allow legal houses of prostitution and, by allowing co-operative brothels, I would free at least some of these unfortunate women from the tyranny of pimps.

I would not shy away from reform in unemployment insurance, since I accept what most people say behind the scenes: that the system could be reformed to deliver more to those who are in need and less to those who are not. Those who attack all changes in the present system seldom explain why it should be acceptable that so much unemployment insurance money currently goes to families with incomes of more than $25,000 a year.

I would support a three-pronged tax reform. The personal income tax should have its base broadened by eliminating most of the deductions for special schemes that mainly benefit higher income groups. Personal tax rates could then be lowered substantially with no loss of revenue. Second, the creaky manufacturers' sales tax should be replaced by a broad-based business transfer tax. Third, important but largely technical reforms are needed to the corporate income tax.

Finances

Much of what I have advocated above would cost money—probably several billion dollars. Mr. Wilson's deficit-reducing plan must be adhered to lest the interest payments on an ever-growing national debt come to take up more and more tax revenue, leaving less and less for other purposes. For this reason, any new expenditures must be matched by new tax revenues.

To do this I would use two sources. First, I would raise about a billion dollars—and increase equity at the same time—by turning all present tax deductions into tax credits. Under the present system, allowances for such things as dependants, old age, and Canadian interest are deducted from each taxpayer's gross income to get taxable income. The value of these deductions ranges from over fifty cents in the dollar, for people with high incomes, to zero for people whose incomes are below the tax threshold. This is inequitable. Converting all of these allowances into tax credits would mean that their values (which would have to be adjusted) would be deducted from each person's tax bill (and a rebate paid if the tax bill was thereby rendered negative). This would make the allowances worth the same at all levels of income.

Secondly, I could raise several billions by reducing services and subsidies to business. The Nielsen task force—remember the high expectations once held for it?—calculated that $4.5 billion is paid out in subsidies to business while $7.7 billion of taxes are not collected, because of special business exemptions. No doubt, special interest groups would complain bitterly when they lost some of their goodies, but there is quite enough money in that pork barrel to finance all of my new expenditures several times over.*

* The views expressed in this article are those of the author only and do not reflect those of the institutions with which he is associated.

JOHN S. MCCALLUM

What one would do as prime minister depends on one's vision of the country. Turning the vision into reality requires not only the right strategic decisions but also a consensus within the country that the vision is where we want to go. Mobilizing people around a vision is the essence of leadership; but even the strongest of leaders cannot indefinitely sustain a vision that does not reflect a community's history, culture, ethics, attitudes and ways.

The prime minister, by virtue of his office, has awesome power "to do"; but to discharge his duties effectively and to maintain the office, he must use this power sparingly, relying on communication, logic, wisdom, common sense, and charisma. No vision has a chance over time in a free country if there is the widespread perception that it is being insensitively imposed on the citizens. No vision has much of a chance, either, unless it is carefully, completely, and consistently presented and reinforced through widely available policy papers and through ministerial speeches, media appearances, and town hall dialogues.

Let me propose this vision for Canada: a democratic country, able to employ its citizens in secure jobs that generate an output of goods and services sufficient to provide a high overall standard of living, while at the same time permitting us to play an important role in the defence of the free world and development of the less developed world.

We have done not too badly, and better than most, at achieving this vision. Recognizing this, what the prime minister should *not* do is probably more important than what he should do. He should categorically not attempt a kind of "ninety days of decision" aimed at turning the country upside down. Such would be far more likely to produce chaos and alienation rather than increased prosperity and harmony. To quote David Stockman, Ronald Reagan's budget adviser, a country "shuffles into the future, one step at a time. It cannot leap into revolutions without falling flat on its face."

First, I would propose an amendment to the Canadian constitution, phasing in a requirement that in peacetime the federal government must match its spending with its tax and other revenues over rolling five-year periods. Because of our huge interest obligations, to move immediately to a balanced budget would bring risk and hardship that would not be justified by the potential benefits. In satisfying the amendment, I would rely far more on spending cuts than on tax increases. The likely effect on the federal deficit and debt of a repeat of anything resembling the 1981-82 high interest rate recession brings the need for a balanced budget amendment sharply into focus.

Such a balanced budget requirement would impose a fiscal discipline on our next generation of politicians which they would not be capable of on their own. John Maynard Keynes provided many insights on the contribution that deficits can make to growth and job creation during a recession, but he did not explain how to get politicians to restrain themselves during the good times.

A balanced budget amendment is important for a number of reasons. There is little peacetime historical evidence that our approach, since the mid-1970s, of having the federal government debt grow at well in excess of debt-service capacity leads over time to a prosperous economy. The amendment would free resources for the more efficient private sector to invest in the state-of-the-art plant, equipment, machinery, product and market development, research, and training that are so crucial to international success in the high-employing industries of the future. Canadians would be justifiably inspired to keep their capital here—rather than shipping it elsewhere, as has been our wont for years; moreover, foreign capital could be expected to look more favourably on Canada. Fiscal prudence in the strong part of the business cycle would leave the federal government with a far greater capacity to stimulate and manage the economy creatively in the weak part of the cycle. The effects on inflation, interest rates, and the dollar would be favourable.

The amendment has that most desirable of characteristics of emphasizing income creation before income distribution. It would force the federal government to use resources more efficiently, thereby moderating such long-standing irritants as politically inspired regional development and the abuse of government services. The user fees for government services that would inevitably follow the amendment would lead Canadians to be less wasteful and more demanding of excellence.

Finally, the amendment would give our politicians a scapegoat for the service cutbacks and tax increases that are already inevitable because of our past profligacy. Asking voters to pay higher taxes, in order to cover interest payments on money borrowed to provide already consumed and forgotten past services, does not go over well in election campaigns. Neither does a restraint program aimed at saving the voters from a financial ailment which they do not understand or even know they have.

This book serves the useful purpose of demonstrating the extraordinary diversity of Canadian public opinion, which makes the prime minister's job so challenging. Diverse public opinion does not, however, count for much when it comes to what constitutes prudent financial practice. Between 1976 and 1984, we were decidedly on the imprudent side. The fact that every senior government in Canada now faces an indefinite future of service cutbacks and tax increases confirms that the next part of our financial journey will be a good deal less pleasant than the last.

Our past financial misconduct imperils our capacity to continue to make social and economic progress; it also threatens what we have already achieved. As we contemplate where we go from here, with our oppressively expensive social programs, we should note historian Edward Gibbon on the decline of the Athenian democracy: "In the end, they [the Greeks] valued security more than they valued freedom and they lost both."

Second, regardless of future temptations, I would greatly restrict federal government foreign borrowing, with the exception of that needed for the short-term support of our currency. Hasty devaluation is not the route to prosperity and international competitiveness. After several devaluations between 1976 and 1984, our share of international trade has declined, unemployment remains unacceptably high, we are not competitive in a host of today's important industries, and, most worrisome, we are poorly positioned in key industries of the future, such as microelectronics, bio-industry, and space age materials.

These are the reasons for keeping foreign borrowing to a minimum. It represents a discipline on government spending. It avoids the risk of large, unanticipated government financial obligations that are associated with untoward currency movements. It greatly reduces the possibility of a future financial crisis. In time, foreign borrowing often gives nameless, faceless international bankers (who are accountable only to their boards of directors) a say in the conduct of domestic policy.

The proposition that federal government debt is not worrisome if we owe most of the debt to ourselves is naive; but if the federal debt is kept within the country, it at least leaves us to determine the options and to make the choices if a financial crisis develops. The foreign creditors' lever for inserting themselves, without invitation, into domestic policy processes is the very real threat that they will withhold credit crucial to local standards of living. Those who think that Canada could never develop a serious foreign-borrowing problem are generally not aware that our provinces and corporations already have serious foreign-debt problems.

Third, I would put great emphasis on a formal trade agreement with the United States that guaranteed preferred access to U.S. markets for our goods and services. Such a free-trade agreement will be painful and costly on several fronts, but it beats the alternative of being picked apart, industry by industry, by a protectionist U.S. Congress and a tired administration. Effective dispute settlement mechanisms are an unpublicized key to an agreement.

What opponents of a U.S. trade agreement are unwilling to accept is that the United States is no longer willing to tolerate the huge merchandise surplus we now enjoy. The Americans argue that merchandise surplus costs them too many jobs, contributes significantly to their burgeoning debtor-nation status, and has only been achieved through an array of unfair trade practices which range from a managed currency to liberal subsidies and preferential licensing arrangements. With over one-fifth of our Gross Domestic Product made up of trade with the United States, and with expanded European and Asian trade being difficult, the only thing worse for our standard of living than an agreement with the United States would be no agreement.

Fourth, I would step up the pace of privatization. Repeated experiments in North America, Europe, and Latin America confirm that government-owned corporations do not deliver goods and services to the citizens as efficiently and effectively as private firms that are competing in free markets where the survival and profit imperatives demand a high level of consumer satisfaction. Government enterprises usually suffer from political interference, mediocrity in the executive suite, slow response times, and market insensitivity.

Unresponsive, uncompetitive government enterprises exact a particularly heavy burden on standards of living in the present rapidly changing, fiercely competitive, international business world. The decisive question on government enterprise should not be what they do for us now but what could alternatively be done with the resources. On this basis, there is a host of privatization candidates in communications, energy, health, and transportation.

Fifth, I would remove financial penalties on provinces that allow extra-billing by doctors. Not allowing people to contribute directly to their own health care promotes inefficiency and waste; in time, it will reduce the quality of health care; and it encourages those who are financially able to seek high-quality care in other jurisdictions, thus depriving our economy of jobs and activity.

Advancing medical technology and an aging population assure a future of rapidly growing health care costs. Our provinces can barely afford their present health care bills. People who are able to do so should contribute directly to their own health care. As with privatization, in health care policy we should put great emphasis on the benefits from alternative uses of the funds, rather than blindly pursuing universal health care, regardless of the costs.

Finally, I would make a series of moves aimed at promoting the work ethic, entrepreneurship, innovation, investment, international manufacturing competitiveness, and rapid adjustment to changing workplace technologies, consumer wants, and input costs. To keep Canadian capital and skilled labour here—and to stimulate worker effort, entrepreneurship, innovation, and investment—I would significantly reduce personal and corporate tax rates and replace the lost revenues with a tax on consumption. To the extent possible jurisdictionally, market-distorting and incentive-sapping devices such as high minimum wages, rent controls, industrial subsidies, corporate bailouts, and equal pay for work of equal value would be discouraged. No new universal government social programs would be introduced, and an effort would be made to tie current programs more to need. Investment-oriented government spending (such as that associated with professional education, worker training, scientific research, and industrial development) would be given a much greater priority.

This type of program has often produced an internationally competitive strong-growth economy with a high standard of living. History is not on the side of finding prosperity in ever-higher taxes, ever-greater government deficits, ever-increasing government intervention in the economy, an ever-increasing number of universal social programs, ever-greater and more powerful government bureaucracies, and decreasing reliance on individual wants and needs expressed in free markets. We shall be a unique exception if we are able to borrow, subsidize, and intervene our way to a sustainable prosperity.

THELMA MCCORMACK

A long career of critical opposition to the politics of both left and right makes it very unlikely that I would ever become prime minister; personally, I would not "make book" on it. But if I did become the PM, the first hundred days would, I hope, put Canada back in the forefront of nations that measure their progress by the degree to which they realize the potential of their people. Our current political agenda does not. Its steady drift towards the deregulation of the economy and the regulation of morality has made us intolerant, narrow minded, and ungenerous towards those less fortunate at home or abroad. My government would reverse this: more social economics and less concern about cultural repression (anti-pornography legislation) and punitive justice (capital punishment).

Three Guidelines
In recent years, the welfare state and Keynesian economics have been subject to extensive criticism, by friends as well as enemies. According to the critics, the policies not only do not work but they create their own secondary problems. Yet they were introduced because policies based on *laissez-faire* economics didn't work either. Recent revivals of this have proved just as disastrous, especially in Third World countries where supply-side economics have made the wretched of the earth still more wretched.

If I have to choose, then, between these two imperfect economic models, Keynes or Friedman, I would prefer the less individualistic, the one that appeals to co-operative solutions and social welfare rather than to personal self-interest, the one that gives hope for a future to all of us, rather than to the few. Beware economists with a nostalgia for the sweat shops, the Great Depression, and child labour of the past!

The second guideline for policies would be the balance between excellence and equity. When in doubt, favour equity, for no democracy ever died of too little excellence, while a great many died because of too little equity.

However, one of the current shibboleths on both the left and the right is that we must choose between equality and civil liberties, between Section 15 of the Charter and Section 2(b). But that is a cruel and unusual choice, for these values are two sides of the same coin;

they flourish together, not apart. E. P. Thompson, the British social historian and peace activist, was once discussing a similar problem, the trade-off between disarmament and human rights. "It is wrong," he wrote, "to say that human rights must be a condition for disarmament: that way we will get neither. It is wrong to say that human rights will be the consequence of disarmament: our friends on the other side have not given us power of attorney to make that decision. Both must take place together, as part of a single process, the making of a democratic peace." The same is true of equality and freedom of expression; like human rights and disarmament, they are inseparable. That is the third guideline.

The Decline of the Macho State
My first act would be to appoint a cabinet made up of persons chosen on the basis of their expertise and androgyny scores. The latter, eminently fair and totally objective, would go far, I believe, in ending the era of the macho state without substituting its opposite and equally offensive alternative, represented in the thinking of REAL Women. With high androgyny scores, we can alter the political culture of Canada without acquiescing, as we have in the past, to the gender bias that pervades our social institutions. The same criteria, incidentally, would apply to the selection of heads of crown corporations. The result would not be Utopia, but it would have a salutary effect on our political culture and the quality of life.

Universal Social Security for Children
Divorce and remarriage are part of the Canadian way of life, norms that reflect our commitment to marriage based on interpersonal compatibility. No-fault divorce was part of the same enlightened direction and was proposed nearly twenty years ago by the Royal Commission on the Status of Women. But in recent years there has been a disillusionment with no-fault divorce, especially in marriages where women have custody of dependent children. (In about half of our divorces there are no children.) Support payments by absent fathers are usually inadequate and often irregular, while the woman who re-enters the labour force finds she is disadvantaged by her lack of experience, her comparatively low level of education, and by wage inequities and other forms of sexism in the workplace. As a result of this constellation of problems, women who at one time supported a provision in the family reform legislation for no-fault divorce are now returning to a concept of culpability.

Far wiser, in my opinion, would be to separate the two issues—the reasons for terminating a marriage and child support—and provide for the basic needs of children through a universal system of social insurance. In effect, this is what does happen when a marriage is terminated through the death of the spouse; children are automatically protected by insurance. Why should children in divorced families be any less protected?

A universal system that would click into operation as soon as the divorce or separation was final (without a means test and with no questions asked) would give children the basic security they need and would spare them the stigmatizing effects of divorce and debt, while the cost of tracing and pursuing former husbands who default on child support would be eliminated. In a recent study of the U.S. legislation to enforce child support, a sociologist found that it primarily benefited middle-class women, who got a good bookkeeping system out of it, while the women on welfare were still on welfare.

The male economists with whom I have discussed social security for children are appalled. Their reasons are interesting and suggest that chivalry may not be quite dead. Almost all say that it would make it easier for men to "fool around" and walk away from their responsibilities. I don't know whether this low opinion of their own gender is the result of their sex-role socialization or their neoconservative economics, but their attitude assumes that marriage is a partnership of unequals. Men typically underestimate the extent to which women might have another concept of the marriage relationship, and consequently they overlook the fact that this vestigial patriarchal attitude can contribute to marriage breakdown. One of the major advantages of the system proposed—apart from its administrative simplicity and the cost/benefit advantage in eliminating enforcement procedures—is that it would contribute to a more egalitarian model of marriage. No-fault divorce backed up with a safe, predictable income for children would reduce the dependency of wives, and to that extent would contribute to a future model of egalitarian marriage, a relationship which is at neither partner's financial or, hopefully, emotional expense.

Nationalization of Data Banks

When François Mitterrand came to power in France, one of his first acts was to nationalize the banks. It was a stunning move, but ever since things have been downhill in France. Throughout our modern history banks have been distrusted, and the stereotype of the wicked banker gouging the poor has become part of our art and part of our mythology of good and evil. (Dante had a special ring for them in the *Inferno*.) But modern financial institutions have less impact on our lives than the information industries do. Our new rogues are not bankers but those "insiders" who are privy to organizational information on pending mergers. What these new white-collar crimes demonstrate is the corruption of our new fiduciary system, where information has become a powerful commodity. The old socialist slogan to nationalize the banks is outdated; it is the data banks we should own and control, for information has become a primary form of wealth, as divisive as the ownership of capital was in the early part of the century and the basis of new kinds of structural disparities.

To be without information, to have less while others have more, means simply that we are unable to participate intelligently in any social or economic planning or to hold others accountable. But in addition to becoming marginalized and excluded from the major decision-making processes that impact on our lives, we may become strangers in our own country, for the data-processing and data-storage systems in the United States are gearing up for activity in international markets. Knowledge about us will be subject to their rules about privacy and "security," which are shaped in part by their defence establishment. At best, we may have to buy it back; at worst, we lose access entirely, and this includes knowledge now being generated by universities, which we think of as belonging to all of the people, to an international community. Ultimately, outsiders may structure our research agenda as part of their co-ordinated plan.

Farewell to Fee-for-Service Medicine
The recent doctors' strike in Ontario over extra-billing went a long way towards discrediting a fee-for-service basis of health care. At one point in those sorry events, women were being held hostage as doctors refused to perform scheduled abortions or to serve on therapeutic abortion committees. Misogyny aside, the strike demonstrated that physicians want the benefits of a social monopoly and a market model of delivery. The time has come to put all of our physicians on salary, as many of them already are.

Some would leave Canada, perhaps going back to the United Kingdom, where Margaret Thatcher is busy dismantling the National Health Service, or going to the United States. But most would stay, especially if the costs of medical education were fully covered. Meanwhile, the relative immobility of many women physicians would take up the slack. And without the entrepreneurial drive, we might be able to build our medicine around more holistic models of health and create a health-care delivery system that could accommodate alternative systems of health care, including greater use of nurse practitioners.

Culture and the State
In Israel there is a running debate about the plants and shrubs that have been growing between the bricks and in the cracks of the Wall, which engineers have said is weakening the structure. One group

argues that these plants should be removed and replanted nearby. Another group argues that if God put the plants between the cracks, He meant them to be there and it would be sacrilege to remove them. I think of this Talmudic reasoning whenever we engage in our continuing debate on the future of the CBC.

The Applebaum-Hébert Report recommended dismantling it; the Caplan-Sauvageau Report recommended strengthening it. But neither of these reports recognizes that the CBC has long ago stopped communicating, that it no longer understands the aspirations and ethos of the people as it did so effectively in the postwar period. Today's CBC defines the public as "they," as the "other," and can't tell the difference between the women's movement and the Girl Guides. The women's movement, the peace movement, and the environmental movement are equated with hobbyists or "interest groups," but either way they are shut out or trivialized.

I give up on the CBC. Let it be "program-driven," as the Caplan-Sauvageau Report recommends. But the cutting edge of our culture will come from elsewhere, from the experimental film and video makers, from the margins of the art world, the political humour of the coffee houses, the small theatres, the university galleries, and the off-beat magazines. The alternative culture is less interested in celebrating Canadian culture than in changing it. It is what the CBC used to be; it was the language of a cultural and social revolution in Canada—just as French, and the issue of French, was the language of the Péquiste revolution. I would like to see closer links between the alternative or countercultures and the universities, but however it is organized it will need major subsidies.

There are other similarly modest proposals my government would try to enact during the Imperial Prime Ministry: making Canada a nuclear-free zone; building a foreign policy around the problems—social, economic and political—of the Third World; eliminating the term "welfare" and substituting the less invidious term "subsidy"; increasing support of research in the humanities and the social sciences, which are less likely to be funded by the private sector. These are some of my priorities.

The items I have listed look more like Dim Sum than a coherent program, yet they do reveal my background. When I was a student, I was very much influenced by the work of R. H. Tawney; in recent years, it has been the theories of gender and cultural liberation as reflected in feminist theory. And still more recently, I have watched and learned from the transformation of a society in Quebec. A year spent in Halifax at Mount Saint Vincent University gave me back that faith in human nature and community that was nearly lost in academic elitism. These are my only qualifications should that moment ever come when *l'état* became *moi*.

DONALD MACDONALD

First, a word about the theme of this book and the question I have been asked to respond to: What would I do if I were prime minister? I have had two opportunities in the past to *try* to become prime minister. The first was in 1979 when I was willing but the opportunity disappeared, and the second was in 1984 when the opportunity came again but I decided not to reach for it. Lest it appear that I am looking for a third chance, I shall respond to a somewhat different question: What would I expect of a prime minister?

A political leader like the prime minister not only has the opportunity to present a specific agenda of policy and law but also has the opportunity to state a broader set of national goals and to bring about a change in public attitudes. One example from my own time in politics was the way in which Pierre Elliott Trudeau achieved a dramatic redirection in the thinking of English-speaking Canadians towards the French fact in Canada by gaining acceptance—by many Canadians in all provinces—for the concept that the French language is more than just something to be tolerated: it is a fundamental element of our national being. Another was the viewpoint that Lester B. Pearson represented of Canada as a knowledgeable and responsible player on the world scene, seeking not just to advance its own interests but also to guide the international community in more rational policy directions.

The two tasks of this kind that I would set for a prime minister in the late 1980s and 1990s would be, firstly, to make Canadians fully aware of the fundamental changes that are occurring in Canada's economy; and, secondly, to awaken the confidence of Canadians that we have the skills and resources to adapt successfully to these fundamental changes.

Compared either with the experience of other countries or with our own history, the four decades between the end of World War II and the mid-1980s were a period of remarkable economic success for Canada. The Canadian economy grew to be one of the strongest in the world, and the economic circumstances of many Canadians were dramatically changed for the better. There were numerous reasons for this economic success, but the most important was the development of Canada's exceptional resource base.

What will happen in the balance of this decade and into the 1990s—and, indeed, what is happening right now—is that the world's demand for more production of Canada's resources has come to an end. The resource sector will always be important for Canadians, but the rate of growth it has known in the past will not continue. If we expect to enjoy continued improvement in our standard of living, and if we expect to engage in the kind of public programs at home and abroad that we would like to, then we are going to have to find a new economic vocation. This is not a popular thought, but it is an inescapable one.

When you have been making something and selling it, and then your customer says, "I don't need it any more" or "I can get it cheaply from someone else," then you have a change that you must adapt to. The correct reaction to this change is not to curse your fate or to blame someone else in your community or, least of all, to do nothing. The only response is to say, "I'll have to find something else to do, something that will give me an income and will pay for the things I would like to do for myself and mine, and for others."

This kind of situation, the end of an economic vocation and the need to begin another, is where Canada finds herself today. The last thing we should be doing about it is nothing (although there are some among us who would persuade us to do just that). We can't afford to assume that things will work themselves out in our favour without adaptation, without effort, or without using our minds. Consequently, the first task that I think our prime minister must discharge is to bring about a better realization, among Canadians, of this fundamental change in our circumstances.

His or her second task would be to try and liberate Canadians from the self-image—sometimes expressed but so often implied—that we cannot excel in the world, that somehow to be Canadian is to be second-rate. Vincent Massey, a proud Canadian, once wrote, with justice: "We have never been guilty of being too sure of ourselves." I am not arguing for a stupid cockiness; but rather for just a little self-confidence based on our capacity for success, as demonstrated by our achievements of the past.

Canada has enjoyed many notable successes of which we can be proud. The building of a nation with a constitutional, democratic structure, which now has a longer period of continuity than many other nations (not just in the developing world, but among the proud powers of Europe) is one such success. Another is the creation of a standard of living that is among the highest in the world within a successful economy—and this despite the most difficult endowments in geography and certainly one of the most difficult legacies of weather. A third is the building of a society with a level of tolerance and civility that bears favourable comparison with any other state in the world. These are all Canadian achievements which should persuade us that we can do and can be almost anything we want—if we are prepared to set for ourselves high standards and difficult goals, and if we are prepared to believe in ourselves.

As well as looking to a prime minister to give leadership in attitudes, let me also suggest to him a policy agenda. I would set five program priorities. (I give these in summary terms, because a more extensive description and argument for them may be found in the report of the royal commission of which I was chairman.)

Firstly, to meet all our other objectives as a country, we must secure our economic base. Canada has prospered in the past because it was able to trade in a world market. To continue this prosperity in the future, we must negotiate more favourable access for Canadian goods and services in markets throughout the world, but particularly in the market of our nearest and best customer—the United States. Gaining this access will have a cost for us, but far less of a cost than if we fail to take the initiative and risk declining into economic stagnation.

Secondly, we must restructure our programs of income security to make certain that in providing assistance and support from public funds, those who are given priority in concern are those who need assistance the most. We have built a comprehensive set of programs to meet the income concerns of Canadians. But these programs do not adequately meet the requirements of those among us who should have first call on our national resources: those who are most in need. We should be prepared to alter other social benefits to make certain this priority is met.

Thirdly, we must orient our programs of education so that Canadians will be prepared for the kinds of change they may expect to encounter in their lives. It is no longer a question of training for a single lifelong career. Most people in the next generation will be faced with adjusting to two or three or more jobs in their lifetime. Indeed, the concept of work itself is undergoing an important change. Our emphasis in education must be not just to train for a specific task but to prepare the work force to adapt to changing opportunities.

Education is closely connected at the university level with basic research. Good education is fundamental to our success, but so is maintaining the capacity to do the fundamental research which is at the source of innovation. Enhancing the Canadian capacity to do the basic work of discovery, and our ability to apply the results in the market place, will also be a key to future economic success.

My fourth task for a prime minister would be to address that quintessential Canadian problem—interprovincial and interregional conflict—which has been so much a part of our history and remains a current concern. In an increasingly competitive world, the inability to resolve conflicts between ourselves impairs our ability to respond to challenges from abroad. One of the strengths of the Canadian confederation has been that we have found ways in our political system to accommodate regional differences. But while Canadians want the kind of regional choice that our system provides, they also expect that these differences will be reconciled in order to meet national goals. We need a new set of institutions which can aid in bringing about a better reconciliation of regional differences.

Finally, Canadians have come to expect of their government that it will play a positive role within the world. Attempting to help others is not a Canadian service that is new to this generation. Missionaries from Canadian churches began to play a significant role in other countries in the last century, as our soldiers have done in this one. I referred earlier to the positive contribution that Canada made, under Lester B. Pearson, to a more stable world community. But the policies and roles that Canadians defined in the circumstances of the 1940s and 1950s need to be redefined in the changed environment of the 1980s and 1990s. Canada has the position in the world, the means, and the inclination to play the part of leadership in seeking the betterment of mankind. We should not be content to leave the conduct of international relations to the Great Powers. Our aim should be to ensure that the interests of the small as well as the great are taken into account within the community of nations.

If the prime minister can meet these expectations, then he will have made a great contribution both to his country and to the world community. His period in office will deservedly be known as one of the "great ministries."

ALEXA MCDONOUGH

I've devoted many waking hours over the past seven years to pondering what I would do if I were premier—of my beloved Nova Scotia. Trying to get from where I sit as leader of a tiny, brave, third-party caucus into the premier's chair to act out these ambitious dreams has taken most of my energies and all the intellectual capital I could spare.

The rude reality of how hard it is to get from here to there and the stark realization of how much easier it is to dream the dreams than to implement them effectively have been important lessons in humility (missed, apparently, in Mr. Mulroney's political upbringing, much to the benefit of the NDP!). Arriving at 24 Sussex Drive by editorial whim rather than through electoral toil is the easier route, that's for sure! Besides, what would I put in all those closets if I were to arrive there in real life?

At last, the great day has come. My New Democrat colleagues and I sit as the Government of Canada. I look around at my colleagues— perhaps the most intelligent, able, resourceful and decent group of men and women this old chamber has ever seen (big improvement over a caucus of three from my days in the Nova Scotia legislature). I think what it must mean to those who worked so long and hard that our vision might be kept alive and growing in the public consciousness. I look around at the other first-timers, no doubt as scared as I am—and as determined, for we have inherited a sea of trouble.

We lead a country battered and diminished by as mean-spirited, mealy-mouthed, and two-faced a government as Canada has had to endure in a long time. Productive workers have been tossed on the scrapheap, sacrificed to the god of the Bottom Line. The numbers of hungry children and homeless families have increased. Young people are idle and understandably restless, many like lost souls turning to senseless crime. Soup kitchens, food banks, and emergency shelters springing up in every city symbolize a seeming contradiction between people's generous impulses and the nation's inability to organize itself to meet the most basic of human needs. Every day a little less of Canada is ours. Month by month our independence seeps away.

I am conscious of being leader of a party elected more out of desperation than understanding or hope. Demonstrators on Parliament Hill this morning seemed a little less angry, but what if we should fail them?

I look around the chamber to those back benches where *they* sat almost alone or in their tiny minorities. I need no reminding that those social democratic pioneers transformed Canada, nevertheless, in ways that make every hospital patient and senior citizen glad, and cause the young, when they are privileged to go abroad, to plaster big Canada labels and red maple leaves on their luggage, lest they be mistaken for their more backward southern neighbour.

No, we will not fail them. As prime minister, my certainties are theirs. Canada and every other country has the right to life, liberty, and the pursuit of happiness, its own way. "Might makes right" cannot be allowed to reign in any neighbourhood, especially if that neighbourhood encompasses the globe—or the whole "universe," to bring it up to date.

Canada has the right—and a responsibility, surely—to put its own house in order, to follow its own destiny under international laws (perhaps as leader in a coalition of non-aligned states). Under my government, Canada will not support, openly or covertly, those who stick their noses into the business of other countries (e.g., profiteering from Vietnam). It will not engage in holy wars against either the right or the left, but it will participate eagerly in internationally sanctioned action to extend support to members of the human family who need it.

Canada is, to use a cliché, a land of incalculable resources. We have able people. There is an inexhaustible list of things needing to be done and of needs and desires to be met. By defining these and setting out to meet the needs, we get rid of unemployment—or at least dramatically reduce it, which in turn allows us to begin making a dent in the deficit. A country has to be crazy to let good workers go idle or to waste $20-an-hour abilities on $4-an-hour tasks. My government's statistics will never report smugly that an engineering graduate is fully employed as a seasonal waiter in a fast-food outlet.

As a new government, we have arrived with a long list of things that must be done, preferably at once. The caucus, the cabinet, and I have—with vociferous arguments, of course, in the best NDP tradition—mapped out our priorities. First, as in any family, the children must be taken care of. The nation's children must be fed at nutritionally adequate levels, of which many are now deprived. They must have shelter and protection. But this is an automatic reflex with NDP governments. My ministers can certainly be trusted to take care of it. They can be left to set the child-care wheels in motion. They will tackle with pent-up energy the whole terrible issue of poverty and misery in the midst of affluence.

My own special task begins with trying to assure the survival of Canada in every sense of the word. We must guard against being vaporized by our unsettling neighbours or by even crazier members of the nuclear club. We must strengthen our backbone in dealing with those who take advantage of less developed countries or less well defended nations. My government will speak up for the right of all nations to live freely within their own boundaries, but it will also co-operate with international authorities in the protection of the persecuted wherever they may be.

If our chief trading partner remains adamant about erecting trade barriers, or commands our support of its foreign policies as a condition of doing business, we may have to raise new trading partners from scratch. Nova Scotia has a foster village in Ethiopia, and if it thrives as it seems to be doing, the time will come when it will no longer be a dependant, of us or of anybody. Perhaps we have not only saved lives but found a trading partner—a customer and a supplier—as well as a prototype for future mutual assistance.

My government is proud that Canada has generally been well regarded internationally. We will move to repair what damage has been done by the Mulroney government's lap-dog adherence to certain American policies. We will take a firmer attitude towards superpower encroachment. To succeed, we will need to use the traditional skills of women more fully in dealing with confrontation and conflict. I look forward to the day when our caucus will have equal numbers of women and men. Politicians who are jealous of their macho image or are insecure about their own self-worth are less than fully effective as negotiators. Our efforts to maximize women's participation are finally paying off in electing more female parliamentarians—not as fast as we'd hoped, but enough to make a difference.

The task that will be the most fun and must engage us all is that of putting together the gigantic jigsaw puzzle of Canada's remarkable resources, its plentiful supply of workers, a bottomless pit of things that need to be done, and a long line of eager consumers. There can't be many countries where unemployment makes less sense than it does in Canada. I don't pretend that government, not even an NDP one, can do all this at once or alone. But suppose we entice the people of Canada into working together with us to solve this fascinating puzzle. From listening to "Cross-Country Check-Up," it's clear that there are a great many Canadians out there who are thoroughly frustrated because their knowledge, expertise, and ingenuity are never called upon. And among them they know every nook, cranny, and opportunity in the country.

A top priority task for my government will be to reassure Canadian financial and business interests. We are not intent on disrupting or destroying anything; only doing much more and much better with what we've got. Nor did we come to power empty headed about how we'd proceed. Other social democratic countries have managed to maintain low rates of unemployment while simultaneously controlling inflationary pressures and achieving impressive income growth and high rates of production—a balancing act that can only be pulled off if you involve every sector of society. With "jobs, jobs, jobs" and no strategy still fresh in their minds, Canadians seem eager to get involved in giving it their best shot. If we can get the structures in place early so as to ensure maximum participation in the partnership, then the labour market strategies, the incomes and investment policies, and the regional development programs will fall into place.

Our government must, I believe, conduct more small but sometimes daring experiments to test new ideas. We promise, however, that we will never order thousands of mailboxes without trying them out first on a couple of ten-year-old would-be vandals and a senior citizen with arthritis and bifocals. Nor will we ever fund a plastic coffin factory (as was done in Nova Scotia in the name of regional development) without a customer survey to discover whether anybody would be caught dead in one!

My government knows that the future does not belong to those with the biggest defence budgets. Both of the superpowers—the United States and the USSR—are now badly crippled by their defection of science and technology to the military. Maybe, like Japan, we can slide by them, almost unnoticed, while *their* brain power is out to lunch and their capital is tied up in less and less productive activity.

We must concentrate on those things that we most urgently need to know or that show the greatest promise for our health, happiness, peace, and prosperity.

I and my government long to know (and are prepared to research as an urgent priority) how to achieve greater productivity while getting more fun out of achieving it. We know that people will work tirelessly and happily if they love their work. (Would I be your prime minister today if that weren't true?) Look at the awesome effort, the intolerable discipline, and even the physical pain of the competing athlete or the ballet dancer; or the overwork of an executive addicted to her desk, or the artist enslaved to his painting.

Canada has shown some flair for high technology, and we will support research for this, as for much else, including clever, nonlethal methods of forcing those who would step on our sovereign toes to back off. We will stir up our inventors, both professional and amateur. Incentives will be offered, particularly for devices that fill an important human or industrial need; for schemes that generate large numbers of jobs with limited capital; and for goods that are particularly appropriate to the needs of emerging countries.

It goes without saying that we will support the arts and culture, but we will add an exciting new dimension. While Canada certainly does have artists of international acclaim, for every Karen Kain, Robertson Davies, or Maureen Forrester we have let thousands go to waste or have forced them to go south. Suppose Rita MacNeil had, far earlier in life, received the attention she and her talents deserved. Or suppose Glenn Gould's genius had cropped up in a family that only laughed and scorned his oddity; Canada would never have known how it had been impoverished.

So my government is setting up Operation Alert, offering sizable rewards for information leading to the discovery of children and adults who have remarkable potential in any sphere, and for schemes to ensure the fostering of their exceptional promise. The Tory government of Nova Scotia in 1985 gained general approval for donating a million and a half bucks to a racing yacht that scarcely got off the ground. Canadians can surely be persuaded to invest in talent trusts and human resource development with far more certain pay-offs. (But we must be prepared to argue, as David Suzuki did so convincingly at our 1985 federal convention, that research and development pay-offs, whether human or high tech, don't always produce in four-year election cycles!)

The challenges our new government faces are awesome, but so are the opportunities. Our every move will be inspired by the belief that Canada is more than a unique experiment worth preserving: it is an experiment that has only just begun. And if we are to realize our true potential as a caring, daring nation, we need all Canadians to participate. It is exciting that my cabinet and caucus are more representative in their ethnic and cultural diversity, their anglo-francophone and bilingual mix, and their socioeconomic background than any government in our history. That, in itself, will help more Canadians feel more involved; and a more representative government offers the potential for a nation to be more democratic, economically and socially as well as politically.

My government will do its best to erase the memory and to repair the damage of the mean-spirited political ideologies and economic policies of the last decade. We will not be driven by a ruthless competitiveness that puts greed at the top and humanity at the bottom. We intend to offer Canadians a chance to work together in jobs that use their talents—educated, energetic, with the best research and the benefits of technology to back them up, and with the vast resources of Canada to play with, limited only by a responsible concern for our children and for future generations.

For our government to be effective, we must be open and honest with Canadians. This will be politically hazardous, but it will be necessary if the Canadian people are to be involved in charting Canada's course. And no matter what political parties may offer voters in the future, Canadians having once been active in government will never again tolerate governments that shut them out!

PATRICK L. MCGEER

Canada is a country struggling to maintain a First World standard of living and First World social programs in the face of Third World economic leadership. If I were prime minister, I would provide this First World economic leadership by creating a high-technology industrial sector competitive with those of the United States and Japan.

Japan's wealth from high-technology trade has now made it the world's number-one exporter of capital, with a momentum that is just beginning. The 3.5 million man-years of industrial research it has completed in the past decade will ensure Japan's economic future for the next decade. The Americans and West Germans come closest to the Japanese in the pace of economic gain, because they possess the next two largest industrial scientific work forces. (The United States still leads all nations in standard of living, of course, because of its additional advantage of natural resources.) Canada has minimal participation in such high-technology economic activity, because it lacks a significant industrial research force. During the past decade, Canada completed just over 3 per cent of the amount of industrial research Japan completed, or about 110,000 man-years. Thus, there is very little new technology in the bank for exploitation and jobs in the next decade.

Industrial research is the essential forerunner of such development. Just as it is necessary to erect a dam before electricity can be generated or to build a railroad before freight can be moved, so it is necessary to complete research *before* the population can benefit from new manufacturing enterprises. Neither the end result nor the pace of development can be predicted for any given discovery from industrial research: on average, about a decade passes between laboratory success and full commercial exploitation.

In contrast to Canada, Japan has almost no natural resources. But it has proved that industrial scientists are a much more valuable asset to a nation than resources are—or, for that matter, lawyers, accountants, bureaucrats, or politicians. For more than a generation, Japan has been training its brightest young people to be scientists and engineers, and locking them into permanent careers. They now make up an industrial research force of 350,000 that is unmatched in sophistication by any other nation.

A senior General Motors executive described to me his whimsical plan to counter this force, especially as it applied to automobiles: for every thousand Japanese cars sold in the United States, the Japanese would be required to supply one engineer and to accept one American lawyer. He theorized that U.S. industry would improve and that, before long, Japanese industry would be as tangled in red tape as U.S. industry. I would not try to sell this plan to Canada, even though it is said that Canada is a country run by lawyers. (Certainly, we have an adequate supply of them. Ontario alone has as many lawyers as the whole of Japan.) But, as my top priority, I would immediately establish policies to provide Canada with as many scientist-inventors and engineer-developers per capita as in Japan.

To put it another way, I would correct the situation in which we have too few people inventing and developing goods in relation to the number available to manufacture and sell them. Exporting resources will not keep our people busy, nor will it generate adequate wealth. We have one of the highest unemployment rates in the Western world— over four times that of Japan. In the past decade, our dollar has declined dramatically, reducing the relative value of savings and earnings of all Canadians by roughly one-quarter. During the 1960s and 1970s, federal and provincial governments concentrated on social planning. In a vague sort of way, they assumed that economic growth was automatic—just as many Third World countries did. Now we are faced with huge annual government deficits, non-competitive taxation, lagging investment, and confusion as to where to turn for our future well-being.

Scientific research can be our economic salvation, but it cannot come without some sacrifice, because it will need to be supported for at least a decade before an economic pay-off can be anticipated. Policies will need to be introduced that have as their objective the recruitment and support of an industrial scientific force about five times the present size. This support must continue until the results of the research can be translated into new production and new jobs. To reach the same per capita level as Japan, about 700,000 man-years of industrial scientific research will be needed over a decade. Canada should then be internationally competitive. Once secured, the expanded industrial system will finance its own research and be able to supply sufficient taxes to support the country's social programs.

If I were prime minister, therefore, I would immediately introduce a Technology Incentive Program (TIP) to accomplish these 700,000 man-years of industrial research and to tip the industrial scales in Canada's favour. TIP would have three components, each of which is of proven effectiveness.

The first would be a tax incentive system, modified from the Scientific Research Tax Credit (SRTC) scheme that was introduced briefly at the federal level. The second and third would be the expansion to a national level of two highly successful initiatives that I introduced into British Columbia when I was science minister: a Science Council grant system and the Discovery Foundation concept.

The SRTC scheme, which the federal government flirted with and then abandoned after a few months, could have provided us with much of the industrial muscle we need. It was instituted in the dying days of the Liberals—almost as a deathbed repentance for the years of scientific neglect. But it was so ineptly managed that the newly elected Conservatives labelled it the greatest tax scam in Canadian history and then cancelled it. Only about half the money diverted from taxes actually found its way into science, because large amounts were siphoned off by professional consultants, both legal and financial, who commanded huge fees and then arranged for the placement of a significant proportion of the SRTCs in the hands of individuals who had no intention of doing research. More than a billion dollars went to these unscrupulous people. Nonetheless, the money that did find its way into legitimate industrial science will ultimately produce a handsome dividend for Canada.

Since the abuses of the scheme were easy to identify and correct, why was the scheme abandoned? Officials in the federal Department of Finance had originally estimated that $200-$300 million per year of tax funds would be diverted to research as a result of the SRTC program. Instead, it appeared as if the figure would be ten times as large. In their view, this investment in research was far too costly, and therefore they recommended cancellation. Canada is now stymied because bureaucratic leadership will not forego taxes and corporate leadership will not risk profits in order to do research.

The centrepiece of my TIP would be a modified tax transfer system, which would incorporate the attractive features of the SRTC plan but would eliminate its abuses. Companies selling research tax credits would be required to take some equity in the receiving company and also pay back taxes if the receiving company reneged on its research commitments. The plan would recognize that established corporate leadership in Canada lacks experience in research and has no intention of embarking upon it. It would further recognize that new companies must be developed to recruit the researchers—companies with a different attitude towards technological advance. Since these start-up companies would not yet have the profits to finance their own research and growth, the plan would permit them to use the profits from mature companies that would otherwise be paid in taxes.

If sustained, the program would redirect about $4 billion per year in taxes towards industrial research, as well as attracting an equal amount in equity from around the world. It could be expected to produce roughly 400,000 man-years of industrial research over a decade—more than half of our requirement to achieve adequate industrial growth. It would have the additional benefit of introducing the growth potential of research to many existing corporations which currently have no belief in its value to them.

There was an important side effect of the SRTC scheme that should generate considerable optimism about this particular component of TIP. A significant number of projects involving foreign discoveries were transferred to Canada for exploitation because of the SRTC incentives. The implication here is that by implementing sound policies, we can benefit industrially from discoveries made beyond our own boundaries.

The remaining scientific effort required to produce the necessary 700,000 man-years would come from existing industrial research, together with expansion to the national level of the B.C. Science Council grant system and the Discovery Foundation concept.

The B.C. Science Council gives grants to scientists whose applications have met the high professional standards of peer review, industrial applicants being given priority where possible. An independent consultant's evaluation of the results after the first five years of the program found that there had already been a four-fold return to the economy of the grant money spent, with a twenty-fold return being predicted through the lifetime of the technologies developed. A follow-up report estimated there had been an eighteen-fold lost opportunity from other meritorious applicants who had been turned down because of lack of funds. Based on this favourable experience, I would greatly expand the program, making $400 million a year available to provincially created science councils across the country. This would assure the strong support of science in all parts of Canada and could be expected to produce another 60,000 man-years of scientific effort over a decade. It would greatly enhance the efforts of the National Science and Engineering Council, which primarily supports university scientists.

British Columbia's Discovery Foundation is an independent society that was created to support entrepreneurial efforts in high technology. It operates research parks at each B.C. university, a venture capital fund, and multitenant research buildings in which new companies can start their industrial work. Several dozen small high-technology companies have been incubated in these facilities. Their success rate has been 95 per cent, compared to the typical North American survival rate of small businesses of less than 30 per cent. Some of these corporations will grow into multimillion-dollar enterprises, but only time will tell which ones. The sums involved to make this a national scheme would be modest, because the activities would soon become self-supporting. I would initially allocate $100 million per year to start provincial foundations but would phase this out over a decade. A further 100,000 man-years of industrial scientific effort could be derived from this source. Maintaining the existing industrial scientific force of 14,000 for a decade would make up the remainder of the necessary 700,000 man-years.

I realize that this scientific research program is not the heady stuff of populist politics, and I would not promise my followers re-election on the basis of such a program. As a recently defeated provincial politician, I can provide first-hand evidence of this program's limited electoral value if dealt with on an orphan basis. On the other hand, our country was built by pioneers who made sacrifices for the generations that followed. I believe that Canadians would be willing to carry this tradition onward by making small sacrifices for the decade it would take to put Canadian science on its feet. A national political leader has an unequalled opportunity to explain such a program to the public and thereby gain their support. The stakes are too high to ignore the challenge.

GEORGE MANUEL

As one who believes in the sovereignty of our "Indian" nations, my first task as prime minister would be to work out the ways to make this possible. I would persuade my colleagues to join me in a renewal of our "original" compact, called the Gus-Wen-Tah or Two-Row Wampum. As far as I can determine, during the four hundred years that a foreign culture has attempted to democratize us, Canadian society has not found anything comparable to the Gus-Wen-Tah. In this arrangement, we agreed to share our lands, living side by side with the newcomers, who were to govern their own people with their own governments and laws; and we were to govern ourselves with our own governments and laws.

Our nations across this Great Island, now called North America, continue to have an obligation to the Creator to care for and protect our lands for seven generations into the future. This obligation remains a sacred commitment, and I would immediately work with the Indian nations, the provincial governments, citizens' groups, and conservation/environmental groups to develop a nationwide plan for land protection as a top priority. I would conform all federal laws to this plan, in which protection of the environment would require legislation that would allow nature to renew and replenish our polluted waters, the earth, and the air. I would depend on our elders to advise me of the best means of land use in order to provide for the needs of all our citizens. I would involve our elders in Canada in a program of education with our youth on the importance of the environment and would instil in them a desire to protect all aspects as an obligation to future generations.

I would ask parliament to recognize the aboriginal title, rights, and treaties of all aboriginal people, including our inherent right to govern and make laws within our territories for our people. These would be the basic principles by which aboriginal and non-aboriginal institutions would relate. Since aboriginal laws are based on natural law and respect for life, there would be no conflict for Canadian citizens. Aboriginal laws are developed to harmonize with nature and mankind. The new laws on land protection and use of resources would not conflict with aboriginal law, nor would they violate people's rights to survive in the areas where they live. Protecting our lands is protecting our national interests. Without clean air, water, and soil, we will not survive at all.

Protection of our lands will mean reviewing our participation in international efforts to increase Canada's military involvement in alliances such as NATO and American agreements on defence, involving Star Wars or other military initiatives. I would question the wisdom of pursuing this course and would recommend that we diminish our support or withdraw from these efforts. In their place, I would attempt to strengthen international peace by working to outlaw nuclear weaponry and every experiment involving germ warfare; to eliminate toxic chemicals; and to develop education programs that would encourage our youth to work in fields that ease hunger and suffering caused by natural disasters. I would encourage all nations to support a massive international program that would enable young people to travel and learn in other nations through peace and respect. Within Canada, I would develop a civilian force to work with the poor and less fortunate in our society and to work with the military to help our citizens develop survival skills for emergencies and to train the young people.

Because of the ravages created by colonialism and the psychological use of techniques to oppress people, I would commit Canada to the United Nations covenant on decolonization, condemning colonialism in all its forms, and would support groups fighting this form of oppression. This includes the black people in South Africa, the people in Northern Ireland subdued by the British for centuries, the indigenous people oppressed by foreign governments in their homelands such as Australia, New Zealand, Polynesia, northern Scandinavia, and all the countries of Central and South America. I would not condone terrorism. But I would set an example within Canada and would apply pressure to the governments of these countries to recognize the right of these oppressed peoples to self-determination and their right to live in dignity. I would encourage the United Nations to allow these indigenous nations to take their rightful place among the family of nations and to take part in developing international law which would encompass their rights. To prevent the continued exploitation of people, I would work on new trade initiatives and close doors to corporations and multinationals that exploit a country's people for profit.

To put meat on the bone, I would review Canada's dealings with all these countries and would reconsider our political relationships in those areas where people are being denied their rights. This would include a hard examination of our relationship with Great Britain, Australia, New Zealand, the United States, France, the Soviet Union, and any nation prepared to build its riches on the backs of weakened people. I would sponsor forums where these people would freely meet to confer and express their views, not only to their own governments but internationally, so that we can build an understanding of their humanity and realize why armed conflict has in some cases become their only option.

At the international level, I would promote and support research into new processes that would allow nations to settle internal strife and external threats of domination, and to get what they need through peaceful coexistence. I would not support either confrontational or clandestine international politics, yet I would take a strong position regarding any violation of Canada's territorial integrity. Meanwhile, I would encourage a re-examination of world philosophies where it is clear that their intent is to survive through the destruction of other people's cultures and beliefs.

I would support similar "peaceful coexistence" research within Canada and would arrange for forums where our citizens could meet to exchange ideas and have an input into the processes for change. These forums of free exchange would be a way of obtaining recommendations for government policy changes on matters that are of concern to the general public. I would encourage education programs on citizens' rights.

Another of my major concerns is the plight of the young people in our society today—Indian and non-Indian. I would put our youth as a top priority and would ask the elders of Canada to assess the problems of our young people and to recommend changes to our approach and to our government policy which would lead to the whole health of our children. I would work to develop programs where our elders—Indian and non-Indian—would be able to communicate, socialize, and assist our youth in their growth and development. I would also look to the wisdom of the elders for guidance in foreign policy and for the training of our diplomats in statesmanship and peaceful relations with other nations.

Within Canada, I would increase support for the advancement and development of our cultural foundations. I would concentrate on the arts, literature, and communication. I would allow artists a free expression of their talent by providing financial support and by making it easier for artists from other countries to share their talents with us. I would work to have our culture as aboriginal people take its rightful place within the nation as an expression of our nationhood. In this sense, I would eliminate the Indian Act as a destructive tool for our identity and would replace it with laws that reaffirm and recognize the true identity of each of our First Nations in Canada.

Through free enterprise, I would work with businesses to provide a strong economic foundation by alleviating poverty. I would ask businesses to adopt specific depressed areas of the country as a return on their use of the lands, which belong to everyone. Businesses would be freer to generate revenue; but as their contribution to our growth, I would ask them to adopt the people of a depressed area and assist them in recreational activity, training, education, etc. The goal would be to contribute to the whole health of a particular segment of the community or particular area of the country. By this process, I would eliminate the practice of charities competing for business dollars and businesses using money as political leverage. The assistance given by any business would be limited to the place it had chosen. Whatever resources accrued to it would become a resource to the community, to the extent that the business itself was not threatened. Tax-break considerations would be developed on this basis.

In addition to working to rebuild the whole health of our people—whether young, old, jobless, poor, or weakened in some way by the way the country is presently run—I would work to find a fairer method by which segments of our society would share the country's burden. I would meet with the leaders of labour unions, with women's groups, groups representing the physically and mentally handicapped, refugee groups, the unemployed, and others who have been disadvantaged, in order to look at the socioeconomic and political pressures that are not at present being adequately addressed by government policies, and to seek guidance in finding a fairer way of sharing the country's burden. I would support research into the contributions these groups have made towards the enhancement of people's rights or the alleviation of poverty; and I would examine ways by which these groups could continue to play their roles while being protected from oppressive agencies. I would also encourage international exchanges with similar groups in other countries so that the various groups could learn how people in other parts of the world fulfil this important role of promoting and protecting the rights of the ordinary person.

In all of this, I am promoting the belief I have that we must be creative if we are to overcome old prejudices. We live at a time when "big" is endangering us all and when no one is allowing the ordinary person to have a say in correcting the huge problems created by "big." We have neither the government nor the leadership to encourage the creativity of our people to resolve problems which the government has been unable to solve. Each government adopts the errors of the past, as well as the processes which created them. But we can find other ways of achieving the same goals for peace and for living in harmony with one another. I believe that if we strengthen our people and provide them with opportunities to participate in governing, we will set down a stronger foundation for our nation's survival. We are surely finding that Machiavelli's approach to governing has its share of takers but that it wreaks destruction on human dignity.

ROBIN MATHEWS

I would have a single, major purpose for Canada upon which all policies would depend. The purpose, fully discussed at election time, and subsequently carefully presented to the population, would be to release Canada and Canadians so that they can realize the potential they have increasingly been prevented from realizing. Canada is like an animal tethered to a stake by its master. It is permitted to go in a circle carefully set out. Horizons are defined by the length of the rope. If the circumference of freedom changes, it does so because the master decides to shift the stake. Indeed, the animal—unless prodded or alarmed—comes to believe the master is very generous for permitting it such a nice, green, secure patch of its own grass to eat.

Canada is a unique country: uniquely spacious, uniquely beautiful, uniquely harmonious among its various peoples, with unique potential as a force for harmony and peace in the world, and uniquely blessed with the wealth of culture provided by two "founding" white nations and a number of aboriginal nations who have not, even yet, been fairly acknowledged in the Canadian mosaic. Finally, it is a country uniquely blessed with natural wealth and with a population that is intelligent, educated, and in good health.

But governments of Canada have acted like animals tethered to stakes. They have denied Canadian uniqueness—to pretend we are British, to pretend we are U.S., or to pretend we have no identity at all and are foolish to claim one. In denying what we are, Canadian governments have fallen prey to other people's solutions for Canadian problems. They have fallen prey to other people's desires to use Canada. Indeed, they have invited ordinary Canadians to deny the very structure of the society that Canadians have built.

Only recently, a major spokesman for free trade said that if Canada does not effect a free-trade treaty with the United States, we will have to look forward to the bogey of significant state involvement in the development of the Canadian economy. But we have had this condition historically; and we have had it in order to keep a measure of independence from the United States in Canadian enterprise—and in the uses enterprise is put to in relation to the good of the people of the country. Yet the statement that we should fear our own government as a participant in the Canadian economy was made as if no one would disagree with it and as if there was no evidence in Canadian history to call it into question.

How would a program operate to release Canada and Canadians into the realization of heretofore strangled potential?

It would, of course, operate through policy and legislation—to be discussed. But it would begin, first, in general discussion of who we are, where we've come from, and what we hope for as a people drawn from many parts of the world. This kind of discussion would go on during election time. But it would continue in two ways afterwards: first, by a genuine policy of openness in government; and, secondly, by prime ministerial and MP contact with the population.

Much talk is currently expended on the subject of openness and accessibility. But there is an advertising adage (unfortunately, originating with the public relations experiments of the Nazis) which applies to Canada today: that you talk most and express most concern about things you have no intention of dealing with in any concrete way. Governmental secrecy about public business in Canada has reached a bizarre level, and there has never been so much talk about the need for openness and straightforwardness.

We are presently asked to put into power governments which don't have the slightest intention of telling Canadians their real values or their real programs. The so-called free-trade negotiations are a ghastly example. Unmentioned, except negatively by the party that gained power, free-trade negotiations then became the most important government activity. The government appointed a continentalist to be chief negotiator and then backed him in a policy of absolute secrecy. What free trade was to mean to the Canadian people was kept a stumbling, fumbling, on-going uncertainty, purposefully maintained.

Quite apart from the fact that the matters negotiated were the business of Canadians, an honest government, working for the people of Canada, could only have gained strength at the bargaining table by being able to say that the Canadian people knew and supported the program being put forward on their behalf. Governments that hide major matters from the people are governments that intend to deceive the people. We think of the Reagan administration as outrageous in its deceits about arms sales to Iran and secret assistance to the Nicaraguan contras. But the calculated secrecy of the Canadian government on free trade may turn out to be a far greater deception, destroying our sovereignty and damaging our capacity to survive—under the argument that to discuss the negotiations honestly with the Canadian people might endanger victories Canada might otherwise achieve at the bargaining table.

As prime minister, I would spend an hour every three months on national television telling Canadians about government policies, about Canada, about the complex and demanding experiment this country is. I would write my own talks completely. I would never announce anything that might pre-empt the rights of parliament. And I would be happy to have the other political leaders get equal time to answer or to present different subjects for discussion.

Such a program of speaking directly to Canadians would be necessary because Canadians are at present invited to be confused about their identity, and I know that confidence about identity is a prelude to firm, consistent, imaginative, constructive action. I am convinced the Canadian governments we have known in the recent past have been terrified that Canadians will take hold of their identity. In 1967, when governments had to participate in celebration of the fact of this country, the Canadian people revealed an intense longing to be permitted a positive, constructive identity. Yet as soon after Expo 67 as possible, Canadian government embarked on a subtly self-denigrating, anti-nationalist posture. The Liberal party pushed forward as prime minister a man who despises nationalism and whose government began the first steps and studies towards free trade with the United States.

It is in the face of these past realities and present disharmonies that the Canadian people deserve to be spoken to directly and candidly—as a new experience for them, and to help them understand legislation.

My Government's Policies
In a sense, everything begins with the economy, in our case an economy still largely in foreign hands. I would begin a ten-year buy-back plan, a first stage, in which Canadian government would target industries for repatriation. When purchase was announced, government would share ownership with foreign and Canadian investors, to cut costs of purchase and to involve Canadians in their own enterprise. Foreign capital would be welcomed: Canada would be open for business; but foreign capital would not be permitted to have owning or controlling shares. Foreign capital would be used, for a change, to help repatriate Canadian enterprise rather than to take it over as part of foreign profit-making and policy fulfilment.

Canadians would have to have explained to them, I think, that foreign ownership doesn't simply mean a loss of visible profits. It means a loss of policy-making power. It means the purchasing of parts, patents, managerial expertise, and lease agreements outside the country to suit foreign head office practice and the policies of a foreign government.

At the same time, I would launch a new policy on research and development. Any country that is going to guarantee a decent standard of living and independence for its people must—in our day and age—

contribute a portion of its economic wealth to research and development. Canadian governments, for the last twenty-five years, have taken it for granted that Canada will be an economic colony. And so Canada spends less than the vast majority of Western industrialized countries. My policy would call upon free enterprise, state enterprise, and tax money to guarantee a huge leap in research and development activity in Canada.

In the arts, taking for granted that they are also part of the economy, I would initiate in a revolutionary way. I would create a fund of between $15 and $20 billion that would be managed by Canada's canniest investment experts. This sum would be the on-going basis for the budgets of the CBC, the Canada Council, and the National Film Board for the next ten years. The money managers and the executives of these organizations would be independent, but they would be given a clear and explicit mandate: to invest profitably, to increase Canadian involvement in all creative activities, to sell to the world where possible, and to begin sound creation of a Canadian feature film industry, a Canadian textbook industry, and an international (Canadian) music industry.

At the end of ten years, appreciation upon investments, world sales of arts products, profits from the taxes of an increased arts workforce, and the confidence engendered in the arts workforce in the country would show our cultural identity as being a good deal more secure. What is more, by the end of ten years the original fund might have grown a great deal larger than predicted. An industrial base would have been founded from which to develop and enlarge cultural activities at all levels in the country.

Presently, Canadians waste money because the budgets of "arts" operations are always threatened and are always short term, anti-Canadian, and unstable. Private enterprise would be encouraged under the new arts policy. But broadcasters who violated CRTC rulings on Canadian content (as most do now) would be removed from operation. Symphonies that failed to show they were really training young Canadians, seeking Canadian music, and taking it abroad would lose budget allocations. Open to the world, Canadian arts and culture institutions (and universities) would be invited to show that their cosmopolitanism was based in a demonstrated respect for the energy, talent, potential, and achievement of Canadians.

Critics will say they have never heard such folly as borrowing the amount of money I have suggested. But careful investment can make a good deal more money than interest costs. Moreover, the normally budgeted money for the CBC, the Canada Council, and the National Film Board could be used in general revenues and so increase the amount of money available to government.

194

If Canadians are to be released so that they can realize their potential, then women must become full and equal partners in the society, without any question; the original peoples must be declared part of the family of Canada and must not (as now) be the victims of big development; and unions must cease to be "international." Without interfering with their independence, I would urge and help unions in Canada to become Canadian unions.

If Canadians are to be released so that they can realize their potential, then Canada will have to renegotiate all defence and military treaties. I would begin to return Canada (as Canadians want it returned) to working genuinely for peace and for peacekeeping. This would mean that military pacts like NORAD and NATO would have to be seriously reconsidered. Indeed, I would attempt to take Canada into some totally new international agreements. First, I would attempt to negotiate bilateral treaties with both the United States and Russia. Carefully staged and launched, they would deal with the Canadian Arctic, with non-aggression treaties, and with shared space and territory surveillance. I would strive to make Canada a place where both Russian and U.S. people could meet because they would be guests of Canada on Canadian ground working on mutually advantageous projects.

I would begin to make serious treaties of exchange, cultural assistance, education, and technology-sharing with all Latin American countries. Canada is currently wasting goodwill, wasting opportunities to develop trade, and wasting our human obligation in our hemisphere, simply because the United States does not want to see strong Canadian–Latin American ties. But strong Canadian–Latin American ties would not only enhance the lives, the economies, and the cultures of all parties; they would also put great pressure on the United States to rethink relations with Latin America. At present, that part of the world is a military training ground for the U.S., a market to exploit ruthlessly, and a source of emotional gibberish about Communist threats in the Western Hemisphere.

In external affairs, Canada is an animal tied to a stake. It can only forage where its master sets the stake. But a dynamic Canada, working on the Pacific Rim, entering new trade and friendship pacts with the USSR, opening up to Latin America and mutually developing technologies with that part of the world, rethinking military treaties with the United States, and reorganizing strategies of energy and power development with that country (as well as negotiating strong and truly effective environmental conservation agreements)—that would be a Canada for which it would be just to say a new page had been turned.

If I were prime minister, Canada would enter its most exciting years; and when I was through being prime minister, Canada would be a self-respecting nation, founded on justice and equity for its own people and on an identity that could only be fulfilled in harmonious relations with others and with deep regard for the oppressed and the neglected in the world.

JOHN MEISEL

Although it would be tempting to concentrate on only a few objectives and apply one's energies more or less exclusively to their realization, this strategy, beloved of many experts in management, does not work in the real world. In a democracy, all leaders are partly led. So I would pursue a number of policy priorities while allowing for numerous lurking and unexpected issues to intrude into my agenda. The following would be among my most pressing goals: the creation of a regime encouraging the fullest possible development of our human and material resources and of a fair, humane, and effective social welfare system (privatization and the interests of the market would be low priorities); a genuinely peace-oriented, independent foreign policy (the survival of humankind, as opposed to the survival of the Pentagon); and the adoption of measures designed to strengthen Canada's cultural and economic distinctiveness (the fact that it costs something to be oneself would be squarely faced). The trick, of course, is to spell out the details of each of these policies—a task that would take infinitely more time and space than I have available, even if I knew how to achieve it. I don't. The one thing I am sure of, however, is that I would wish to pursue my ends in a manner that was radically different from those adopted by my prime ministerial predecessors.

The keystone to my multifaceted program would centre on nothing less than the ethical and moral foundations of politics. Some argue that the necessarily flawed conditions under which a prime minister must operate involve "givens" that he cannot but accept and can perhaps exploit. I reject this view as a facile cop-out: it overlooks how profoundly our prime ministers have come to dominate our political life and how deeply they influence its values and folkways.

I do not for a moment claim that we once enjoyed a golden age in which political morality—of governments and of the public—offered exemplary models of public-spirited rectitude. Our proximity to the United States has always influenced our political history; our non-ideological approach to public issues has made for a political style in which patronage, self-seeking, opportunism, and the buying of votes (directly or through the expenditure of the taxpayers' dollars) have long been commonplace. Although the forms in which these practices have occurred have changed, the substance has not altered substantially. A larger proportion of public servants (but by no means all) may be hired through competitive examination; public tenders may be called before the spending of public funds; and general programs, allegedly applicable to clearly specified situations, may be developed; but in practice we still continue—and in a way even extend—the clientelist politics typical of the early years of our history.

The shortcomings of governments in political morality take many forms, ranging from the espousal of policies that are insensitive to the requirements of a humane and caring society, to the seemingly benign neglect of the public interest for partisan advantage. I am here concerned with the latter. It may, at first glance, appear relatively trivial compared to the great ethical issues confronting societies and governments, but this impression is misleading. Political morality of the bread-and-butter kind envisioned here, on the part both of citizens and rulers, affects the health of the political society, the degree of trust people accord their governments, and ultimately even the goals which societies pursue not only in the public but also in the private sector. The means, as has rightly been said, enter the ends and transform them. The decency, fairness, and rectitude of the daily political process therefore ultimately affects the very essence of the society and its polity.

Citizens as well as governments are usually implicated when transgressions occur (although there are exceptions), but since we are here concerned with the behaviour of prime ministers, I shall deal largely with lapses initiated by governments. Five kinds are particularly common:

– partisan favouritism,

– policy decisions prompted by expediency,

– manipulation of the public mind,

– unnecessary, profligate government expenditures,

– feather-bedding by the political class.

Let us look at each in turn. Firstly, the notorious patronage appointments by Pierre Trudeau at the end of his reign, to which John Turner became an accessory, are only a particularly visible and dramatic instance of an ongoing process. Brian Mulroney's apparent outrage at this wholesale rewarding of Liberal politicians acquired a pharisaical and cynical hue in the light of the blatant and brazen partisanship and favouritism displayed by his own government in subsequent appointments. The awarding of all manner of government positions and contracts to the faithful, practised by the Liberals, continues under the

Tories. And increasingly, at the present time, the government party resorts to raising money by selling access to the key decision makers, including the prime minister. It is now common for political fund raisers to organize dinners or lunches with party bigwigs for people who, at egregious prices, thus buy the opportunity of rubbing shoulders with the party brass. In the case of the government party, this means members of the cabinet and their advisers.

Rewarding people not on their merit but according to how effectively they have ingratiated themselves with the government party and/or how good they are at buying contacts with the mighty creates public cynicism. The system is manifestly unfair to those who are unable to play it, and it undermines the trustworthiness of the government. A discredited administration cannot hope to elicit the willing support and co-operation of the public. This, in turn, materially diminishes its capacity to govern well.

Secondly, the practice of deciding policy not on the basis of how it will serve the public interest but on how it will serve the party in power (beloved of all our government parties) leads to the inefficient allocation of resources and causes the government process to be perceived as discriminatory. Two types of such behaviour are particularly reprehensible. One consists of ministers directing large public expenditures towards their own constituencies. The behaviour of Lloyd Axworthy, Allan MacEachen, and Brian Mulroney are well-known examples of this practice. The other involves the awarding of large government contracts in regions where the party in office needs to build or consolidate its electoral support.

Third, the manipulation of the public's mind at its own expense reflects a dishonesty somewhat different from those invoked so far, but it is equally pernicious. What is involved is the use of the colossal government advertising budget for the purpose of winning support among the voters. This started after World War II, when it was effectively applied—particularly in the ethnic press—but it has since been widely used. While the publicity involved does not specifically mention any particular party, it unmistakably conveys the idea that the government in office is efficient and worthy of support. The advertising agencies—which, incidentally, grow fat as the result of this self-serving use of the media—then work for the government party in subsequent elections on highly favourable terms.

Fourth, there has not only been a dismaying long-term increase in the size of government expenditures but also a disturbing qualitative alteration. The sums involved are relatively minor, but the impact on the way government is carried out, and on the manner in which it is perceived (by the governors and the public alike), is far-reaching. Our ministers, and particularly the prime minister, have come to acquire many of the trappings formerly associated with the perquisites of monarchy or of oriental potentates: they have lavishly equipped offices to suit the alleged taste of their occupants; they make unnecessary use of executive jets, moving everywhere with an impressive phalanx of assistants and lackeys; they conduct public events, such as visits by official callers, in the manner reminiscent of a *bon viveur* during the *belle époque*. This tendency has received a boost from Prime Minister Mulroney's preening style, but it started during the Trudeau years.

Do not misunderstand me. Not every minister (or deputy) has fallen into these extravagant ways, and there is nothing wrong with senior members of the government being given the resources and conditions of work to ease the discharge of their crushing burden. But the spendthrift manner in which recent governments have approached this aspect of their role reveals an attitude that ill accords with what have traditionally been the virtues of Canadians and of their public life. The conveyance of our prime minister and his court in fleets of limousines and aircraft (and all that goes with it) does not fit our values, and it offends those who are aware of the state of our economy and the large number of people suffering as a result. This emulation of the behaviour of the rulers of certain comic opera republics (or superpowers, for that matter) is not only ridiculous but displays an insensitivity to the need for integrity in all aspects of public office.

Most of the blemishes noted so far are related to one another; the final one is no exception. It concerns the feather-bedding we contrive for former politicians and civil servants. The political class has created a vast new army of government hangers-on—mostly former civil servants, ministers, or MPs—who feed from the public trough by working on contract, acting as consultants, or generally benefiting from their connections with those in government. Some are doing legitimate work, of course, but many are engaged in influence-peddling or have simply abused the rules guiding early retirement by earning higher incomes from government service after retirement than they did before.

The increasingly large and powerful role of consultants, lobbyists, expert advisers, etc., with former links to the political or administrative arms of government is a dangerous and often immoral addition to our governmental process. It generally by-passes the usual channels of decision-making and accountability, and it is also frequently used to enrich former politicians or bureaucrats at the public expense. It, of course, thrives on the less appealing features of excessive partisan favouritism, mentioned earlier, and on the unrivalled capacity of the public service to look after its own.

To catalogue all these shortcomings of our governments, past and present, may seem an excruciatingly oblique way of approaching what I would do if I were prime minister. But it has been necessary to go through this litany because one of my major resolves would be to stop any further decay of public virtue and, more important, to try to bring about conditions in which politicians and other citizens would come to demand and apply a higher level of public morality.

Lest I should be accused of being both naive and utopian, let me hasten to admit that I am perfectly aware that my goal may be impossible to achieve. The conditions responsible for the status quo may be so immutable, and perhaps so closely linked to simple human nature, that no amount of effort can make any dint in the fallen status of our political morality. But one cannot be sure. On the contrary, it is reasonable to assume that if our political leaders, and especially the most powerful among them, were to recognize the problem and vow to tackle it, reform would be possible. We have been dragged down by them; the same influence could elevate us.

So even at the risk of failure, I would endeavour to discuss these issues earnestly and frequently with my party, my ministerial colleagues, and the public. Brian Mulroney inscribed national reconciliation into his political program, and he has made a persistent effort to sell the idea and apply it. I believe he has had some success in bringing it about. It would be equally possible to espouse the cleansing of the political process as among one's principal goals and, by argument and deed, to begin an era of reform. A passionate, determined, and diligent effort might put us on a new course.

It is, of course, obvious that pious hopes and merely well-intentioned argument would not get me far. A thorough rethinking of the structure and performance of political parties would be required, as well as a re-evaluation of the current practices and procedures of the public service, particularly of the upper mandarinate. Political education would claim my attention; I would attempt to induce all governments to recognize the importance of the issue raised here and the need to cope with it.

A zealous commitment to reform would have to be made *before* I was chosen as party leader, and the support of significant elements among my colleagues for a purification platform would have to be mobilized. An inspired, massive effort at public persuasion would be required, and a resolve to remain impervious to the cynical scoffing of sceptics. In addition, my sights would have to be set at a realistic level. The best I could hope to achieve would be to place the item on the public agenda and to begin a reorientation of our practices. A fundamental, permanent reform would take generations. But unless a start is made—and made seriously—we shall continue to slip down to a slimy, stinking morass. If I were prime minister, I would try and launch a turnaround.

WILLIAM R. MORRISON

If I were prime minister, I would adopt policies that would remove one of the most glaring inconsistencies of Canadian life—our attitude towards our North. Every time Canadians sing the English-language version of the national anthem, extolling the "True North, strong and free," they are perjuring themselves, either wilfully or unconsciously, for the truth is that our North is neither strong nor particularly free, and we certainly do not stand on guard for it.

If the North is defined as the Yukon and Northwest Territories (the northern parts of the provinces have been neglected too, but that is another story) and if the history of these territories is examined, it becomes apparent what a sad job our country has made of managing this magnificent legacy. Even its acquisition was haphazard. Part of the territories was acquired by Canada through the transfer of the Hudson's Bay Company's lands in 1870, and the rest ten years later, when Britain turned over its rights to the Arctic islands. Yet when Canada was given the Arctic, some members of parliament objected to the transfer, on the grounds that the land was worthless and might be expensive to administer. Britain virtually had to force Canada to take the gift of hundreds of thousands of square kilometres of land.

For the first quarter century after Confederation, my predecessors— and Canadians in general—ignored their North, giving it merely a token government from Ottawa. A few official voyages were made to the eastern Arctic, but there was no national presence north of the 60th parallel. As late as 1905, the annual budget for the administration of the Northwest Territories was about $5000, most of it spent on tiny grants to church mission schools.

Because neither Canadians nor their leaders had any interest in the North and refused to spend more than a pittance even on exploring, let alone administering or developing it, almost all of the more remote parts of the region were first explored by citizens of Great Britain, the United States, or Norway. This led on occasion to embarrassment, and even the potential for loss of territory. For example, several large islands in the High Arctic—Axel Heiberg and the Sverdrup Islands— were discovered around the turn of the century by Otto Sverdrup, a Norwegian. Our claim to these islands was so weak that we eventually had to buy off Sverdrup's rights to them, and only the fact that Norway did not want the land saved Ottawa from serious difficulties.

What it took to move Canada to assert its rights in the North was generally the suggestion that some other power might do so first, or that foreigners were up to some activity there that might embarrass Ottawa. This was what brought the Mounted Police to the Yukon in 1894, three years before the Klondike gold rush. At that time, there were hundreds of miners, most of them Americans, writing their own laws and dealing with the Indians as if the Yukon were no man's land—which, as far as Ottawa was concerned, it was. In the Yukon, as in the eastern and western Arctic, Canada never initiated a northern policy but always reacted to the presence of others. It was not a case of standing on guard for the North but one of "I suppose we have to do something." This was still the policy during World War II when, during the construction of the Alaska Highway, tens of thousands of Americans operated in the Canadian Northwest totally free of Canadian supervision, until a British official prodded Ottawa to take some interest in the region. The same attitude, to a considerable extent, prevails today.

As prime minister, I would move to change this attitude. Here I would expand on the policy of John Diefenbaker who, whatever his faults as a politician, was the first of this country's leaders to enunciate a policy towards the North—the "Northern Vision" made famous in his election campaign of 1958. Many people have snickered at Dief's northern policy, but in fact he did make a modest start with his "roads to resources"—it was his administration that began the Dempster Highway, linking the Mackenzie Delta with the southern road system, and the railway which made possible the development of the mine at Pine Point. But Diefenbaker's vision proved to be a false start, and his successors have not done much to make the North part of Canada.

Before outlining specific ideas for the North, a word on what I would not do. First, I would not lay mines in the waters of the Northwest Passage, a recent idea which encapsulates everything that is wrong with Canada's official attitude towards the North. Mining the waters to prevent foreigners trespassing is illegal under international law, or should be, just as planting a land mine in your front yard to blow up intruders is illegal. Worse than this, it continues the tradition of Canadian passivity in northern affairs; it appeals to some people because it is cheap and because it requires no human presence—just machines. Nor would I spend half a billion on an icebreaker, unless it could be shown that there was more use for it than just crashing through polar ice, touching at each island once a year or so to show the flag.

What I would do for the North is to make it part of Canada. It sounds simple, but in the first century and a quarter of Confederation, it has never been done, or even really attempted. Here is my program.

First, I would settle the comprehensive native land claims in the North in a manner that would protect the native people while not trampling too outrageously on the Canadian taxpayer. The reason that these claims have dragged on for a dozen years now is that the government has insisted on extinguishment of aboriginal rights, but the native people have refused, demanding instead a true partnership in the future of the North. This is an entirely reasonable position, and as prime minister I would immediately negotiate a settlement of the comprehensive claims, which would recognize the rights of native people to full partnership in the development of the North, including the right to rule on future resource projects. No huge sums would be given to the native people, since they would not be paid off for their rights but would prosper in the future as the North prospered. This important reversal of traditional government policy, which has always given native people no more than a token say in northern development, would be a cornerstone of my program. I would also transfer to the native people the funding and responsibility for managing their own health, education, and social programs.

Second, I would end the fragmentation by which control over northern affairs is split among various departments: Indian Affairs, Public Works, Environment, and so forth. I would create a "super-ministry" of Northern Affairs, responsible for all aspects of the federal presence in the North. At its head would be a minister with the same authority to take action on behalf of the North that Clifford Sifton had in the West at the beginning of the century. Perhaps Jean Chrétien could be coaxed out of retirement to head it.

Next, and central to my program, would be to establish a northern university in the territories, probably in Whitehorse or Yellowknife. A northern-based university would accomplish a number of useful things. It would serve as a permanent centre for people engaged in northern research—no more summers in the north and winters back in the south. Those who profess a commitment to the North could demonstrate it by moving the base of their scholarly activities there. The university would attract scholars and students from other countries and would become an international centre of teaching and research, and a centre for native arts, culture, and education. Its role would be to develop northern and Arctic studies in geology, architecture, climatology, sociology, psychology, and other fields. It would demonstrate to the world our national commitment to the North.

Many faculty and students would naturally gravitate to such a university, but for those who needed extra incentive, I would provide generous tuition assistance as well as travel grants. For years, the government has funded travel for young people among the provinces; I would extend this to make it possible for students to travel and study in the North.

At another site I would establish a military base. At present, the presence of the Canadian military north of the 60th parallel is negligible, though the Canadian forces go there from time to time to carry out exercises. A large permanent military base would do for the territories what the American military has done for Alaska: demonstrate interest in the region and willingness to defend it, as well as increasing the population and providing many jobs for northerners. Canadians cannot be forced to live in the North, but members of the armed forces must serve where the country needs them, and a larger Canadian presence is badly needed in the region. Since Canada's present NATO mission requires northern experience, it seems logical to shift some of the military to the North. Moreover, some military personnel would inevitably come to like northern life and, as has happened in Alaska, would choose to live there at the end of their careers. Thus, this is a measure that would be beneficial to everyone.

In developing the economy of the North I would be cautious to distinguish between projects that have a present and future benefit to the region and those that do not. Short-term resource extraction projects have often proven to be of little value, as the present unhappy story of mining activity in the Yukon has shown. While giving every possible assistance to entrepreneurs, I would not give away northern resources for nothing, particularly at today's low prices; rather, I would proceed very slowly, evaluating and stabilizing them instead of making a small quick profit from them. The resources will still be there in the years when the prices rise to make developing them worthwhile. The North must end its dependence on resource extraction: this is the point of the northern university, which would be permanent rather than temporary and would not depend on the ups and downs of world mineral prices.

I would also recognize that the High Arctic, north of the present limits of Inuit habitation, will likely never support a sizable permanent population. I would preserve it as a wilderness heritage for all Canadians, subject only to scientific research and the military and government presence necessary to demonstrate Canadian sovereignty over it. This would be done by the establishment of a non-partisan review board, with generous research funding and with representation from the scientific and native communities, which would be able to veto any development of the High Arctic that menaced its ecology.

Finally, I would take measures to increase awareness of the North among all Canadians. I would encourage and subsidize the provincial governments to introduce a healthy component of northern studies, both historical and contemporary, into the school curricula. Most Canadians know almost nothing about our North, and the school is the place to correct this situation. There are many ways to acquaint Canadians with their north—one would be for Loto Canada to give away northern tours as prizes. I would also begin a program similar to the *visites interprovinciales*, which was designed to increase friendship and knowledge between anglophone and francophone Canadians. This new scheme would be a "North-South dialogue" (to use a phrase of one of my predecessors) between the territories and the provinces. Many young northerners now travel south, but too few young southerners travel north. I would correct this by means of a program encouraging travel, work, and study in the North.

The North, once experienced, can never be forgotten, and if Canada's northern consciousness is to be raised, it must begin with our youth. Within a generation the ignorance of the North would be at least partially erased, and Canadians would be more aware of the attractions and potential of this shamefully neglected part of the country.

PETER C. NEWMAN

The man or woman who attains the prime ministership of Canada is more than just the first politician in the land; he or she joins a historical continuum and becomes keeper of the national conscience. The office combines terminal authority with soul-wrenching responsibility. It is the ultimate public testing ground of character and intent.

No one in the country can match the prime minister's power, yet the holder of the office soon finds himself shackled like a Gulliver by the tenacious tendrils of economic, regional, social, and religious problems. To govern without offending Canada's divergent elements becomes the major concern at the political summit. Will a vote at the United Nations against French nuclear tests weaken the administration's attempts to bring Quebec into a constitutional entente? Will refusal to participate in Star Wars threaten Ottawa's ability to negotiate reasonable access to the American market for Atlantic fish products?

Despite the fascinating thesis of this collection, I would not ever wish to be prime minister. It has become an untenable office, its psychic clout exhausted by a long cycle of high expectation and inevitable disillusionment. Because so many Canadians expect Ottawa to care for their needs, virtually from erection to resurrection, no politician can fill the office with any hopes of success.

The newly elected Canadian prime minister soon discovers that to remain a unifying symbol to his party and the nation at large, he must dilute statesmanship with compromise, and occasionally even with opportunism. His main problem is to chisel the ability to make major decisions out of the bedrock of others' self-interest—while sidestepping any tendency towards absolutism.

To retain and expand his power, he must blend self-confidence with self-restraint and be prepared to suffer political abuse without inflicting it. To keep from being strangled by the machinery of his office, he must possess the fortitude to look beyond headlines, the intellectual agility to use proffered advice with discrimination—the courage to make tough decisions and accept responsibility for them. He must, above all, retain effective control over his own party. His followers must be genuinely convinced that their fractional differences are worth ameliorating in order to keep him in office. Once this loyalty wavers, the prime minister's authority is fatally weakened.

Although Canada's political system culminates in this one person, and although his arsenal of authority is huge, both the basis and the boundaries of that authority are ill-defined. Technically, the prime minister is merely the chairman of a committee of the Privy Council—"the influential foreman of an executive jury," according to Lord Rosebery, the British constitutional expert. The office of prime minister developed in England during the first half of the eighteenth century after the Hanoverian, George I, had succeeded Queen Anne to the British throne. His inability to speak English and his indifference to the governing process permitted power to gravitate to his ministers, who appointed Sir Robert Walpole, first lord of the treasury, to preside over their deliberations. Walpole's power eventually came to depend less on his loosely defined office than on his force of personality.

Modern Canadian prime ministers draw their authority from a similar source, even if more than a century of custom has significantly strengthened their position. The prime minister's power is based on the fact that unlike anyone else within the parliamentary hierarchy, he carries with him, when he vacates his job, the resignation of his entire administration. He sets the cabinet agenda and decides the most important federal appointments, including ambassadors, chiefs of defence staff, privy councillors, the governor general's staff, crown appointments in the Commons and the Senate, cabinet ministers, lieutenant-governors, speaker of the Senate, federal judges, Treasury Board members, deputy ministers of government departments, and even librarians of parliament. It is on his advice that the governor general summons or dissolves parliament, and he dominates its proceedings. He is the nation's chief diplomat. His anger can destroy the career of ambassadors (or ambassadors' wives). As the final arbiter between the federal treasury and the members of cabinet in charge of federal spending, he controls the government's annual budget—or the size of its deficit.

But as leader of his party, he must also concern himself with more mundane aspects of backroom politics, such as patronage and partisan favours. It is his control of the party machine that ultimately gives him real political clout, as distinguished from the vague constitutional authority of his office.

A prime minister must play all these and other roles simultaneously. What he does in one reflects on the others. A trivial decision that turns sour, a miscalculation in timing, a casual remark blown out of context, can produce graver consequences than the most meticulously plotted policy shift. Woodrow Wilson might have been describing the Canadian prime ministership when he said of the American presidency: "The office is so much greater than any man could honestly imagine himself to be, that the most he can do is look self-possessed enough to seem to fill it."

What the prime minister of Canada is *not* is established by legislative checks and the circumscribing realities of Canadian politics. What he *is* depends on him.

The office is reconfigured by its occupant, just as the job itself frequently transmogrifies the man or woman who holds it. Becoming prime minister has an almost magical power to elevate individuals or to bring out the worst in them. For Mackenzie King, it became a hive of intrigue. Louis St. Laurent acted as if he were chairman of a large corporation. Under John Diefenbaker, who was neither a recluse like King nor a father figure like St. Laurent, the very metabolism of the office seemed to change. He made the prime ministership more accessible to the average citizen and sometimes used its powers in helping the little man overcome the inevitable injustices of stodgy bureaucratic administration. Yet he also brought to his post a flair for self-aggrandizement and turned it into a focal point for the little arts of popularity he insisted on practising. He behaved as if he subscribed to the Islamic idea of power: that a sovereign has the right to govern only until a stronger one topples his throne.

Lester Pearson treated the office as his refuge from a sea of self-inflicted troubles, yet he managed to put in place some remarkably enlightened legislation. He sometimes acted as if he were secretary-general of the United Nations, but in his time it may have been a necessary posture. During Pierre Trudeau's stormy stewardship, this dull, middle-class nation gave birth to two political phenomena, one as novel as the other. The first was Trudeaumania, the cultish response to a middle-aged French-Canadian intellectual which turned politics into a spectator sport, subject to all the vicarious thrills of contest, climax, and sudden death. The second was Trudeaucracy, the conduct of the nation's business in a new technocratic manner, with pragmatic management of the economy rather than any creed or ideology guiding government action.

In the process, Trudeau created a presidential system without its attendant congressional checks and balances. He was extraordinarily clear-headed and realistic about Ottawa's sources of power. On the one hand, he recognized the immense potential of initiative and guidance that existed in the federal bureaucracy, yet he also realized that this great instrument of authority lacked effective centralized leadership. This he supplied by organizing around him a presidential-style office and by bringing order and discipline to the cabinet's operations.

Neither Joe Clark nor John Turner were in office long enough to leave their mark, and it is still too early to assess Brian Mulroney's long-term impact. Midway in his first term, it was possible to predict that the Baie-Comeau politician's chief liability was his basic misunderstanding of the chemistry between a prime minister and the electorate: he was still acting as if his claim to power depended on being loved by the voters. This was nothing less than a monumental and potentially fatal misreading of how the average citizen views political leaders. Love (or hate) is not the issue; it is respect that a prime minister must earn if he wishes to renew his mandate.

Using this criterion, we have had only two great prime ministers: Sir John A. Macdonald and Sir Wilfrid Laurier. There have been four near-greats (Sir Robert Borden, Sir John Thompson, Lester Pearson, and Pierre Trudeau), four adequates (Alexander Mackenzie, R. B. Bennett, Arthur Meighen, and Louis St. Laurent), and four disasters (Sir John Abbott, Sir Mackenzie Bowell, Sir Charles Tupper, and John Diefenbaker).

The kind of respect that produces greatness flows only from deep commitment to a cause, and this in turn requires a sense of motivation unswayed by momentary acclaim or abuse. Any man or woman intent on leading Canada into the twenty-first century will have to champion something more inspiring than the attainment of a basic living standard for his people. He will have to concern himself much more with the *quality* of the lives Canadians lead. His appeal will have to move beyond the welfare state (which offers only palliatives for existing inequalities) and concentrate on the environmental barriers to social progress. His government will have to concern itself primarily with Canadian society's capacity for self-fulfilment.

This will mean expanded state-financed educational facilities, a qualitative attack on Canada's housing problems, a solution that will finally enforce racial and sexual equality, effective measures against traffic congestion and water pollution—in short, an attempt to make life excellent and Canadian society more civilized. This kind of policy thrust will have to include a positive external affairs function for Canada, not as a middle power (a concept which was long ago a victim of the age of nuclear overkill) but as a nation willing to share its bounty and technology with the underdeveloped world. It will also mean redefining our military posture as a country concerned with its (non-nuclear) self-defence, rather than perpetuating meaningless U.S.–dominated alliances.

New political leadership must recognize that the ideologies of traditional Liberalism and Conservatism have been exhausted—that they must be replaced with new initiatives that will bring about genuine economic justice. In shaping this new kind of politics, our future leaders will have to take into account the fact that Canada is becoming not just an urban-oriented country but a full-fledged metropolitan society. The party which first shows itself to be an expression of this new metropolitan ethic will inherit this country's federal institutions. At least some of the leaders of the future will receive their political training in the face-to-face confrontations and coalitions of municipal councils. "This is the age of the urban crisis," J. K. Galbraith has written. "The day is coming when no one will be considered really ready for higher office until he has been a successful mayor."

The function of democratic leadership, it seems to me, is to respect the past, grasp the present, and enlarge the future. My ideal prime minister would be someone attuned to swift change, both economic and social; he would welcome its challenges and delight in finding ways to harness it. He would have that special brand of courage Ernest Hemingway called "grace under pressure," being aggressive without being contentious, decisive without being arrogant, and compassionate without being confused. He would respect ideas but would not substitute them for action. He would be a master of prose but would not become intoxicated by his own. He would be pragmatic, but only up to a point, so that he would always know when to spurn the arithmetic of expediency. He would be articulate and forceful enough to involve the people, including his opponents, in his struggles on behalf of Canadian nationhood.

Such a leader would set out clear national goals for this country, not on the basis of public opinion polls but from a strong sense of national necessity. Instead of participating reflexively in the maelstrom of history, he would be capable of gripping events on the move and exercising the kind of impact that would reveal the character of the country to itself. The very force of his personality would become a unifying influence for the nation at large.

Perhaps the most apt description of the kind of politician I have in mind was given by Norman Mailer, commenting on the leadership crisis in his own country. "It is a hero America needs, a hero central to his time," he wrote. "A man whose personality might suggest the contradictions and mysteries which could reach into the alienated circuits of the underground, because only a hero can capture the imagination of the people, and so be good for the vitality of his nation."

The problem, of course, is that any man or woman can be a hero only for a short time. There is something extraordinarily perishable about heroism, an existential state that can vanish in a season. Canada's prime ministers are like high-wire artists working without a net: one wrong move and their act is over. Still, Sir John A. Macdonald probably had it right when he delivered a casual aside that still stands as the ultimate definition of the prime minister's powers: "Given a government with a big surplus, a big majority and a weak opposition, you could debauch a committee of archangels."

PATRICK O'CALLAGHAN

I've met some folks who say that I'm a dreamer, but to consider running the country would put me in the realm of nightmares, not dreams.

No man in his right mind would want to be prime minister of Canada, because the country is ungovernable. It is the second-largest geographic mass in the world, the world's largest democracy, a nation of political immaturity and untrammelled naiveté, a land of unrealized potential and unreal expectations. It is a nation of compromise, of chaotic impetuosity and bland indifference, of barely concealed prejudice cloaked in the thin cloth of tolerance. It is the snowy-breasted pearl of the northern continent, where nature exaggerates with bold brush strokes the magnificence of its western sunrises and sunsets.

To describe how I feel about Canada, I would naturally have to borrow from an Irish poet:

> You'll burn in my heart till these thin pulses stop;
> And the wild cup of life in your fragrance I'll drain
> To the last brilliant drop.

The irony of those lines by Joseph Sheridan LeFanu, who died more than a century ago, is that they were not written in praise of his native land, or as a throbbing manifesto of loving faith to a lady fair, but were the thoughts of a drunkard on his bottle.

Perhaps there is no irony at all, because Canadians tend to imbibe deeply from the bottle of life without any appreciation of its hangover potential. The beauty before their eyes, the limitless vision of unspoiled promise when the curtain of night has been pinned back by the stars, makes believers of them all until the harsh dawn brings the dregs of unfulfilled dreams and the cold reality penetrates.

Canada is a land to marvel at, to glory in, to speculate upon. But it is also the land of suicidal political tendencies, of two major kingdoms with unchallenged power and eight fiefdoms struggling to force their way into the regal club. It is a land halfway between a colonial appendage of a foreign crown and a New World republic. It has a split personality as befits a nation of uncertain parentage, with under-the-blanket affairs adding strange blood to the mix. It is not a land of beginning again but a land where no one is quite a Canadian, the hyphen denoting a longing for other places, other times.

Unlike Australia, a land built on penal colonies, where the past is dead and buried, Canada is a never-never land, not secure enough in its own destiny to dare shed yesterday's skin. This uncertainty pervades the political structure, adding its own deadening effect. If politics is the art of the possible, then to be a successful politician one has to have an understanding of the compromises that force Canada to accept weak tea rather than strong drink as a potent stimulant.

In recent times, only Pierre Trudeau has been able to bully Canadians into accepting his vision of nationhood. Even at that, he had to wait until his last term in office to impose his will on a reluctant nation. It cost his party the next election, and it left Canada a nation of regional disparities, the provinces bickering amongst themselves and with Ottawa. Trudeau's legacy for a nation he despised more than he loved was a flawed constitution, with a charter of rights that defies logical and judicial interpretation, and a nation that only now, under a Tory prime minister, has produced a constitutional accord that will finally welcome Quebec as a fully fledged partner in Confederation.

Trudeau overdosed on a constitution that few felt Canada needed. And in ensuring the traditional overlordship of central Canada, he earned the undying enmity of western Canada. His vision of Canada was all that the eye could encompass from the slopes of Mount Royal. Despite his autocratic style of governance, he was the most parochial of all federalists. The lesson to be learned from Trudeau's effrontery and arrogance was that the only way Canada could be run efficiently was through a dictatorship. Given time, he might—like Mussolini— even have made the trains run on schedule.

Short of another Trudeauvian dictatorship, the only hope for a prime minister who could come to office with an acceptable program, and actually carry it to fruition, lies in lowered expectations and low-key promises. Canadians suspect the brilliant, the unorthodox, the ebullient, the forward-thinking progressives, because change must come slowly and be given time to sink in. Brian Mulroney's exaggerated rhetoric and torrent of new ideas gnawed at the soul of Canadians, who don't expect Rome to be built in a day—and certainly not before every possible fringe group, backed by taxpayers' funds, has had the opportunity of saying where the Coliseum should be located in this brave new city.

Therefore, to contemplate having the run of 24 Sussex Drive, with or without all those shoe closets, needs the subjugation of any major program for determined change. A visionary with a real grasp of the essentials for Canada's future would never get past the nominating stage of whatever party's coattails he might tread upon. He needs a touch of charisma for the 30-second clip on television, where a moonbeam smile will attract more votes than ideas ever could. He needs the patience of Job (another reason why I could never be a politician at any level, because I have never learned to suffer fools gladly, and most voters are short-sighted or self-centred fools). He needs to be anything other than a westerner, because a westerner, with western interests uppermost in his mind, will never again get elected as leader of anything other than a purely western party. And Albertans are totally outside the pale. They are the outcasts, the urchins one would never invite into a civilized drawing room. They don't know their manners. They don't even touch their forelocks in the presence of their elders and betters.

The system is loaded against the West. A federal structure that excludes from real power all but two provinces carries the seeds of its own destruction. Unless Canada makes a reasonable effort to give Alberta full membership in the federal club, it is doomed. Unlike Quebec, Alberta has never learned to live off the berries in the hedges behind which its guerrillas lie in ambush. Self-survival is an art that Albertans must acquire until the will of Canadians changes to reduce the blatant regionalism that frustrates Alberta by the sheer weight of numbers. It needs a great leap of faith and logic to cross a river that is too wide to be forded. It needs understanding and a broadening of limited perspectives, and there is little indication that such magnanimity exists in the current federal system.

Any discussion of an elected Senate, with equal representation from all provinces, is a subject for hilarity in central Canada. "What does Alberta want?" the central Canadian powerbrokers chortle. "The same powers as Prince Edward Island?" The answer, of course, is "yes"—provided both P.E.I. and Alberta have the same power as Ontario and Quebec. Absurd? Only if you overlook the American and Australian examples.

So we are back at square one. Short of a palace coup and the declaration of a dictatorship, an Albertan could not become prime minister with a fair-to-all mandate unless the political system was drastically altered. So certain assumptions will have to be made if I am now the prime minister and ready to implement my strategy for running the country. To simplify things, let's just wave a magic wand. Don't ask what you can do for your country, just hand me the keys to the government limo and we'll rev up the engine of progress and regional equality. And give me at least ten unobstructed years to bring it all about.

We'll start with equal representation for all the provinces, not only in the Senate but in the Commons as well. And my first target will be all those tariff fences built to protect southern Ontario's industry, with the West as its captive customer. If southern Ontario prices itself out of the western market, let's go back to economic logic so that meat-packing plants will return to the area where the cattle are reared—on the prairies. No more preferential freight rates that make it cheaper to transport beef on the hoof to the stockyards of Toronto.

Let's build some car plants in Winnipeg and Calgary and Vancouver, recognizing that westerners drive cars too and shouldn't be stuck with the cost of bringing their vehicles all the way from Oakville and Windsor. And let's move the secondary oil industries back to Alberta from Sarnia and central Canada, where they use artificially depressed prices for western feedstock. Put them cheek by jowl with the source of all that cheap energy.

We'll get rid of the Ontario-imposed regulation that forces Alberta gas producers to keep twenty-five years' supply of gas in the ground, even though Ontario refuses to pay for it in advance. If Alberta is to be treated as a vast warehouse for Ontario's gas needs, then let Ontario pay the warehouse fee through guaranteed price contracts.

And just to wipe the slate clean, we'll send back to the West the $65 billion plundered from Alberta in the years of the energy wars. Not all that money should go straight into the Heritage Trust Fund, however. Set aside $20 billion for prairie farm assistance. This could be used for support payments in those years when there is a world surplus of grain. A program should be started to buy out those farmers who want to get off the land. When such land is acquired it should be rented out to tenants, who must work the land themselves, holding it only so long as they remain productive and profitable.

If the cost of all this sounds somewhat prohibitive, a new investment fund should be set up, its source of revenue being the hydro companies of Ontario and Quebec. In line with the vast potential of these hydro companies as exporters of energy, they should be subject to the same federal taxing requirements for their renewable natural resource as are Alberta's non-renewable gas and oil fields.

All provincial trade and tariff barriers should be removed so that there are no artificial barriers to trade, services, or employment anywhere in Canada. Obviously, only a dictator could ordain such a change in provincial autonomy. It would need a similar dictator south of the border to achieve the same end to state interference and massive local subsidies. Only then could continental free trade become a reality, with no holds barred.

If all of this is not music to the voters' ears, you can be sure that my policy on social programs will strike an even sourer note. Since this is the time to be realistic, let's begin by putting the knife to the sacred cow of universality.

Our priorities should be clear. No Canadian should be abandoned by the state because he cannot find work. He and his family should be accorded financial help that is adequate for their needs to see that they are housed, clothed, and fed to certain set standards. They should be sheltered from debt collectors and foreclosures, with the state making minimum interest payments, which should be repaid when work is eventually found. All helped in this way would have to demonstrate not only a willingness to work but an eagerness to seek work. All help should cease if these vital components were missing.

The baby bonus should only be paid to families whose income falls below a set level, to be determined and amended by changing circumstances. Subsidized day care should be provided in the same way for all whose income is insufficient to meet the standards set for those out of work. Federal and provincial governments would have agreed standards for quality day care, but the provision of such day care would be left to private enterprise. No subsidy would be provided for such day care for other than those whose income did not meet the acceptable level above the poverty line. However, there would be tax breaks for all using unsubsidized day care, as well as for families where one parent stayed home to bring up the children.

It would not be the philosophy of my government to provide state care from the cradle to the grave. Therefore, all existing social services would be examined by an independent tribunal to determine which were essential and which had exhausted their usefulness. The needs of too many special-interest groups are currently being catered to without any adequate understanding of their justification on economic or humane grounds. We can no longer go on giving money simply because of strident demands by self-interest groups.

A tribunal of five senior judges would be set up to examine all native land claims. The tribunal would be given five years to decide their validity and to adjudicate accordingly. Its findings would be binding on both my government and the native people. If massive funding was required to meet such a judgement, a limit for payment of all outstanding debts (say 20 years) would be included in the terms of settlement. Such a settlement would include the disbandment of a federal bureaucracy to deal with native affairs and the acceptance by the native people of full Canadian citizenship. The only continuing association with Ottawa for the native people, other than as ordinary citizens of Canada, would be the honouring of all treaty pledges for those who stayed on the reserves. This somewhat arbitrary method of dealing with land claims would not include any offer of self-government. The idea of more than five hundred governments in Canada is too absurd to be taken seriously.

Next to the native land claims, the biggest continuing problem seems to be the CBC. We seem determined to make it the instrument of Canadian culture, without having the faintest idea what constitutes Canadian culture. The CBC treats other broadcasters in the same way that the awfully well-bred Briton used to treat the colonials. (Still does, come to think of it.) But at least the colonials are making their own way in the world, while the CBC, silver spoon stuck firmly in its mouth, needs monthly cheques from dear old Dad to survive.

The CBC will never meet its requirements out of the cash flow of its advertising revenues. So let's accept this and take it out of the advertising field altogether. At the same time, let's order it to stop competing with commercial broadcasters for stock foreign programs. The CBC should be the PBS of the north so far as television goes.

The money the government turns over to the CBC should be set by formula, tied to increases equivalent to the cost of living. To help offset the loss of advertising revenues, a 1 per cent tax on all broadcast revenues should be earmarked for the CBC. This would be in addition to the government's annual formula contribution.

The CBC would continue its news and information programming. It should be allowed to continue bidding for major events that are deemed to have overwhelming Canadian interest, such as the Stanley Cup playoffs. For the most part, however, the CBC programming would consist of at least 75 per cent Canadian content, with the bulk being made up of so-called quality programs from abroad which commercial broadcasters might find unsalable to a popular audience. As for CBC radio, it should abandon the "popular music" field to commercial radio. It can't compete, and there should be room on the air waves for an alternative to all that screeching cacophony.

In defence matters, my government would honour all its obligations to the various alliances to which it now pays only lip service. It would immediately undertake an upgrading of our armed services. It would state in categorical terms its claims to the Beaufort Sea and would build an adequate fleet to patrol its northern waters.

My government would undertake an urgent review of the whole system of justice. Too many Canadians are going to jail for offences that do not involve violence. And there is a disproportionate number of native people in our jails; we appear to have a two-tier system based on race. The hangman would be permanently banished from the land.

The whole tenor of my government would be that of less interference by the state. Government must become more accessible to the people. Its bureaucracy must not be allowed to shelter behind governing arrogance to prevent citizens at large from finding out the full range of policy options. The Access to Information Act needs to have some fresh air blowing through it. Freedom of speech and a press completely free of government encroachment must be guaranteed without any caveats.

The starting point for this whole exercise, of course, is that the most urgent necessity for Canada is for a confederation in which each of its parts is equal. This is a commendable and obviously simplistic definition of what is so clearly lacking. We don't have equality, and paradise itself may be more easily attainable.

If you have followed my zig-zag course through the philosophical icefields of western political despair, then it is no major mental exercise to conclude, as I have always done, that I could never be prime minister, because I am non-electable. To put right the imbalances in Confederation along the lines outlined in my manifesto would be akin to blowing up Lord Nelson's statue on O'Connell Street in Dublin on the fiftieth anniversary of the Easter Week uprising. About all that effort achieved was that the pigeons which used to rest on Nelson's statue now flock to Daniel O'Connell. Where would the pigeons roost if Alberta ever brought central Canada down to its own level?

Oh well, if I can't be prime minister, I'll settle for the next best thing. Send me to Dublin as our next ambassador. Then they can build a statue to me alongside Daniel O'Connell. Bring on the pigeons!

GILLES PAQUET

The Prime Minister Must Be a Leader

In the Canadian democracy, the person elected prime minister is entitled to take action without referenda and/or plebiscites and to lead the nation on the strength of the mandate received from the population. This is the *quid*. As a counterpart, the population is said to have received the *quo* from the prime minister during the election campaign: a mission statement about what is to be accomplished during the term of office, a corporate plan stating the ways and means to be used to get there, and the rules of the game to be respected in normal times but also in times of emergencies or crises, should they occur.

This is a sort of implicit contract between the populace and the PM. Some PMS have been trapped in this arrangement and have become mere managers of the public household, labouring under the illusion that they could understand and control the course of events. The results have been pathetic. A good PM is not a naive manager but is first and foremost a leader. This means someone who has, in the language of Isaiah Berlin, the capacity to expose "the false signposts...a sense of what fits with what, of what cannot exist with what...a special sensitiveness to the contours of the circumstances in which we happen to be placed."

The PM as leader must determine the character of Canada as a going concern, through the development of shared fantasies and the imparting of values. Leadership is massively and intrinsically valuational. So a leader must find ways to change the myths and metaphors of the community, to impart a new dream to the populace if the sort of change called for by the continuing external pressures is to ensue. The job of the leader is to define and mold the issues, to educate people about the problems facing the country, to uncover the deeper underlying issues, and to motivate all to develop solutions to these problems, taking the deeper issues fully into account.

This leadership job is both more ambitious and much simpler than the management job that is so often associated with the title of prime minister. Canada may not be manageable from the centre, but it can be led. To lead, the prime minister must first eliminate the "misfits" and must then take measures to improve the way things in Canada "fit."

Eliminating Misfits

The prime minister must be an opportunist who has strong principles; he must scheme virtuously. Any PM has approximately six months' grace to define the style of leadership that will prevail during his term of office. But before he can really hope to accomplish anything, a certain amount of cleansing is in order. A negative code of ethics must be presented as the new civil theology that will be the rudder of the ship of state. This code is based on a philosophy of design. The designer does not know what the ideal form is, but in his search for the least undesirable form, he can eliminate what does not fit. (Similarly, a medical doctor does not speculate on what health is; it is sufficient to recognize illness and to eliminate it as a misfit.) Ethics is to the prime minister what aesthetics is to the designer.

What are these misfits? When asked why he and James D. Watson discovered the structure of DNA when so many others failed to do so, Sir Francis Crick is purported to have said that the basic reason for success or failure in research is that those who succeed have become aware of assumptions they were not aware they were making. The same holds true for a successful PM. If he assumes that he knows everything it is important to know about Canada and that he can control the Canadian experiment, he is bound to fall prey to conspiracies, which already exist, to prevent the leader from leading. These conspiracies have been analysed in the literature on administrative sciences, by Warren Bennis in particular. First, there is an unconscious conspiracy (emanating from the inertia of the system and from the mountain of trivial affairs to be dealt with) to prevent the PM from doing anything whatever to change the status quo. Secondly, there is much moral numbness and petit-Eichmannism, which allows subordinates to continue acting out a role, even though they are persuaded that their action is wrong-headed, or simply wrong.

Both these conspiracies have to be tackled in a prime minister's first days in office—the first type of conspiracy, through the creation of an executive constellation of ministers and staff members, who will be educated in the difference between management and leadership, who will know more than the PM in their areas of competency, and who will protect the PM from getting enmeshed in routine matters; the second conspiracy must be tackled with a strict order that any case of misfit—apprehended or real—must be reported to the PM's staff immediately, and that there must be a warning that any silence on observed misfits or any failure to detect and report misfits will be regarded as a form of petit-Eichmannism and will be punished accordingly.

To some, such declarations may appear of little use, but in fact they would provide the loyal servants around the prime minister with fundamental guidance. To keep their jobs, they would quickly have to develop an acute sense of the difference between routine and governance issues, as well as taking personal responsibility for any action they took or any silence they kept in relation to misfits. This should ensure for the prime minister a form of collective leadership that would be extraordinarily attentive to sound information flows from the population and would be based on a radar system all through the organization directed to informing the PM of misfits, i.e., of events or reactions which appeared to be out of line with the general philosophical thrusts that he had declared to be the government's direction.

Making Things a Better Fit

Such general safeguards alone are not sufficient. The PM must also become a social architect, a designer of institutions that are likely to improve the way in which the existing order fits Canada's needs. This is not an easy task, for there are vested interests connected with each existing institution or set of rules. Nevertheless, in the first six months in office, the PM must announce that some institutions will be eliminated and others will be created, in order to help the electorate move in directions that are desirable for Canada.

First, since the PM cannot claim omniscience, much should be done to improve the communicative skills of Canadians—their capacity to educate themselves about important issues and to communicate to their PM what they wish to impose as limits on his activities. This calls for the practical use of referenda and plebiscites. Such devices, by providing incentives for citizens to invest some time in exploring crucial issues, would be bound to help them develop a stronger taste for participation.

Second, many institutions that have ceased to be important as relay points between the public and the prime minister must be done away with (e.g., the Economic Council of Canada and the Science Council of Canada). New institutions must be created, among them a refurbished Senate, known as the Council of Social Values, which would provide a forum for discussion by individuals, groups, and technical experts on the goals to be pursued. This would be an excellent apparatus through which to educate the PM about goals and objectives; such a forum would also provide a locus for debates about global change and long-term socioeconomic trends—matters that are unlikely to receive a serious hearing anywhere at present.

Third, in order to help improve the general quality of the House of Commons, a modification of the electoral process should be introduced which would allow one-third of the members of the House to be selected from a priority list established by each party on the basis of its proportional share of the popular vote. The very best minds and souls each party was able to mobilize would be ranked on these lists. Such a system would have several advantages: it would improve the quality of the discourse on most matters in the House of Commons; it would ensure that the best minds from all parties were in the House; and it would smooth the transition between governments of different parties, since each meaningful party would continually maintain a contingent of very good participants in House of Commons work.

Fourth, since three out of four Canadians live in one of three metropolitan areas—Toronto, Montreal, and Vancouver—it would be essential for the PM to create an Advisory Board of Metropolitan Governments so that the leaders of these major centres could have a direct say in shaping Canadian policy. Such a board would help the PM think through what the policy of the federal government should be in the distribution of its activities throughout the country. For instance, there is no good scientific or economic reason why the national scientific laboratories of the National Research Council are located in Ottawa to the extent that they are. The presence of federal laboratories in different areas of the country might play a developmental role in the different regions (for instance, as enrichment to local universities); they might also serve as an antenna to gauge better the evolving vocations of the different large metropolitan areas. This forum could serve as the locus for the development of a policy of decentralization and deconcentration of the federal administration, based on the complementary roles of the different metropolises and provinces within the Canadian socioeconomy.

Envoi

One is reminded, when spelling out one's priorities, of the lyrics of an old jazz ballad: "The difficult, I'll do right now. The impossible will take a little while." The above proposals are simply difficult. Others might appear impossible. They would be topics for discussion at the meetings of the Council of Social Values. Should one abolish the Bank of Canada? Will Canada dare to face its responsibilities vis-à-vis the Third World? Can the education system be reformed in Canada to promote the learning of many languages, the development of tolerance, and the transformation of Canadians into some sort of new Phoenicians? Can this dream of unity in diversity, of Canada as a community of communities, be propounded more effectively? Is the day coming when a garbage collectors' truck will be heard majestically broadcasting Vivaldi or Vigneault as it goes its rounds in the streets of Montreal or Toronto? And can one person, who is allowed temporarily to hold the rudder in Canada, do anything to promote the realization of these or any other objectives?

For myself, I consider such leadership possible. A good example of it was provided at the local level by an unsung hero of the National Capital Region—Douglas Fullerton—who transformed a frozen canal into the longest skating rink in the country and who allowed Ottawans to discover that they wanted to ride bicycles along those marvellous lanes throughout the city. He is one of the group that Robert Townsend regards as the best type of leader: people do not notice their existence, and when their work is done the people say, "We did it ourselves." The work of the prime minister in Canada should be what Fullerton did writ large.

In the past, we have had prime ministers whom people have hated and despised, or have feared, or have praised and honoured. These may be regarded respectively as fourth-best, third-best, and second-best PMS. Now we may be ready for the best, a PM who would hardly be noticed because he—or she—would allow Canadians to do their own thing, while innocuously helping them to go beyond their limits. On such a PM's business card there would be a simple inscription, borrowed from a TV hero of yesteryear: "Have gun. Will travel." This would serve as a reminder that if and when the ride gets tough and the optimal amount of coercion turns out not to be zero any more, the PM will be ready.

ART PHILLIPS

A prime minister has a great deal of power. He can spend his time pussy-footing around, worrying about his own re-election, or he can shake things up. I think Canada needs some shaking up.

Post Office Reform

In recent years, the prize for the worst-run enterprise in Canada would undoubtedly go to the post office. In spite of deterioration in service and enormous price increases, the post office still manages to lose money. What's wrong?

In the era of single-digit postal charges, Canada used to be proud of its postal service. But in recent decades, management and unions have been at each other's throats. Inefficient work is a badge of honour among militant unionists. And management is so blockheaded as to try and sell the second-rate service of group boxes as if it were an improvement. There is a way to motivate the post office to perform better. If I were prime minister, I would make the following changes:

- freeze all postal rates at the present levels for five years;
- freeze all postal wages at the present levels for five years;
- not allow any further reductions in levels of service (but permit improvements);
- reduce the present subsidy to zero in five annual steps;
- change the board of directors of the post office so that there would be five government appointees, one from each region of Canada, and five employee appointees, one from each region of Canada; the ten directors would then select an eleventh person as their chairman;
- finally, and most important, 50 per cent of any profit made would be shared on a pro rata basis by all the employees.

Suddenly, all the employees would realize that they are responsible for the business and that the better job they do, the more they earn. I guarantee that over the next five years the post office service would improve dramatically, the employees would all be much happier and more efficient, the number of employees would probably decline but the average employee would earn more, and we the taxpayers, through our federal government, would be earning a tidy profit instead of subsidizing a second-rate service.

If this sounds like a pipe dream, it's not. I've seen it happen time and again in business enterprises when the employees participate in the decision-making and earnings of the enterprise. If it were ever done, we would all wonder why it hadn't been done sooner.

Parliamentary Reform

Parliament, as it presently operates, is essentially irrelevant. The public sees this but tends to shrug and say, "That's politics," because there seems to be no better alternative.

Surely we can do better. Surely we can devise a system where members actually discuss issues, listen to each other, and draw conclusions based on something other than political party divisions. Surely regional interests can be better represented and individual members of parliament can play a significant role.

The controversy in 1986 over the awarding of a CF-18 maintenance contract to a Montreal firm highlighted the frustration of eight of the ten provinces with the present system. All political parties (and this would include the New Democrats if they became a serious force) pay an inordinate amount of attention to the interests of Ontario and Quebec, because they feel that elections are won or lost in those provinces. Because of the strong party discipline in our system, this effectively silences the voices of the representatives from other provinces. The adversarial tradition of our parliament also stifles intelligent debate. If the government pursues a policy, the opposition feels it must oppose it. As the *Globe and Mail* recently put it, "Critical judgement must be suspended...; hyperbole in the service of opposition is no vice."

I served a few months in the federal parliament as an opposition Liberal MP from Vancouver Centre in 1979-80. I was struck by how boring parliament was for all but the political junkies, and how useless it was. It could be better. I had previously served eight years in the Vancouver city council. By comparison, the council was a model of intelligent debate and constructive decision-making. Members actually listened to what others said and occasionally decided their position *after* the discussion. What was the big difference? Municipal councils do not normally have an organized system or tradition of government versus opposition. They do not sit in two groups opposite each other like rows of school children.

The first reform I would make in parliament would therefore be to change the seating arrangements completely so that the members sat in a large semicircle, arranged geographically. This would be a step towards getting members together across party lines and in reflection of their regional interests.

The second reform I would make is to call every vote a free vote, except specific votes of non-confidence. This would also encourage MPS to cross party lines and express their views and those of their region.

Third, to give individual members a more significant role, I would allow private members' bills, if co-sponsored by a government and opposition member, to be debated and voted upon in the normal way. At present, only government bills are treated seriously.

Fourth, I would remove the government's right to call an election when it chooses. There should be fixed election dates every four years. If every vote were a free vote, minority governments would continue to govern normally, without precipitating an election. Members could vote their individual preferences. Party discipline would be much less confining.

Fifth, I would abolish the Senate. It performs no useful function.

Sixth, I would allow members to file written reports for the record, as they do in the United States. Then they wouldn't have to stand up in front of an empty chamber, reading a speech to a nonexistent audience, simply to get it printed in Hansard. Parliament would not have to sit for all those extra, wasted months.

Finally, we need better people in parliament. The country would be better served if there were fewer career politicians—narrow, single-purpose people whose only interest has been politics, from university, through the executive assistant route into elected office. These people are skilled at politics but lack outside experience, outside interests, and motivation. They are desperate to keep their jobs because, in most cases, they could never hope to do as well in the outside world.

To get better people into government, I have three additional suggestions. In the first place, more outstanding individuals should be brought directly or quickly into the cabinet as a matter of common practice. People like Lester Pearson and Pierre Trudeau were singled out by previous prime ministers and their path into cabinet made easy. Cabinet should not just be a reward for longevity in parliament or for party loyalty.

Secondly, we should lower the salaries of members of parliament. Years ago it became fashionable to suggest raising salaries to attract better people—and I confess I thought we would get better people. However, time has shown that higher salaries have had the effect of attracting career politicians. Parliament has become increasingly silly and irrelevant as it has become increasingly populated with purely political people. We need more people who are prepared to give a few years of public service and then move on.

Third, the length of time parliament sits should be reduced. Parliamentary business could easily be conducted in one fall and one spring session, leaving members about half the year to return to their communities. At present, members become so "Ottawa-ized" that they lose touch with the real world in the rest of Canada.

With better people, less partisanship, and meaningful roles for members, parliament could be made relevant and respectable again.

Financial Reform

Governments throughout the world do a very poor job of controlling their expenditures. Politicians like to spend money and feel it helps them politically. And all taxes are certainly unpopular. So governments increasingly spend more than they raise in taxes. They borrow the difference and leave future generations to pay the interest and repay the loans.

All sorts of elaborate rationalizations have been developed to legitimize government deficits. For years, politicians claimed that deficits stimulated the economy. If that were so, our economy would be experiencing a hyperboom. The truth is that deficits are the result of political cowardice and the desire of politicians to cling to office. History has shown that when deficits eventually get out of hand, governments resort to printing money, and runaway inflation is the result. It is important that we bring our deficit spending under control before this happens. It can be done, and in fact it used to be done. Until the late 1960s there were many years in which Canada's federal government ran a surplus, and the deficit was never very much in the other years. Governments went crazy in the 1970s during the inflationary period, and we are now faced with having to pay the consequences.

Municipal governments manage their finances much better. This is not because municipal councils are more intelligent but because they don't have the same freedom as federal and provincial legislatures to spend money without having to tax the citizens. If they had the same freedom, they would be just as profligate. Moreover, municipal governments are required to balance their current income and expenditures each year. They are also required to ask voters to approve the borrowing of money for most capital expenditures. As a result, they borrow less and spend it better.

To reform the federal financial mess, I would apply these same rules to the federal and provincial governments. Some may say, "But you can't do that." Why not? The real obstacle is that the federal and provincial politicians would not want to establish such rules limiting their own behaviour. The public should demand a voice in such matters as a democratic right. The politicians are not ultimately responsible for the repayment of the debt they incur. The taxpayers are. So the taxpayers have the right to be presented with the facts and to say yes or no before the government incurs debt.

The citizens are not stupid. They vote for things that are important to them. Give the voters all the information in terms of what the various alternatives will cost the average person in present and future taxes, and they will decide intelligently. Such a system would be far more democratic and much fairer to future generations than the present system is.

Tax Reform

For decades, politicians have been talking about simplifying the income tax system. Meanwhile, it has steadily grown more and more complicated and unfair. Now the United States government has surprised us all by actually reforming taxes radically. The U.S. tax system will, in the next two or three years, eliminate most of the tax shelters that existed and will also substantially reduce personal income tax to a maximum of 28 per cent. The benefits of these changes will be enormous.

First, the tax system will be much fairer. It's not just that "the rich will pay more." Some high-income taxpayers have been paying a great deal of income tax while others have been paying little or none. That's unfair. In the future, the tax burden will be spread more evenly and fairly. Secondly, tax evasion and avoidance will be much less profitable. All those intelligent lawyers and accountants currently involved in trying to beat the tax laws will be able to apply their talents to more productive work. The economy can only benefit. Thirdly, decisions to spend or to invest will be made more intelligently. The tax consequences won't be wagging the investment-decision dog. When you have two kinds of dollars—pretax and aftertax—which are so drastically different in spending power, it distorts everybody's thinking.

We should bring in similar tax reform in Canada as soon as possible. If I were prime minister, I would phase out all tax shelter deductions except registered retirement savings plans. RRSPs are not really tax shelters. They are simply individual pension plans, and nobody seriously suggests that money being put into a pension plan should be taxed as current income.

We should also lower our maximum income tax rates to around 30 per cent combined federal and provincial taxes. This would encourage people to earn more, discourage the evasion and avoidance of taxation, and bring fairness back to the system.

I would make one other radical change and include all inheritances as income. I would not allow any trusts to be set up to defer or eliminate inheritance taxes. Contributions to charities would have to be confined to approved charities. Some provisions might be made for dependency situations, but, essentially, inherited income should be looked at for what it is—an unearned benefit for the recipient which should certainly be taxed no less than earned income.

That would take care of the first term. Now, for my second term. . . .

WALTER G. PITMAN

Prime ministers can have as much long-term influence by what they are as by what they do. Action, in Ottawa, comes from such a mélange of commissions, committees, task forces, boards, and caucus and cabinet meetings that no modern prime minister can happily reflect on many examples of personal legislative or regulatory intervention that have really made a difference. History is truly ironic, and prime ministers are remembered most clearly for changes that were not to be found in their haziest imaginations when elected. But an enthusiasm, a style, a perception that translates itself into a signal for transformation—that is the real opportunity for change presented to a prime minister.

It is in this spirit, which may be termed either cynical or idealistic, that I would choose to take symbolic action if ever the circumstances transpired to transport me to Sussex Drive. As a single act of immediate consequence, I would declare March 21 as Canadian Artists and Authors Day. It would be an annual festival of song, dance, words, drama, image, and texture. It would be a day of rejoicing and a celebration of the talent, the creativity, the sensitivity, the insight of Canada's artistic community.

Many Canadians grew up in a country whose school system's curriculum was obsessed by Dickens and Shakespeare, Magna Carta and the Wars of the Roses. Other Canadians have come from lands rich with their own culture and customs. The need to recognize that all of us live in neighbourhoods filled with fellow Canadians who are writers, composers, craftsmen, painters, and sculptors has never been greater. An Artists and Authors Day could focus every Canadian on the presence of these people, who deserve to be recognized and respected—but more, whose thoughts and visual expressions should be understood and reflected upon. I have chosen March 21 for obvious reasons. In a northern land it is our signal from the universe that rebirth and renewal are at the heart of creation.

It is strange that when we wish to celebrate on July 1 our continued existence as a nation, we invariably turn to our singers, musicians, and dancers to create the occasion of joy and thanksgiving. Yet rarely do we focus on the art and the artist; always we use—and, sometimes, abuse—those who well serve our own interests. This is extraordinary in a country which in a few short decades has witnessed an explosion of the arts. This explosion fortuitously came at the highest point of crisis in our national life—a time in the 1960s and 1970s when one of the founding communities was imbued by a perception that it felt uncomfortable and at a disadvantage in a union with the English-speaking majority.

Marshall McLuhan said, "The artist picks up the message of cultural and technical challenge decades before its transforming impact occurs. He, then, builds models or Noah's arks for facing the change that is ahead." At that time of a breakdown in consensus, our artists built the "ark" by writing the novels, the poems, composing the music, making the films, and choreographing the dance which helped us to understand each other across this immense geography, and particularly across a linguistic and cultural rift.

Today, Canada faces the other McLuhan challenge, the technical challenge. Our writers and playwrights are grappling with the effect of technology on the human condition—not only in the narrower context of techno-stress imposing itself on us individually, but in the way that technology is influencing our collective life. Canada's creative people are wrestling with this pervasive force as it threatens to disrupt the nation's economy. We had an enormous advantage when economic well-being came as a result of easily accessible raw materials, energy sources, and capital. At that time it was possible to import our technology from the United States (through the mechanism of the multinational corporation) and our technologists from the polytechnics of the United Kingdom and West Germany. Indeed, economically speaking, "the living was easy."

Today, the only resource that really counts in an internationally competitive information economy is the creativity of its people. Whether we talk about creative management, marketing, or product development, we are addressing the same issue. Canadians have given only lip service to the need for research and development and for high-level technical and technological education—and we are paying the price in the 1980s. However, creativity is a seamless garment; the motivation, the insight, and the innovative spirit that produce a great opera or magnificent porcelain also produce industrial design achievement and exciting, inventive management and production techniques.

A day devoted to Canadian artistic creativity would make this link—and would send a message to every teacher and educational administrator that the future will belong to those who identify and nurture creative energy.

It would be imperative on such a day to ensure that Canadians are made aware of some basic facts about the arts which challenge the long-held perceptions that such activities are on the periphery of the market places of this country. It would be essential to transmit the data revealing how many hundreds of thousands of people work in the arts and in arts-based industries, and how much the arts contribute to the Gross National Product. It would be an opportunity to remind Canadians that the revival of the tourist industry to levels of the 1960s and 1970s (in terms of the share of world tourism) can only come from a more visible artistic expression. It is surely understood that tourists can no longer be attracted and captured by visions of mountains, lakes, rivers, and trees. It is now conventional wisdom that people in other lands want to experience the Canadian perception of the human condition; that is, how we view the quality of the environment, how we look at the question of nuclear war, how we explore issues of alienation, loneliness, sexism, racism, and all the other walls that men and women have to climb day by day. And it is our artists alone who can show our visitors this—in our galleries, theatres, and concert halls.

But the economic arguments in favour of Canadian Artists and Authors Day must be subservient to its central purpose: the celebration of the contribution that artists and authors make to the intellectual and spiritual life of every citizen. In essence, this day could be a recognition of the role of every Canadian in supporting the arts; for each of us has, through our taxes, encouraged this unique growth since the 1940s. One remembers how little artistic activity could be found in Canada before World War II. It was the Massey Commission that reported a "hunger for the arts" and recommended the establishment of a funding agency which would emulate the recently founded British Arts Council and would develop programs to assist Canadian music, theatre, dance, literature, film, and visual arts. Thus, the Canada Council came into being.

Today, there are funding agencies or arts councils in several provinces, and there are cultural ministries in every province. As well, cities across Canada are now establishing arts councils and identifying municipal tax money to be passed on to artists and arts organizations. Over the past three decades, millions of tax dollars have been used to support theatres, orchestras, publishers... a host of activities. Compared to the millions of dollars supplied to the corporate world for its perceived needs, this is an infinitesimal and inconspicuous response, yet it is enough to have changed the face of this country dramatically.

Ultimately, resources would be found to ensure that on Artists and Authors Day there would be opportunities for people throughout Canada to see and hear live theatre, dance, and music, and to meet our novelists, poets, and non-fiction writers. Such activity would soon be supported by special grants from all levels of government, and it would certainly be appropriate for special broadcasts on television and radio (both private and public). We might learn how important the CBC has been to the cultural life of this country through its nurturing of composers, writers, actors, directors, playwrights—and to what extent all of our electronic media depend on the existence of a critical mass of such talent.

This intense focus on the arts might convince more Canadians that the arts are not just entertainment, not therapy, not economic exchange, but that they are the ultimate communication, the ultimate learning experience.

People have come to Canada from every corner of the globe and we have learned how to live together. Our cities are inhabited by representatives of every imaginable culture, wearing every imaginable costume, eating every imaginable type of food, speaking every extant language, and praying to every known deity. Racism is not unknown to Canadian newcomers—visible-minority immigrants have been abused and humiliated, as they have in every country. But racism in its most violent and destructive form has been contained. Our police, our social workers, our teachers, our professionals have learned to serve in many different styles, using a variety of models. The greatest influence in the war on intolerance is the presence of the arts of every land in all their glory. Multiculturalism as a term has been abused, but the fact of our mosaic has saved us from the excesses being experienced in so many other parts of the world. Artists and authors come in every language and culture—and so it must be on Artists and Authors Day.

There may be some who will regard my proposal—the creation of a day of artistic recognition and expression—as the trivialization of a magnificent invitation to express myself as the prime minister of a substantial nation. Indeed, we live on the edge of the precipice of total annihilation. Unless that problem is solved, all the suggestions to be found in this volume, along with all the hopes and aspirations of every Canadian, will be obliterated in a few minutes. But where has this singular truth been expressed more adequately, more convincingly, and in more different ways than in the work of authors and artists of every discipline?

It is in those moments when we revel in the sights and sounds of the citizens of every nation-state—on stages, in orchestra pits, in picture galleries and exhibitions—that we understand how much we share as humans on the fragile planet that we call home. We are left breathless by the power and clarity of an East European orchestra, and Chinese citizens weep at the sound of a Canadian contralto singing Mahler.

Nuclear war will not be diverted by artistry—it will ultimately be decided by the political leaders and their aides. But such great universal decisions for peace and disarmament do not emerge from a vacuum but from the widespread realization that, as world citizens, we hold a common aspiration to survive in dignity, to live in harmony. On Canadian Artists and Authors Day, it would be appropriate to encourage and fund an exchange of artists, particularly with those countries whose world politics we find unattractive, so that the full impact of the arts as a peaceable activity could be felt.

Such a day might be a Canadian first step towards the ideal stated by the Canadian Conference of the Arts: "The world must once again put culture and the arts in the centre of public policy as they are at the centre of human activity. The needs are manifest, the rewards are clear—a better world, a more meaningful life for all citizens, new ways to tackle problems."

Only one day.... But surely a start.

W. GUNTHER PLAUT

The invitation to imagine myself as prime minister has forced me to arrange my diversified beefs about Ottawa and its political hothouse into a few manageable categories. I presume that as PM I would also be the head of one of the political parties, and this stretches my imagination to the breaking point. It also reminds me that while I might persuade the country to adopt all (or some, or maybe one) of the following policies, I would have a much tougher time with my party caucus. After all, its members have the sacred obligation of striving for re-election whereas I, their leader, strive only for the right and the good....

I shall assume, however, that by dint of charisma, superior salesmanship, threats, promises, or whatever the PM uses to bring everyone round, I would get the go-ahead from caucus for a priority program of ten policies, which I would then lay before the nation. I am fully aware of the difficulties and of the likelihood that I would fall short of my goals. But I would comfort myself with the thought that laying my ideas before the public and engendering wide-ranging discussions about them would have its own benefits and could be considered an achievement in itself.

So here they are, arranged not so much in order of importance as in categories of general and specific programs.

Identify the Greatness of Canada
Every speech that I or members of my party make will in part aim at convincing Canadians that they live in a country of great achievements and even greater potential. Such achievement and potential, however, have little to do with natural resources, economics, politics, or even hockey. They will refer, in my policy statements, to the fact that we are a mini-universe of the earth's populations. We are making a success of having people of every background and culture live next to each other without having to surrender their own heritage. We are one example of all too few in the world where diverse cultures are encouraged to persist rather than to be absorbed, acculturated, assimilated, and melted down in a pot of national conformity.

Lead Instead of Follow

I shall tell the country that I do not aim to be re-elected, either by my party to its leadership or by the voters at the polls. I shall therefore not arrange my program in response to what the voters are likely to approve. To be sure, I shall try and persuade them that what I am doing is good for the long-range health of the country. I shall expect, however, to discharge my responsibilities primarily in accordance with my convictions, and to do so irrespective of the pollsters and their products.

At first this will be a hard bill to sell to my caucus, but I rather think that in a short time they will find out that the ordinary Joe and Jane really want a leader and not a pulse taker. When the pollsters confirm this, as I think they will after a while, my party will be on side. This will help to repair the popular image of the politician as a person whose greatest goal in life is to be re-elected and who therefore will make any promise that will assure him/her of success.

Stabilize the Process of Governing

After choosing the members of my cabinet, I shall announce that there will be no sporadic shuffles designed to spruce up the administration's good looks. Such repeated shuffles do more harm than good. It is difficult enough to learn the complexities of any ministry and department, and it takes at least a year to familiarize oneself fully with its multifarious tasks.

Such stability will also enable the ministers to make their civil servants toe the line and carry out the policies that the elected officials have laid down. In the ordinary way of doing things, cabinet ministers get moved around like chess pieces. Bureaucrats are then the only stabilizing force in government, and it is usually *their* policies that are being carried out.

Not so in my administration. Ministers will keep their jobs unless they goof, or unless it becomes obvious that they are unsuited for their assignment, or unless they request to be relieved. Frequent reviews of their performance will be an important task of my personal staff.

Upgrade Backbenchers

Traditionally, an enormous amount of talent is wasted by relegating lots of capable people to the anonymity of the back benches. The obligation to vote for the leader's policies makes them rubber-stamping figures rather than independent representatives of the people who elected them. Cutting the backbenchers loose and giving them freedom to vote their conscience is only an occasional practice today—as, for example, in the discussion of the death penalty. I would increase the number of free votes to at least ten a year in order to give every member of the House of Commons the opportunity to deal with many more issues on the basis not of party discipline but of personal knowledge and conviction. This would also give the voters a better chance to assess the person whom they had sent to Ottawa.

Appoint Outsiders to the Cabinet
With few exceptions, only members of the Commons are appointed to cabinet positions. This convention has often forced the prime minister to choose unsuitable persons from parts of the country that would otherwise be underrepresented. While I shall not adopt the American system of having all cabinet members chosen from outside the legislature—which is necessary there because of the separation of powers—I shall look for half a dozen of the most capable persons I can find and make them my ministers. They will be assisted by junior ministers who will answer questions in the House.

Such leeway of choice will also make it possible to have in my cabinet members of minority groups, who somehow do not seem to find their way to the seat of power. This will help to unify the country and will give additional millions of citizens the feeling that they too belong.

Appoint a Federal Ombudsman
I shall push for the institution of a federal ombudsman (male or female). Provinces already have such guardians of the public interest, who give the average person the opportunity to complain about governmental ineptitude or unfairness, whether real or imagined. Often the ombudsmen turn out to be "fixers," in that they bring to the attention of civil servants certain inequities which, once acknowledged, can usually be rectified.

This would mean that there would be vice-ombudsmen in all the provinces and territories. It would be their task to look into federal matters: beefs about crown corporations as well as the whole gamut of the federal civil service. While this will add more bureaucrats to the payroll, it will in effect save us money in the long run and moreover will be another instance of confidence-building for the whole people.

Reduce Federal Spending
Having just added to the deficit, I shall now proceed to several radical economic suggestions:

- Each ministry will have to reduce its staff by 5 per cent in each of the years I am in office. Should my term last four years, this would mean a reduction of 20 per cent, and therewith a sizable dent in the deficit.

– The principle of universality is a sure vote-getting ploy, but its unjustness is palpable, and besides, the country can't afford it. If we generally tax on the basis of ability to pay, why is the method no longer applicable once a person reaches a certain age? If my income tax is over a certain amount, I obviously earn enough not to need the government's handout. To be sure, there is the "grandfather clause" which would probably apply. People have planned their lives in a certain way, knowing that they will be getting a cheque at the end of the month. So if I could not abolish universality for those already receiving these monies, I would start with those not yet retired and would give them a five-year lead for planning. This is one of the measures that would be vastly unpopular at first, but once the people saw that their leader meant what he said, they would also see the justice and necessity of this proposal.

– Mandatory retirement is unjust—and probably unconstitutional as well. It deprives people of their right not to be discriminated against on the basis of age; while the provinces deal with most such cases, there is enough employment in the federal service to warrant the introduction of a federal law.

– I would sell unprofitable crown corporations to the private sector but would retain the CBC.

– I would take a serious look at instituting a flat tax.

Take a New Look at Immigration
Believing that true independence will not come to Canada until it has a more substantial population base, I would order a review of long-range policies that deal with immigration to this country. At present such policies are arrived at in an *ad hoc* annual manner, in response primarily to employment levels at home. There is no clear conception of what kind of numbers are really desirable for Canada in the long-range view, and no realistic attempt has been made to expand our population. Yet there is good reason to believe that if Canada had another 10 million citizens, its home market would be so substantially enlarged that the economy would benefit enormously, and in turn we would become less dependent on the United States with its vast number of people who outnumber us ten to one.

Obviously, such a dramatic increase in our population would not and could not be accommodated in a few years, but it could take place over several decades. The process has to begin some time, and a study of whether, how, and when such an influx could be encouraged would be undertaken at once.

I would also challenge the Canadian people to confront a problem they have so far avoided—or, rather, which the government has refused to put on the public agenda. I would ask: If we expand our population, what will its national components be tomorrow? How will we be sure to preserve the democratic character of the country? How will the special situation of Quebec be safeguarded? How will we deal with residual racism in Canada?

These and related questions are fraught with emotion and preconceptions, and are therefore traditionally avoided by government. I would release the study which I submitted to the Feds in 1985 and which they have so far refused to publish. At the time, I asked a series of questions and challenged the government to put them up for public debate. As prime minister, I would proceed to pull the matter out of the closet, where it currently rests.

Confront Increased Pollution
The federal government should enlist the co-operation of the entire Canadian public in cleaning up our badly polluted air, water, and food sources.

For instance, the current fad of making hard and soft drugs the core of our public worry has diverted us from looking at smoking as the number-one addiction which threatens both the individual and the environment. I would advocate the prohibition of smoking in any place accessible to the public and would then tax the production and consumption of tobacco to such an extent that the former became unprofitable and the latter too expensive. The temporary profits that government would derive from this policy would be used to enable tobacco farmers to switch to other crops.

Of course, such a program is likely to encourage smuggling of American or other foreign-made smoking materials into Canada. But this problem will be contained in that public consumption of tobacco will be illegal, and smoking will therefore be confined to the privacy of people's homes.

Establish a Department of Peace
We have a Department of Defence, but we do not have an equally prestigious Department of Peace. The very institution of such a department would signal to the public that we mean to take the promulgation of peace seriously. I shall not here describe what precisely such a ministry might undertake, but there are a few areas that will bear immediate exploring: revising the Charter of the United

Nations; exploring the idea of world federalism; establishing a federal peace academy that would train Canadians (or others who wish to attend) in the arts of peacemaking. The inclusion of a minister of peace at the cabinet table would do much for the temper of our discussions and the direction of our policies.

To conclude, I am not unaware that my ten-point policy statement would cause me to be dubbed a radical, a dewy-eyed dreamer, an anti-politician, or whatever. In other words, I'd have a tough time selling my policies. But since I would have campaigned for them and would, presumably, have been elected to carry them out, I might have a chance. If not, it will surely be better to have dreamed and lost than not to have dreamed at all.

RICHARD ROHMER

If I were prime minister of Canada, my time in office would be a period of change. The goal would be to achieve a dramatic change in the form and substance of the federal government.

First, I would restructure the cabinet, partly adopting the American system. In the United States, the president has the right to step outside the ranks of politicians to select a cabinet from among the best, most able, and most qualified men and women (in his political judgement) whom he can find—even people who are not of his own political persuasion. The result is that, by and large, the U.S. cabinet is made up of outstanding individuals who are responsible only to the president—except for their occasional requirement to account to certain committees of Congress.

A similar ability to select cabinet members from outside the House of Commons exists for the prime minister of Canada, but it is seldom exercised. As a matter of custom, the prime minister must select his cabinet from among members of his parliamentary caucus. This constraint is added to by the need to provide regional representation in the cabinet. Even though the regional representatives are often inept, without special skill or talent, they are all too frequently given senior cabinet posts of high responsibility.

I would overcome these constraints by selecting ten cabinet members in the American manner—the best-qualified Canadians I could find. To make them eligible for a cabinet post, I would appoint them to the Senate. However, this would be at my pleasure in that, on appointment, they would give me their open-as-to-time resignation; and they would automatically cease to be senators when parliament was dissolved for the purpose of a general election.

I would have no more than thirty cabinet ministers altogether. The ten from the Senate would be able to hold any portfolio except those that by their nature require a member of the House of Commons. For example, the deputy prime minister could not be a senator. Each senator minister would be accountable to the House of Commons through an associate minister, who would be an elected cabinet member (possibly with a portfolio of his or her own: a double-hatted individual).

By creating this form of senator minister, I would be able to induce into public service citizens who, for personal reasons, would never choose to run for election as politicians. In this way, I would effectively upgrade the quality and credibility of the antiquated British cabinet system, moving it into the reality of modern times—without any legislative changes!

Secondly, I would regularize my attendance in the House of Commons during question period. As the leader of the government, the prime minister carries an inordinately heavy administrative, political, and ceremonial load. To take the time for the daily question period, together with the preparation and briefing for it, is far too onerous. Moreover, when the prime minister is in the House during question period, he is the lightning rod for all manner of attack—often personal—by the opposition; and with the House performances now being shown on television, any lapse on the part of the prime minister tends to lower his image in the eyes of the public.

For these reasons, I would advise the House as follows: I shall appear for question period every second Wednesday, unless there is what I consider to be an emergency. Furthermore, I shall answer only reasonable questions and only those that are submitted in writing to my office by 6 P.M. on the previous day, dealing with them in the order they arrived at my office. It follows that I shall also answer supplementary questions. And I shall, of course, give priority to questions submitted by the leaders of the opposition parties.

As prime minister, one of my principal goals would be to establish long-range policy objectives for the social, economic, and cultural enhancement of the nation. The target would be to create policies that would go beyond the normal four to five years of a majority government.

A model for this type of planning can be found in the work and recommendations of the Mid-Canada Conference. Its final report was published and presented to the Government of Canada in 1971, following three years of in-depth effort by a cross section of interested Canadians, who paid to participate in the conference or were invited to take part because of their special skills. The objective of the conference (in which some hundred and fifty Canadians took part over the three-year period) was to examine the need for and feasibility of creating long-term policies and plans for the orderly development of the mid-Canada region—the Boreal (or Northern) Forest, including the Mackenzie River region to its mouth on the Beaufort Sea. Task forces of conference members were created to deal with, among other things, environment, social impact, transportation, communications, natural resources and land use, industrialization, and urbanization.

244

The conference recognized that the Boreal Forest, some 2.5 million square kilometres in size, is capable of providing a livable environment for many millions of people, and that long-range policies and plans could feasibly be prepared for the orderly development of this sector of Canada. The conference's prime recommendation was therefore that the Government of Canada, in conjunction with the provinces and territories, should create an organization to carry out the necessary planning. This process might well continue for a full decade before comprehensive plans were produced; but against these plans, government policies would then be created whereby all sectors of the fabric of the nation would become involved in their implementation.

The Mid-Canada Conference recommended that in the national interest it was urgent that such policies and plans be created. Yet no action was taken by the government of the day or by those following it. If I were prime minister, the recommendations of the Mid-Canada Conference would be taken seriously and would be implemented.

A "mobile" House of Commons would be another of my objectives. One of the major problems in maintaining the unity of Canada is its vastness. This gives rise to regional disparities. The most difficult of these is the concentration of population, industrial strength, and political power in central Canada. To try and overcome some of the psychological damage that occurs in the Maritimes and in the West because of the perception there that Ottawa favours and pays attention only to central Canada, I would make the House of Commons a mobile institution. By this I mean that I would put forward legislation permitting the House to sit, for given periods in the year, in the capital cities of the ten provinces, on a rotating basis. There would be two such sessions each year outside Ottawa, each not to exceed six weeks. Today's communications and transportation technologies are suitable and adaptable to the House sitting anywhere in Canada. The members of the government would readily be able to keep in direct touch with their main staff in Ottawa.

The benefits would be twofold. First, those members of the House of Commons who had never been in the province or place where the House was sitting would perforce have a far better understanding of the problems of that region. Secondly, the people of that province and region would be able to have direct access to the various committees of the House, and indeed to its membership—however limited that access might be.

A new defence policy would be another priority, and I would see to the restructuring of one of the core elements in our society, namely the military. It is absolutely essential that there be new policies and objectives for the Canadian Armed Forces. The following statement is the basis of a defence white paper that would be created if I were prime minister.

A 1990s White Paper on Defence

This proposal is based upon:

1. the need to provide clear direction and motivation for the CAF;
2. the requirement to delete commitments and tasking that are beyond the capability of the CAF;
3. the opportunity to provide a new dramatic role for the CAF as a "rescue and disaster aid" force that can provide aid and relief in natural disaster events anywhere in the world *without* any increase in O & M;
4. the need to cap and, if practical, to reduce the CAF budget—or divert savings to urgently needed capital equipment; and
5. the desirability of increasing the size and effectiveness of the Primary Reserve.

THE WHITE PAPER PROPOSALS

Roles of the Canadian Forces

The primary role of the Canadian forces is the defence of Canada. Secondary roles are:

1. to provide reserve land and air forces to NATO in Europe and Norway in the event of hostilities;
2. to participate with the United States in continental air defence through NORAD, the North American Aerospace Defence organization.

It is also a primary role of the Canadian forces to provide, on the direction of the government, emergency relief aid to those countries that suffer national disasters. The Canadian forces will no longer attempt to carry out military or naval tasks that are a mere duplication of U.S. tasks. Instead, they will concentrate on those defence tasks that are dictated by the geographical position of Canada in relation to all potential threats to its sovereignty and having regard for the nation's vast land mass, its many thousands of kilometres of coastline, and its extensive ice-covered Arctic waters.

Implementation

To complement the above statement of roles, the following steps, among others, are to be initiated:

1. The army units (4 Canadian Mobile Brigade Group), three fighter squadrons, and all other units located in West Germany will be redesigned as NATO units held in reserve and will be relocated at bases in Canada but will become fully air mobile so that they can be returned immediately to Europe or dispatched to Norway in the event of hostilities. The role of the designated army units will be renegotiated with NATO, and the resulting re-equipment that will permit air mobility will follow.

246

2. The fighting units of the Canadian army (Mobile Command) will become air mobile in all aspects, in order that they can be transported quickly to any region of Canada, with emphasis on the Arctic sector; or transported to Europe or such other place in the world as the government might direct.

3. In addition, designated units of the air-mobile army will be trained to undertake emergency relief and rescue aid in any country where a natural disaster has occurred (e.g., Mexico City earthquake) and will bear no arms when carrying out such tasks but instead will be equipped with portable hospitals, bulldozers, emergency food supplies, and all the necessary gear required to carry out the relief and rescue task.

4. The Canadian air force (Air Command) will acquire such additional heavy transport aircraft (used Hercules on the world market) to conform to the tasking of the air-mobile army.

   All of its current fighter aircraft except the CF-18s will continue to be retired from service as delivery of the CF-18s progresses. Of the CF-18s to be ultimately delivered, one-third will not be operated but will be held in ready reserve.

   The air force will establish and conduct sovereignty operations in the Canadian Arctic. It will provide tactical air support to the air-mobile army with transport and fighter aircraft as required.

5. The Canadian navy will relinquish the Atlantic submarine warfare (ASW) role to the United States and NATO navies. The navy will be equipped with at least four Class-8 icebreakers fitted with state-of-the-art missiles and electronics gear and weaponry to perform sovereignty tasks, as well as ASW and other defensive roles, in Canada's Arctic waters and in the nation's other coastal reaches.

   The frigate program will be abandoned and will be replaced by four hunter killer submarines for under-ice Arctic sovereignty and defence tasks. Four destroyers will be retained until the submarines are commissioned but then will be phased out. All other destroyers will be decommissioned forthwith.

   A six-minesweeper building program will be initiated.

Personnel

In order to carry out the above roles and tasks, there will be a realignment in the numbers of regular force and reserve personnel. In the next twenty-four months the regular force will be reduced from 83,000 to 50,000 and the reserves will be increased from 20,000 to 50,000.

The reserves will be constituted in a new organization called Reserve Command, which will be provided with a budget separate and apart from that of the regular force. Reserve members will be provided with incentive pay and pensions, as are their U.S. counterparts.

The reserves will be equipped with the same equipment as their regular force counterparts whom they will augment as units (as opposed to individuals) in the event of an emergency or hostilities. Reserve units in regions of the nation where unemployment is high will receive priority in all aspects.

Finally, there is one major area that cries out for a change for the better. It is in our overall relationship with the United States. By "overall" I mean not only trade but the recognition and respect that is due to Canada but is rarely if ever paid by a congress and a people who regard this nation as a mere colonial appendage to the American way of life.

If I were prime minister, I would make a major effort to educate the people of the United States and their governments about Canada and its people. The medium would be television. The method would be persuasion and saturation, combined with a tough, independent stance at any bargaining table where it is necessary to sit down to do business with our American "friends."

If I were prime minister. . . .

Thomas K. Shoyama

A host of complex, difficult issues continues to crowd the public policy agenda in Canada today. They range from matters of substantial economic policy, through problems of political and institutional organization and process, to emotionally charged questions of intense, personal concern. But if I were prime minister, I would try to focus upon urgent economic and social problems, giving the highest priority to four interrelated areas. Briefly put, this would encompass a much more vigorous effort to increase job growth, a continued all-out push on the "two-track" trade liberalization front, a balanced but no-sacred-cows drive towards comprehensive tax reform, and integrated with this last, a radical overhaul of the national income security system.

The first priority would go to the achievement of faster employment growth. Since the downward plunge of the economy in 1981-82, the number of jobless people in Canada has never fallen below a million people. Today we seem stuck with an unemployment rate of more than 9 per cent, and despite five years of apparent recovery, every forecast—official and otherwise—sees an indefinite continuation of this sorry situation. Yet our society in general, and governments in particular, seem ready to live with this waste. We seem to accept it with indifference at worst and at best as inevitable, in a manner sadly reminiscent of the catastrophe of the 1930s.

There is, of course, a rhetoric about the importance of more jobs and an emphatic self-congratulation over the fact that the rate of employment increase in Canada over the past few years has been among the highest of all OECD countries. Accepting this as a measure of good performance and good intentions, nevertheless a real problem remains. As an immediate modest target, we need to bring down the rate of unemployment by at least two or three percentage points. That means an increment of growth that would put about 300,000 more Canadians back to work, over and above the normal annual increase.

How to bring this about? It will need a co-ordinated wide-ranging strategy—and one that may carry serious risks. It will need both deliberate government leadership and the participation and support of the 90 per cent of Canadians already at work in gainful employment. But in a country like Canada, with its resources of nature, people, and capital, its high average levels of income, and its political and constitutional strengths, there is no excuse for perpetuating the tragic misery and huge economic losses involved in an unemployment rate of 9-10 per cent in general and 14-15 per cent among 2.5 million young people.

Fortunately, in some respects at least, the situation is favourable for an all-out effort to alleviate the problem. The rate of inflation has been and remains under reasonable control. Interest rates at home and abroad have come down to their lowest level in fourteen years. The exchange rate is strong—perhaps unduly so for optimum international competitiveness. The real fiscal deficit at the federal level has been reduced to the point where recent tax increases may be imposing a fiscal drag on the economy. Federal demands on the country's savings and upon an inflow of foreign funds are currently at relatively modest levels. At the same time, the rate of personal and corporate savings remains high, and international confidence in Canada appears to be inducing a strong inflow of both portfolio and direct investment takeovers.

Most fundamentally, across the country wage and salary earners alike appear to have reconciled themselves to some reduction in real income under the stress of adverse external conditions and the underlying structural shifts which have been accelerating in recent years. There is a more general recognition and acceptance of the adjustments in technology, work practice, and industrial organization that seem to be necessary to maintain and improve productivity, international competitiveness, and employment growth. However, new investment, both private and public, continues to lag, and something is urgently needed to push the economy up to a higher level of equilibrium and fuller employment of our productive resources.

Broadly speaking, a significant increase in domestic demand now seems to be warranted. An important, initiating part of this can and is only likely to come about from a carefully allocated increase—not a decrease—in public expenditure. Some of this needs to be directed to the improvement of the health, education, welfare, and environmental services which appropriately and inevitably form a larger part of the consumption budgets of an affluent society. For the same reason there is a case for increased allocations to the arts, cultural activities, and recreation. Increased attention should obviously go to publicly supported research, technology, and resource development, which, if not quickly profitable, promises longer-run economic gain. There is a special need for old-fashioned, non-recurring capital investment in public infrastructure at all three levels of government. The job and income increases thus generated—and particularly for the younger and better-trained part of our unemployed—will stimulate and multiply demand throughout the private sector.

All of this requires both fiscal and monetary expansion, and involves the serious risk that the increased demand would tend to flow into higher incomes for those already employed, rather than generating stronger employment growth. This would be particularly true if it combined with a reversal in the exchange rate to add upward pressure on prices. But if higher inflation, together with improved job security, threatened a new price-wage spiral, there would need to be a rapid and vigorous incomes policy response. Hopefully, this might be negotiated on a voluntary consensus basis. But if not, there would be a strong case for a period of temporary controls. Here the 1975-78 experience has indicated that such a policy can be both effective and acceptable if it is shown to be a vital part of an overall strategy to provide needed new jobs.

A concurrent, bold move toward freer trade can and should be an interrelated part of economic policy. Fortunately, this is already a priority item on the government's agenda.

Here, as has often been argued, the first emphasis should be on full and vigorous support for the multilateral negotiations, opening Canada's market to all comers in return for increased access to Canadian exports worldwide. The inclusion of the agricultural sector in the new round of negotiations is an important two-way street, with appreciable net national benefits being the prize at stake. Similarly, the emphasis on broader and more effective codes for the levelling of the non-tariff barriers adds greatly to the complexity of the negotiations, but it also adds to the potential for freeing up the flows of world trade.

However, it has been recognized that the range of issues, the number of players, and the diversity of interests and concerns make the prospect of early and significant agreement problematical. This is one of the main reasons for the vigorous pursuit of a bilateral agreement with the United States. As much as anything, however, the most compelling motive is simply to give the Canadian economy a large and challenging jolt. Over the twenty-five postwar years of almost uninterrupted growth and prosperity in Canada—due as much as anything to good luck, the bounty of nature, and an exceptionally favourable external environment—attitudes and expectations as to secure and rising incomes seemed to become embedded in the national psyche. But the wrenching dislocations since the early 1970s have shown the overwhelming need to stimulate and develop our own internal sources of strength. Much of this, and the potential for it, will come sharply into focus under a comprehensive free-trade arrangement with the United States.

Clearly, such an arrangement will be neither a panacea for our ills nor an unmitigated disaster. However, both the positive and defensive gains have been well documented. On the positive side, lower prices to consumers for a wide range of goods will free up expenditures for domestic expenditure. Lower costs for producer equipment and supplies will help to make the economy more competitive. There will be casualties and major problems of adjustment for regions, industries, and firms on both sides of the border, but experience strongly attests to the fact that trade liberalization can lead to stronger job and income growth. The objective in the negotiations is to reach the kind of detailed agreement that offers the potential for a fair sharing of the net gains in employment and income. That is why almost every industrial sector, not excluding the Auto Pact, has to be on the table and why exceptions have to be kept to the minimum.

On the defensive side it has been stressed that the main need for Canada is to achieve greater order and restraint by the United States in its protectionist use of a wide array of non-tariff barriers. In particular, Canada's concern is to assure greater market access, with appropriate discipline and rules applying to countervail and injury duties on both sides of the border. With the ground rules better defined and set, and the administrative procedures objectively carried out, investment and locational decisions can respond to longer-run economic judgements rather than to political concerns. And there is no reason to believe that Canada would labour under inherent competitive disadvantage under a carefully negotiated regime. Neither would there be any compelling pressure to move towards fuller harmonization or the dovetailing of social, fiscal, labour, or cultural policies across the border. The focus is on the trade relationship and not upon a common market or economic union which might call for more far-reaching forms of integration.

The third high-priority economic policy area is also firmly on the government's agenda. This is the call for comprehensive tax reform. Here the general directions and philosophy have been set out with considerable rhetorical eloquence. Some preliminary steps, such as the tax credit to alleviate the potential burden of a broader federal sales tax, have already been initiated. But the concern is that when push comes to shove, as it certainly will, the government's commitment to fairness, effectiveness, and common sense may be rapidly eroded.

The case for a broadly based consumption sales tax is impressive, notwithstanding its tendency for regressive impacts (i.e., its tendency to bear most heavily upon the lowest income groups). But the welfare state, conferring vital public services in health, education, welfare, and many other areas, warrants at least minimal contributions from all its beneficiaries. The government revenue budget also needs a large, stable core, which will be capable of growth as the consumption of these public services expands. The proposed business transfer tax, which has the side benefit of taxing imports as fully as domestic goods, seems to fill the bill. At a minimum, it will be needed to replenish the revenue loss from the decline in customs duties resulting from a freer U.S. trade deal.

As for the corporation income tax, the finance minister has emphasized the need for a more neutral system, freed of as many of the special preferences and complexities as possible and closely integrated with the personal income tax. This has nearly always been the goal of tax reformers but has rarely been achieved. It is an inherently complicated field at best, and a case can always be made in a market economy for the preservation of corporate savings and for inducements for reinvestment. Perhaps the best safeguard is one of process—a reliance upon objective analysis and expert judgement as to the balance of objectives, with minimal deference to the abundance of influential special pleaders.

Similarly, on the personal side, much is being made of the need for greater simplicity as well as for lower marginal rates. A great deal of this is overblown, although the strongest case can be made for the elimination of several special shelters. An obvious particular here would be the courageous reversal of the capital gains exemption. Another would be the inclusion in taxable income of the very large expansion of lottery winnings. A further move required is to revisit the field of death duties or of wealth taxes, now singularly ignored by both levels of government.

Significant change in personal income taxes brings forward once again the related issue of the income security system. Here the rationale, broad directions, and illustrative program designs were all documented in the reports and research studies of the Macdonald Commission.

The essence of the proposal for a form of guaranteed annual income—labelled as a universal income security program by the Macdonald Commission—involves the consolidation of a group of categorical aid programs, together with a set of personal income tax exemptions and credits, to provide a broader system of support and supplementation specifically targeted to the poorest and lower-income individuals and families. This would be at the expense of the upper-middle-income and richer groups, all within the limits of public spending already established. This further redistribution of income would provide significant benefits to the poor, but only at such minimal levels as not to erode incentives for employment income and personal responsibility. The existing system of old-age security pensions would remain intact, because of the role it has long played in retirement income planning. The overall structure could and would desirably be integrated with a reformed personal income tax system. An important role would remain for the provinces, again within the limits of their present commitments, to provide additional support and social services for those unable to work.

The proposals also include, but also facilitate, major changes in the unemployment insurance system. In this they are paralleled or supported in important respects by the inquiries and report of the Newfoundland and Forget commissions. Specifically, however, savings from a rationalization of unemployment insurance would be used to finance a special program of adjustment and mobility assistance. This would be a vital part of the domestic arrangements put in place to ease transitional dislocations flowing from a freer-trade agreement with the United States.

There is little, if anything, new or strange in the above four-part strategy for economic and social policy in Canada today and now. Indeed, most of the ideas, objectives, and program detail have been actively explored and documented throughout the past decade, and even much earlier. This is both a burden and a major advantage. But if the thinking itself is all quite familiar, the actual changes envisaged are radical and far-reaching. They upset as much conventional and accepted doctrine as they do jealously guarded positions and privilege. The obstacles and resistance to be overcome on all sides, whether technical, administrative or, most of all, political, are more than daunting to even the most foolhardy prime minister. That is why these proposals belong to this volume.

NICK SIBBESTON

As we approach the end of the twentieth century, Canada is faced with many complex and difficult problems. If I were prime minister, I would focus my agenda on dealing with three main topics: the renewal of the economy through regional development, the extension of social justice to all Canadians, and the redefinition of Canada's role in international affairs.

It is somewhat of a cliché to say that Canada is not a single economy but a series of regional ones, linked together not by common interest but by east-west transportation links. Attempts to build an integrated economy have in the past resulted in policies that benefited the industrial core of Quebec and Ontario at the expense of smaller regional economies. The de-industrialization of Atlantic Canada, despite millions of dollars in federal incentives, and the failure to develop industrial bases in the West to take advantage of resource wealth are symptomatic of the centralist thrust of economic development in Canada. These problems are complicated by the natural north-south links between various regional economies and U.S. markets. When combined with the very real barriers to interprovincial trade, this has further fragmented the national economy and created an outward-looking development mentality.

For economic renewal to occur, the focus must shift away from the centre and towards the regions, with policies that will nurture integrated self-sustaining regional economies, whose boundaries are set by natural geography and not by provincial borders. This would require a degree of provincial co-operation that does not at present exist. As prime minister, I would not only use federal policy to support this co-operation, but I would also act as a mediator for the resolution of provincial and regional differences.

At the same time, it would be important to build linkages, both infrastructural and non-infrastructural, between the various regional economies. While these links should be established on the basis of relative advantage, they must establish a relationship between equals rather than the dependent relationship that currently exists. Barriers to interprovincial trade must be reduced, and a rationalization of the economy that would see the centralization of some industries and the decentralization of others must be allowed to occur. This could only be accomplished, of course, through a comprehensive national industrial strategy. The creation of such a strategy involving all sectors of Canadian society would be of primary importance.

Of particular importance and interest to me as a northerner is the need to realign the economic vision in Canada. It would be healthy if the Canadian economy looked less to the south across our border for economic opportunity and more to the north, where the potential for economic growth lies untapped.

The Canadian North is a vast storehouse of wealth and resources. The development of these resources over the next twenty years could and should be a primary engine of growth for the entire Canadian economy. As prime minister, I would bring to Ottawa a new northern vision that would focus our energies on unlocking these resources for the benefit of all Canadians.

In order to accomplish this goal, there would have to be a significant investment on the part of Canada to build the necessary links between north and south. This investment, however, would be well worth it. The creation of a northern economic strategy would result in benefits flowing to many different parts of Canada along these transportation and communication links. Unlike other economic developments, the creation of a northern economy would not be confounded by the natural north-south links that interfere with efforts to build a national economy along east-west lines. Rather, geography would aid the process, and many jobs and opportunities would be created in southern Canada as a result of northern development.

The opening of the North would have both short- and long-term benefits. The construction of necessary infrastructure would in itself create many jobs and would significantly reduce unemployment rates in the country. Projects subsequently established in the North would create wealth and jobs through the exploitation of the resource wealth. A secondary benefit would be the creation of an exotic tourist attraction that would not only bring visitors from around the world but would also keep Canadian tourist expenditures in Canada.

I have already indicated the importance of expanding trade within Canada. At the same time, it must be recognized that internationally Canada is a trading country. It is in Canada's interest to reduce unreasonable barriers to trade, but freer trade must be sought as a means to an end and not as an end in itself. Economic benefits from enhanced trade must not be achieved at the cost of Canadian social and cultural values. As well, the focus of enhanced trade should be worldwide and not simply on what is already Canada's dominant trading partner. Significant benefits would accrue to regional economies through improved trade relations with Pacific Rim and European countries.

256

In sum, my economic policy as prime minister would centre on the creation of strong regional economies linked through improved inter-regional trade. A major thrust for economic growth would be the opening of the North to development, with benefits from that development being shared by northern residents and Canadians in all other regions.

One of the fundamental ideals that has characterized the development of Canadian society over the last fifty years is the belief in social justice that has permeated much of our economic and social policy. As Canadians, we have tried to build a country that balances individual freedom and collective responsibility. This balance between individual and group rights is enshrined in the constitution and, as well, is reflected by the conscious efforts of governments and citizens to bring all segments of the Canadian mosaic into society as equal but clearly unique and distinct partners. Bilingualism, multiculturalism, and the recognition of aboriginal rights are all key components of the Canadian pluralism. In a different and more pragmatic way, the creation of an elaborate social safety net can be seen as another manifestation of the partnership between individual and society that exists within Canada.

The purpose of a strong economy is surely to secure for all citizens the support they need to live full and rewarding lives. I would use economic renewal to strengthen our social security system and to bring about a real redistribution of wealth that would end poverty once and for all. At the same time, I would seek alternatives to the welfare system that would restore to people their dignity and productivity and would encourage all Canadians to contribute to the good of the country. The establishment of a new frontier in the North would be an important psychological boost in creating this new attitude in Canada.

The job of creating an egalitarian society has not yet been completed. Two major goals have yet to be achieved. The first is to eliminate discrimination between men and women within society. The second, which is particularly important to me as a native person, is to bring aboriginal people fully into Confederation through the recognition of aboriginal self-government and the settlement of land claims.

Women must be permitted to participate fully in the Canadian economy, and their efforts must be recognized through measures such as pay equity. At the same time, the federal government must provide support to the family unit so that the increased involvement of women at all levels of society does not result in undue stress on family structure. The contribution to the general good of women who choose to stay at home with their children must be recognized through the tax and pension system if true equality is to be achieved.

The establishment of aboriginal self-government and the settlement of land claims in a fair and expeditious manner would finally end the system of dependency that has burdened Canada's native people since the founding of this country. Moreover, it would bring aboriginal people fully into Canadian society as equal partners in Confederation, capable of governing their own lives and standing on their own feet. In particular, the settlement of land claims would give them the economic power they must have to restore their dignity, preserve their cultures and languages, and participate fully in Canada.

In the North particularly, aboriginal people must be able to benefit from and be involved in economic development. The opening of the North will radically change the lives of the people who live there. They must be able to exercise some control over that development, and they must reap the rewards that are created.

The extension of social justice must include, therefore, a strengthening of the social safety net so that economic security can be seen as an intrinsic right of all Canadians. It must also include the recognition of the individual and collective equality of women and aboriginal people within the context of Canadian Confederation. If I were prime minister, I would use all the influence and authority at my command to bring about this vital realignment of Canada's constitutional structure.

Although economic renewal and constitutional reform would top my agenda, also important would be the reaffirmation and to some extent redefinition of Canada's role in world affairs. Canada can be justly proud of its record in the international arena. Positions taken by previous governments with respect to human rights and assistance to the developing world have placed Canada in a positive light in world opinion. As prime minister, I would continue in this tradition.

The development of the Third World is clearly in Canada's interest. Political stability in developing countries, and hence in the world economy, can only be achieved when the problems of poverty and inequity have been overcome. Canada can play a larger role in reaching these goals through an expanded foreign aid program and by developing innovative approaches to assistance which would place control over development fully in the hands of the recipients. Money, of course, is not the only answer. Economic development must go hand in hand with political development. Canada must continue, indeed expand, her role as a defender of human rights and freedoms throughout the world. I would reinforce Canada's role in the United Nations, the Commonwealth, and other diplomatic channels to achieve this second goal in international affairs. Having put our own house in order with respect to aboriginal people, I would be able to make a strong moral case for the just treatment of oppressed people around the world.

Canada has always played an important role in the field of peace-keeping. Like many northerners, I am concerned about our present policy with respect to international military alliances and, particularly, the nuclear arms race. In 1986, the Legislative Assembly of the Northwest Territories declared the North to be a nuclear-weapons-free zone. This symbolic gesture indicated the abhorrence felt by most northerners for the proliferation of nuclear weapons. If I were prime minister, I would end the use of Canadian territory for the testing of cruise missiles and other hardware whose sole purpose is the delivery of nuclear weapons. I would also develop an independent defence policy that would allow Canada both to protect its own sovereignty and to serve as an intermediary between the superpowers in their disputes and discussions.

I believe that I would bring a unique northern vision to the office of prime minister. In the North, we have had to find innovative solutions to the many problems facing us. Our society north of the 60th parallel is composed of many minorities living and working together, in relative harmony, to build a better world. The model of multicultural co-operation could be applied to the greater society of Canada—and, indeed, to the world. For, after all, the world itself is naught but a community of minorities, a community that must learn to work together peacefully and justly.

STUART L. SMITH

There is a limit, of course, to what a prime minister can really change. In a democracy, it's a safe bet that what will happen tomorrow under a new prime minister will not be greatly different from what happened yesterday under the old one. We frequently call for leadership; but except in crises, it seems what we really want is someone to carry on the status quo in a reassuring and competent manner.

Still, a prime minister can leave a mark, provided he or she is strongly motivated and is prepared to push hard in one particular area, leaving virtually everything else to colleagues. Even then, institutional, economic, and political considerations set boundaries on the degree of reform that is possible.

Limiting myself therefore to one area, what would I try to accomplish? To put it in one sentence, I want to marshal the intellectual resources of Canada in the strategic modernization of our economy.

After decades of procrastination, we must face the change from dependence on our raw materials to a reliance on our brains—an inevitable shift from natural resources to human resources. Only the strategic repositioning of each industrial sector, based on the most advanced knowledge, can assure prosperity for Canada, prosperity essential to our continued existence as an independent nation.

If support for such industrial changes is to be found, Canadians will first have to be convinced of the underlying thesis. I don't know if there is such a thing as a reassuring alarmist, but the prime minister would have to be such a creature. The future has no vote—citizens want governments to prop up operations that exist now, however uncompetitive they may be. Since the new realities of world economic patterns are not yet understood by our people, much of the prime minister's job would be to educate Canadians on the subject. We need a change in the very culture of the country. Canada must not only throw off its colonial mentality with its associated inferiority complexes, but it must become a learning society, one that prizes knowledge for its own sake as well as using it competitively. Canada must also take steps to reduce its near total dependence on United States customers and must become, little by little, a Pacific nation, concentrating greater efforts in regions where enormous future growth can be expected.

The reason such drastic change must be made is that we face a serious threat in the medium-to-longer term. After all, even with the "benefit" of a 72-cent dollar, our financial position remains marginally respectable only because of two classes of exports: our resources, and automobiles and auto parts (under the Auto Pact with its production guarantees). These items make up for a very serious weakness in manufacturing, especially in the higher value-added, sophisticated end of the spectrum. In fact, with only a few exceptions, the more advanced the manufacturing, the worse our weakness! Autos and resources are the real export base at the moment.

Yet in the face of foreign competition, the future of the North American auto industry is not at all clear, nor can we rely forever on the sanctity of a political document such as the Auto Pact. As to resources, there will still be ups and downs, though things do look rather gloomy over the longer term.

The main thing to understand is that new technology lets you get more function out of less resource product, less raw material. We see this every day with downsizing, conservation, durability, recycling, greater fuel efficiency, and so on. Even beyond this, new technology permits new synthetic materials to be substituted for our traditional resource materials. Many new and advanced substances are being made, offering characteristics that our present natural products just can't match. Composites, ceramics, plastics, and even more exotic combinations replace metals and wood. Yet in general our metal and wood suppliers are not engaged in massive research programs into new materials and products; for some of them, when times are tough, research is the first thing they cut.

If all this were not enough, we Canadians now have to face new and severe competition from other countries with similar resources. Some of these countries need foreign currency so badly that they seem willing to keep producing even at very low prices. We in Canada are still competitive and we are trimming our own costs, sometimes very ingeniously; but the downward pressure on prices keeps us at a survival level, not at the level of prosperity we're used to. Finally, we also have to take account of some longer-term supply problems caused by such things as poor forest management, soil erosion, or overfishing.

All in all, it should be painfully clear that with the arrival of a new, technology-driven world economy, we cannot maintain our standard of living by relying on our present traditional mainstays. Nor can we turn to routine manufacturing to save us. For various reasons, we didn't open the country earlier in this century to an additional 30 million immigrants, and during the heyday of manufacturing we therefore never had the market to be a manufacturing power. Then, when we could have used our tariff wall as a temporary shelter allowing infant Canadian firms to grow to become exporters, we were satisfied instead to let it be a means of attracting branch plants, despite the problems of foreign control that came with them. One can only assume that in view of our natural resources, Canadian leaders never thought we would need manufacturing for export purposes; branch plants, with the jobs they brought, were good enough. Now it's too late. Even if we wanted to build Canadian plants to do standardized manufacturing, such an option is essentially closed to high-wage countries like ours.

This option is closed because newly industrialized countries have broken what was a kind of Atlantic monopoly. With rapidly improving education and management ability, people in Korea, Taiwan, and a dozen other places can employ low-paid workers and use new technology to produce standardized products far more cheaply than we can. Except for the few factories that use no labour but only robots, advanced countries will gradually lose the production of standardized products.

Canadians must understand that there is one way we can still prosper, and that is by offering new, advanced products and services that are deeply dependent on up-to-date knowledge, research, and technology.

Canada spends a fortune on education and we certainly have excellent science. Despite this, we are still not ready to compete in a number of these advanced areas. This is because it is hard to make the jump from being suppliers of crude bulk commodities, sold by the tonne, to being international marketers of ultra-sophisticated goods and services. As a resource-dependent economy, we have developed certain habits appropriate to these circumstances; they are not the ones we need for getting into the new higher-technology industries. Such habits become part of the very fabric, even the culture, of the country; they are very difficult to break. We can take pride in our society as a civil and decent one wherein we have learned—better than many other places—how to divide our wealth with reasonable fairness; but we have never had to learn how to work together to create new wealth in complex enterprises.

As bulk-commodity producers, we have the habit of using only a limited amount of research. The number of researchers in Canadian industry is very low in comparison with other advanced countries. Selling large orders to big buyers such as governments, we have not had to learn much about international marketing to individual customers in distant lands. With so many of our foreign-owned companies being branch plants of the kind that have no mandate to export and that rarely develop or design new products here, we are not very experienced in design or product development. Since higher-technology goods are somewhat new to us, we don't always know how to finance them; our financiers are among the world's best in dealing with tangible assets such as real estate, mines, or even corporate takeovers, but dealing with things like intellectual property is still new ground for them. Until recently, our universities were not usually asked to work closely with our industries, the way they do in the United States, so these university-industry linkages are still comparatively underdeveloped. We need more entrepreneurs, both inside and outside our business schools; we need more people with seed money and venture capital to back them. As it happens, a large proportion of the (inadequate) venture capital we do collect actually goes for investment to the United States! All in all, the changes needed in business, in education, in government, and among citizens generally are wide-reaching and represent almost a cultural transformation, with many casualties. But failure to change will bring even more drastic consequences.

The United States has its own problems, but if there is renewed U.S. industrial success, it will be based on new goods and services that do not need our resource products in the quantities that were required by their old, smokestack industries. They won't be so dependent upon our resources; even a 72-cent dollar will seem overvalued. Either we make the new investments and the changes of habit that we need to compete in new industries and new markets, or we shall find ourselves desperately trying to catch the coattails of our huge and more dynamic neighbour, even as we have less leverage with which to bargain. The implications for our sovereignty are obvious and are already beginning to surface. A serious decline in our living standards or in our ability to provide good jobs for our people leads first to a demand for access to U.S. markets, on any terms; the next step is access to U.S. jobs, on any terms. This is the underlying threat Canada faces.

We must find a way to bring about change in our country. But we shouldn't depend so much on our commodity producers; they cannot move easily into new industries, products, and markets, given their heavy investment in current enterprises. They want to stick to the business they know, trying to survive by cutting costs and improving production methods. As to our manufacturers, many are just branch plants and many others are in endangered, labour-intensive sectors like clothing and footwear. We have to count on our advanced manufacturing and service industries. But to develop these—like it or not—we Canadians have no choice but to use government in some way. Unfortunately, governments prefer to rescue the past rather than to build the future. Even more unfortunately, governments by their very nature lack the proper incentive structures to operate efficiently in the world of business. Therefore government can be a catalyst, a partner, a purchaser, and a supporter—but it should not, in my view, be an owner or a competitor in these advanced sectors.

My plan would be as follows. First, I would inform Canadians about what our challenge really is. I would then call together all sectors of industry, one by one, in relatively small groups and with knowledgeable experts. Each sector would be helped to examine its foreign competition, its potential foreign markets, and the direction in which new technology would be likely to take its products and methods in the next ten years. Specifically, each sector would be helped to define its challenges in knowledge, research, and technology, and a renewal plan would be drawn up. Foreign-owned companies would participate, provided they had appropriate export mandates. In each case, the plan would involve both individual and co-operative research, as well as technology development or acquisition; it would be funded, to a varying extent, by government, but it would be accomplished either in industry or under the direct control of industry. If industry groupings or sectoral organizations were lacking, they would be set up for these consultative, strategic purposes. I would emphasize particularly the role of government as a potential first purchaser of new research-intensive products and services.

These discussions would certainly reveal gaps in our industrial structure where we lacked companies to compete in important areas of potential economic growth. To fill these gaps, the government would be prepared to invest with private partners, preferably Canadian, to create potential world-class enterprises. The government position would be that of a minority shareholder, in addition to giving the purchasing guarantees and development support I have already described.

Some will think we need more government ownership and control; I would simply point to the poor record of such ventures and declare my preference for privatization wherever possible. Others will think that I rely too much on government; I would ask them to examine the United States, whose high-technology industries and venture-capital system thrive to a large extent because of government contracts, especially those for research and production in defence and space programs.

I would create an economy in which industry starts to make a much greater demand for research and technology and for trained people. Priority would then arise for the retraining and the continuing education of workers, including long-overdue "paid educational leave," as well as for closer liaison with university and government laboratories, and better access to international sources of technology. It is such demand by industry that would lead directly to stronger linkages with educational and scientific enterprises, both at home and abroad, linkages that would at last enable us to get commercial value out of our excellent intellectual base. A direct result would be greater public appreciation for research and learning in all their forms.

Please make no mistake about what I am recommending. I am speaking of many billions of dollars of both government and private investment in the strategic, technology-driven, consultatively planned renewal of this country's industries, sector by sector. Depending on how they are defined, there may be 150 to 200 such sectors! The task is difficult, maybe even impossible; but if we do not try, we shall lose by default.

World economic changes could mean that many Canadian communities will find it increasingly difficult to survive as their resource base becomes less valuable. Canadians in these locales must be helped to make the adjustments necessary to find other sources of income and, where necessary, to find other locations. We must ease the pain, but we should not try to hold back the inevitable, especially if in so doing we use up the dollars needed for the successful diversification of the economy.

Largely because of our rich natural resources, we have enjoyed prosperity and have been able to afford the sovereignty to do things our own way in our half of this continent. As a result, our country is still the best place on earth in which to live. We have a civilized society with a low crime rate. We have a diversity of language and cultural traditions. We have humane social programs that mitigate against the alienation and frustrations of modern civilization. Our politics are not seriously affected by fundamentalists and by gun worshippers. Our nationalism is modest and friendly. Our people are respected everywhere. And our natural environment is not only bountiful; it is still breath-takingly beautiful.

Failure in our economy would bring with it a demand for jobs and benefits in the stronger economy to the south (just as Newfoundlanders needed the opportunities Canada afforded). Unthinkable as it is now, union with the United States might then be seen as the only hope for hundreds of thousands of unemployed or underemployed Canadians.

All Canadians will favour preserving our national identity as long as it allows us to create and develop our own special, caring society. Our natural resources have taken us a long way. What we need now is the leadership to mobilize our considerable human resources to meet tomorrow's challenges.

STUART A. THIESSON

Really not knowing just how much power a prime minister wields within a parliamentary democracy, I nonetheless have some priorities.

Commitment Towards World Peace

Canada has an important role to fulfil in assuring that peace in the world is maintained, but we are caught between a rock and a hard place. It is not a happy thought to realize the possibility of each superpower developing nuclear defence systems designed to detonate one another's ICBMs over Canadian territory.

Canada must be a nuclear-free zone, and as prime minister I would make it so. If U.S. aircraft fly through our airspace armed with nuclear weapons, we can only be looked on by the USSR as hostile territory. We have already compromised our global influence as an honest broker for peace by permitting the testing of cruise missiles in our North and by rubber-stamping SDI (Star Wars). The youth of our nation must be appalled as they bear an increasing burden of apprehension about their hopes for a secure future.

Social Issues

No person in this nation should suffer the indignity of hunger and the lack of adequate clothing, shelter, and health care. There are thousands who live in ghettos. Often they have insufficient means for nutritional diets. Millions live below the recognized poverty line. Children become the prime victims. We are perpetuating a culture of poverty that encourages a growing number of social problems and crimes. Increasingly, the "better off" in society are developing a siege mentality. As prime minister, I would financially support urban governments and voluntary social agencies to provide proper hostel accommodation and other needed amenities for the homeless and indigent. Anyone living on the street would be doing so by preference.

The mushrooming of food banks in our urban areas is a reflection of a deteriorating social system. The demand placed on this service has begun to assume permanent characteristics far beyond the original intentions of the voluntary agencies that conceived the notion. If food banks are to emerge as a necessary institution in our social fabric, some restructuring will be needed. The catch-as-catch-can reliance of the operating agencies on the charity of ordinary citizens and on food wholesalers and supermarkets represents an insecure method of providing adequate food to the needy. It would be preferable, through federal-provincial co-operation, to guarantee the provision of basic domestically produced food—such as canned meat, fish, fruits, vegetables, milk, milk powder, cheese, eggs, flour, butter, margarine, potatoes, apples, and cereals—for distribution through the food banks in exchange for food stamps issued through the welfare system. These would in part supplement welfare payments and they would be a better way of ensuring that nutritional food was made available to low-income persons, and particularly to their children.

A glaring discrepancy in our value system is the outrageously high prices for food demanded of northern residents. It makes no sense that government-controlled liquor can be sold in the North for the same price as in southern cities while food is many times higher in cost. As prime minister, I would subsidize food transportation to settlements in the territories and to isolated northern areas of the provinces.

Transportation

In my view, the two major railway companies in Canada need to be integrated into a single system. Railways should serve as instruments of regional and national development. It is ludicrous to regard them as competitors or to become preoccupied with improving their efficiency and profitability by allowing reduction of service and increased hauling rates at the expense of rendering other sectors of the economy less profitable and efficient. The profits of railway companies are often not reinvested within the domestic railroad system. At the same time, they receive massive public subsidies. They are exercising far too much power in determining the future configuration of our rural communities.

Increasingly, railway companies have abandoned communities across the country and have reduced and restricted their operations to long-distance bulk movement of basic commodities such as coal, potash, and grain, and to container and piggy-back services. Rising transportation costs have been transferred to the public through massive costs associated with highway construction to meet the needs of the trucking industry. Meanwhile, the railway companies' self-serving television commercials tell us how great they are, while at every opportunity they replace workers with more technology and compromise safety standards. Deregulation is not the answer! My administration would undertake fundamental reform of the railways.

Industrial Strategy

Exactly where are we heading in the relentless pursuit of technology to displace people from gainful employment? The private governments of the corporate sector are managing our resources for greater profitability and for economic concentration and control. Public governments are handed the bills for environmental and pollution problems and for social program costs associated with unemployment and retraining. Additionally, there is the strategy of already profitable corporations demanding public grants, tax breaks, interest-free loans, and other amenities to locate in certain areas of the country. This approaches blackmail as a determinant of our nation's industrial strategy and regional development objectives! Moreover, it does not make much sense to collect taxes from wage earners and the middle-income classes for recycling to an already well-heeled corporate sector. My government would play a far stronger role in determining industrial strategy.

Resources are the most important source of any nation's wealth. Simply permitting their exploitation in exchange for job creation is not sufficiently rewarding to the long-term interest of the nation. While management of resources is a provincial jurisdiction, we have, for example, witnessed an increasing number of concessions to oil companies that substantially reduce income potential for the public sector. As prime minister, my objective would be to strengthen public ownership and the development of resources.

Credit Policy

The role of credit in development objectives cannot be overlooked. The nationalization of our banking system may be the only way in which priorities in the use of credit can be properly directed. The opulent buildings erected by our chartered banks throughout our major cities in the past twenty years far surpass the economy's needs for banking services. And they provide testimony to the expenditure of wealth that has been misdirected in terms of national needs and priorities. Do they really expect us to believe they compete?

If I were prime minister, I would revamp the credit system, offering low interest rates on development loans for basic wealth-creating resource industries such as farming, fishing, and lumbering; another tier of rates would be established for long-term home mortgages, while there would be high interest rates on the purchase of luxury consumer items. Rates for savings of individual depositors would reflect a weighted average of loan rates.

Some may regard these proposals as naive, but the current power of the banks over the destiny of thousands of farm families and small businesses is nothing less than obscene.

Agriculture

Agriculture is one of the nation's most important renewable resource industries. Food production is still one industry that is Canadian-owned. The annual value of farm production is about $20 billion, half of which is exported. It generates employment directly and indirectly for at least 15 per cent of our labour force.

The current policy thrust in Canada is to continue the industrialization of food production. This policy direction is predicated on the continued application of technology and capital to replace labour. It is motivated by the desire to encourage specialization in those commodities in which we are deemed to have a comparative advantage in world markets. Although our export trade in agriculture creates a handsome surplus for our balance of trade, the pressure is to increase it further. Specialization is encouraged to produce more for less. It's a cheap food policy at the farm gate level, and it is causing the farm population to decline and is destroying our rural communities.

Farming in Canada has grown and flourished through the close assimilation of its land and people. This relationship has created a close mutual dependency and a foundation for a rural value system steeped in respect for the land and the demands of nature. Industrialization is destroying this relationship. We are not emphasizing diversification and self-sufficiency. We are experiencing increasing problems in soil erosion and salinization. Farmers are forced, by market pressures of high production costs and declining prices, to sacrifice good farming practices. The national economic impact of the various types of soil degradation now in evidence was estimated to reduce farm Gross Domestic Product by almost 10 per cent in 1984.

Unlike many other industries, agriculture requires policy considerations which strike a closer balance between economic and social needs. The massive substitution of capital to replace labour that has already taken place in farming has failed to create economic security in the farm community. As prime minister, I would reorder the priorities so as to slow down the rate of exodus from rural areas. We need to be concerned about the future shape of our farming communities, about the very real problems that confront young and beginning farmers in the intergenerational transfer of farm land. Because of the recapitalization of land in every generation, many young farmers have been unable to repay their loans when faced with high interest rates and declining prices. Some alternative forms of land tenure and acquisition need to be introduced, otherwise the ownership of productive resources will increasingly become concentrated in fewer hands. We need to provide the opportunities for more farm family units of production—not fewer as has been the trend since the 1940s.

269

I have already referred to farm credit, transportation, and food-supplement policies. There is additional scope for increased self-sufficiency in the production of a number of horticultural crops. In 1985 we had trade deficits of $57 million in cheese, $28 million in mutton and lamb, and $55 million in poultry and eggs. We possess the resources for greater diversification and self-sufficiency. What apparently is lacking is the will.

The present domestic market selling system is a poor determinant of value for farm products. The recurring cycles of "boom and bust" that plague our livestock industry are a case in point; countervailing measures are needed. By contrast, there is considerable stability in dairy and poultry products because of administrative pricing and supply management programs. But the farm marketing programs need to be strengthened. Although stabilization and income insurance programs have been developed at the federal and provincial levels, notably for red meats, federal procrastination has given rise to the balkanization of red meat support programs, with the "have" provinces vying for larger market shares of domestic production at the expense of "have not" provinces.

While stabilization programs will continue to be required, domestic marketing structures must be strengthened with the objective of developing pricing structures that will better reflect the market value for farm products across the nation. As a step in this direction, a national red meats marketing agency needs to be developed in co-operation with the provinces. A further and immediate priority is the structuring of an eastern Canada potato marketing agency to end the stranglehold the industrial and trade sectors now hold on potato producers. Quota values, where they exist for current supply-managed products, should be phased out, since they cannot logically be justified.

The Canadian Wheat Board, as a farmer-financed crown corporation, has served as an excellent export marketing agency for our western wheat, oats, and barley. Through price pooling, it has brought a degree of price stability to grain markets with the minimum of expense to the federal treasury in years of normal world market conditions. The concept of the CWB needs to be extended to include all grains and oilseeds marketed in Canada. All these measures would be implemented if I were prime minister.

Trade

Trade is an important element of the agricultural sector. About 50 per cent of the value of our annual production is exported, most of it grain. We have an efficient farming sector, which is often in competition for world markets against subsidized producers in other countries. Current trading practices of the United States and the European Economic Community are threatening this competitive position. This is another of the problems I would tackle.

Much of the success of our international grain trading can be attributed to the efforts of publicly funded agricultural research through Agriculture Canada's research branch and through our universities. Today, agricultural research is in trouble because of budget cuts, despite the fact that investment in research has resulted in an annual pay-off anywhere from 30 to 200 per cent. I would make support of agricultural research a top priority to enable Canadian producers to retain their competitive position in world markets.

While 50 per cent of our agricultural production finds its way into world markets, the U.S. market receives only about 22 per cent of our agricultural exports, as compared to about 75 per cent of our total national exports. Canadian agriculture has a great deal to lose in any free-trade arrangement that might be negotiated with the United States. While we must and will continue to trade with the United States, the free-trade route holds no promise for the survival of Canadian agriculture or for much of our industry. As prime minister, I would immediately withdraw from such discussions and look towards negotiating mutually beneficial sectoral agreements.

The emphasis of our agricultural trade strategy has been to serve commercial markets. Many developing nations simply do not have the necessary cash or credit, but they may have products or goods they can exchange. The possibilities of developing and facilitating countertrade to expand our agricultural exports should be actively pursued. Trade must be a two-way street—and it would be under my government.

To conclude, it has been a privilege serving as prime minister, if only in fantasy. Much needs to be done, and there are still many glaring priority omissions. So if you should elect me .... And why not? After all, Ronald Reagan is seventy-six!

WILLIAM THORSELL

If I were prime minister, I would live in a big stone house with an attached indoor swimming pool in a rather small and isolated city. Every day would begin with fifty laps in the water and end with something interesting on the stereo and someone wonderful sharing the headphones. In between, there would be a lot of wasted time and posturing, a good deal of drudgery, and some fun. One thing for sure, there'd be no solitary spin through the ravine on my elegant ten-speed bike in the early morning sun. Too many weirdos around; too many things to do.

What's the point of being prime minister without some money to spend? Without money, it's hard to express your personality, your ambition, or your prejudices (portrayed to the public as your "vision"). You just sit there playing damage control, looking weak compared with Ontario's premier, and pronouncing on the evils of American foreign policy, which isn't worth giving up bicycle riding for and will probably lead to defeat in any case. So the first thing I'd do is get some money to spend, which isn't easy when you're running $32 billion a year in the hole.

However, as prime minister with a majority, I would reek of power—far too much to call Canada anything but an authoritarian democracy or a democratic monarchy. So if I can't convince everybody in cabinet and caucus to accept my views, I can still extract their acquiescence. These sundry and motley MPS, fatally infected with ambition, rise and fall at my pleasure—no mean basis to act as a majority of one, politely.

I want more money, but I must also shave the deficit—so I plan to spend *and* save, which suggests the skills of Merlin. (Short course: If I don't control the deficit, higher debt service charges will eat into the money I want to spend, and therefore my reason for being. Big recurrent deficits may also undercut the dollar, fuel inflation, and keep interest rates relatively high—which hurts the poor and unemployed, not one of my policy goals.) I want to spend and save, so I'll have to rejig some big-ticket items.

That does not include my commodious house and swimming pool, which is a small-ticket item in the scale of things, except to me. I like to entertain at home and plan to host vibrant dinners for people who aren't in politics (effect and cause), stage a few drawing-room concerts, and throw some theme parties in the garden when Ottawa isn't awful as well as dull. Every nation needs vicarious experiences to enhance its sense of self. With this prime minister, Canada would get some stylish times at 24 Sussex to round out its popular myths of open space and global moral superiority. (I said "myths.")

So I have to rejig some big-ticket items—my sacred thrust. Since 60 per cent of federal program spending comes under social development, that obviously means social development. And that means no more federal cheques for families who don't need them, so I can write bigger federal cheques for families who do *and* write more federal cheques for other purposes (after a 10 per cent tithe on all money saved to help control the deficit).

Then I'd throw in tax reform to reduce marginal rates. The whole package, which might include higher consumption taxes, would be designed to stimulate private-sector growth and add a little more to my revenue. (I'd also cap the defence budget, focus the troops on Canadian territory, and remain within existing alliances. We might consider internationalizing the Northwest Passage in exchange for demilitarization of the Arctic.)

When I was done with pernicious universality and stimulative tax reform, the comfortable would be less comfortable, the less comfortable would be more comfortable, the discomforting deficit would be less discomforting, and I would have a little more money to spend. Naturally, I'd go on television to make all this perfectly clear, extolling my logic, applauding my morality, and plucking at heart strings, all the while reducing my opponents' criticism to mash by humorous asides. Then off to dinner at home with the people from Stanford University who say they're on the trail of anti-matter as the ultimate energy source and wonder if Canada wants a piece of the action. (We do.)

With more money to spend, I'd have to decide where to spend it. I have a bias towards assets that grow in value (like learning to read). I'd start with education because Canada doesn't stack up well when it comes to forming human capital—our natural resources are depreciating in value and there's a technological revolution out there. I'd use the federal spending power to bring more order and sense to our schools, colleges, and universities. (Education is too important to be left solely to provinces in a country that is already very small.)

Ultimately, students would have to work longer hours in better institutions, and that would give them a higher return on time. (Like tax reform, reform would give them a higher return on effort.) I'd encourage exchanges across the land to drag young people out of their regional wombs. "A decade in pursuit of excellence" might capture the theme.

Again, I'd go to television and milk every parent's certitude that his or her child shows special promise. I'd dare the provinces *not* to come together under my leadership to give Justin and Melissa the only security that really works in a shrinking world—sharper knowledge and better habits. I'd also increase funds for basic research in all academic fields, along with a science policy linking business more closely to R & D. I'd insist that a vote for me is a vote for your children. Could you turn me down?

Then I'd head to 24 Sussex for a soirée featuring Maureen Forrester and Arthur Ozolins in recital, followed by a light dinner where each of the fifty-seven guests moves to a different place after every exquisite course, including California white wines for the people from Ontario who don't realize what their government is denying them.

Freer trade would be upon us with my clear support, bilaterally and multilaterally (I'm a cosmopolitan nationalist). As freer trade generates passionate, fearful talk of absorption by the Americans, I'd have a good excuse to increase federal support (moral and monetary) for Canadian culture—with strong incentives for better administration. (I need an excuse, because a lot of ordinary Canadians have ordinary interests, among which haute culture is not one. I need the nationalist clamour to support my own elitist tastes.) What better time to expand on culture, history, and identity than during a toast to Forrester and Ozolins after everyone is flush with the blush of chardonnay? A purple ending to an excellent day.

Unfortunately, some days grate. We're eliminating regional benefits in unemployment insurance and tightening up the rest of the program. In chronically brackish regions, we're tying new income support schemes to family circumstances, so people who don't need public money don't get it. It's all part of a discreet but powerful policy to encourage younger people to move where the future offers better odds of independence. I trumpet another highly controversial theme: Everywhere in Canada is home. Nature is change.

Certain tiresome premiers are lambasting me for being a heartless ogre, but I keep talking about the long-run interest of our youth and growl, "Some heart, some ogre." I make a point of speaking in a different province every week, just to remind everybody that I represent Canadians too. (Two deputy prime ministers—one anglophone, one francophone, one woman, one visible something—give me time to wander.) In parliament, the nerdish opposition is filibustering, so for the second time this month on different issues, I am personally speaking at length during an evening sitting of the House. (I prefer to speak about *my* agenda during regular sitting hours than their agenda

274

during question period, so I play down question period, denying that I do so.) If I have to use closure against them, they will at least get the satisfaction of the prime minister in the trenches. When I decide to win, I do it hand to hand and go home dirty.

Day care is another fuss. A lot of people want a new universal social program. Not compatible, I say, with my sense of the plausible. We're too poor not to build on what we have. Instead, I'm giving provinces a little more federal money for day care on condition they expand existing systems (where demand warrants) and meet certain standards. Some women's groups say they'll get me for that. I say, God won't: She, too, understands the deficit.

After a bad day, I like a good film. With Michael and Mugdha in tow, I sneak off in a tawdry 1975 Plymouth Fury, shadowed by the RCMP in a 1984 Toyota Tercel, and arrive at a public cinema just after the lights go down. When the lights go up, we mingle with the Volk, who are surprised that the prime minister is so short and homely and acts so ordinary. I have discovered that not acting is the secret of political success, except when you have to be nice to bores (which did not afflict me when I attended the Contadora signing ceremony for the Central American stability pact).

The routine, hypocrisy, venality, and intensity of the job soon get to me, and I don't feel enough nationalism, idealism, or greed to carry on. I just can't take being PM very seriously. I contemplate desirable alternatives and realize that, if I were prime minister, I'd rather be on the editorial board of the *Globe and Mail* (all talk, no action).

NORMAN WARD

My initial reaction to the discovery would be pure shock, and I'd begin with a few days' rest somewhere incognito. Never in my chosen profession did I seek to climb the power ladder, and I've often wondered why a person would work for years to get a Ph.D., so that he could teach and write about his favourite subjects, and then agree to become a department head or associate dean or—in extreme cases— vice-president or worse. I used to say, when offered the slightest administrative advancement, the hell with it; but prime ministers aren't free to talk like that, I suppose.

While recuperating, I'd use my first days as prime minister for a few major decisions. Should I wear a bow tie for public appearances? Should I keep a diary? Should I become a father while in office? Should I answer questions clearly? There's one point I've already settled: I'd want to be the first prime minister to be criticized for spending too much time in the Commons, actually behaving like a member of parliament.

Once I'd recovered from the surprise of being at the summit, I'd want to find out what caused it, and I expect I'd learn that the "what" would be a bunch of "who's." Even I know that you don't get to be prime minister without somebody going to a lot of trouble, and since in my case I'd be totally innocent, it must have been somebody else. I note that in the now-forgotten election of 1984, a Mr. Mulroney, who won, received for his personal campaign in Manicouagan nearly $92,000 from 261 contributors, 146 of them individual supporters. His chief rival, Mr. Turner, raised over $41,000 from 183 supporters, 149 of them individuals. Another aspirant, Mr. Broadbent, got nearly $40,000 from 82 hopefuls, 75 of them individuals and two of the remainder being trade unions. Which means that, not counting the work of thousands in party and other organizations across the country, well over five hundred people helped to create one prime minister from three leading contenders in 1984.

So I'd want to know who worked for me, so that I could keep them out of the Prime Minister's Office. I'm going to have enough problems without further assistance from people whose judgement is so bad that they contributed money to my constituency campaign. The only post-election role I can envisage for them is in a rogues' gallery of selected supporters (and opponents, if I have any) in the prime minister's residence. One of my predecessors, I recall, kept his mother's portrait on his study wall and, when stressed, would sit beneath it singing hymns. My people will get darts thrown at them.

This brings up a problem: How, then, do I pick my principal advisers? I don't really mean the cabinet, because no prime minister ever has a completely free hand in picking his ministers. If the party whose victory has put me in office has turned up only one female MP from west of Ontario or only one bilingual Protestant of any sex from Quebec, I'll have to make them both Honourables even if they're dolts. And, besides, every one of my ministers worth a hoot will have his (or, yes, her) own little barony to service in the best feudal traditions and won't be able to give to my affairs the single-minded attention I'm going to need. And deserve. After all, I am the prime minister.

Still, all my ministers from the House of Commons, at least, will have some political experience, and I won't have time for advisers untouched by first-hand knowledge of the hustings. It's true that our political system is based in part on some weird assumptions, such as the notion that a person who can win a nomination and then an election is automatically qualified to handle an entirely different job, that of a representative. I don't want in my Prime Minister's Office a gaggle of advertising types and poll readers, who may be experts in telling me why I'm up or down 5 per cent but whose political acumen has never been tested—and, for all I know, may be a minus quantity.

If it's peculiar to think that a successful candidate will necessarily make an acceptable MP, how much more peculiar would it be for me, an inexperienced prime minister, to rely on techniques that may be fine for determining how many citizens wear only the tops or bottoms of their pyjamas but cannot show me the elementary difference between a policy that is popular and one that is bad for my country? In my search for advisers, I may be driven to revive an ancient and sensible practice whereby I take on as cabinet ministers a few wily old politicians who had the ill luck to be personally defeated last time around.

Anyway, as prime minister I've got to get trusted advisers somewhere, and I'll assume I have them. Where next? No doubt, I'll have got my job after a good deal of babbling about the top issues of the day, and even as I take my oath of office my ears will still be ringing with shibboleths like job creation, free and/or freer trade, the status of women, regional disparity, native rights, and deficit reduction. I mention these because they're all in today's newspaper, but they all have one striking common characteristic: I don't really know much about any of them, and even where I have some knowledge I haven't a clue to any practical solution to the problems each involves. As long as I was a private citizen that didn't matter, but as prime minister I'd be surrounded by people who claim that it matters like the dickens; and every one of them would have solutions.

What I'd need, obviously, is to be fully informed—possibly a revolutionary innovation in itself—and I'd start by setting up a series of high-powered cabinet committees, loaded with advisers, to provide me with the answers to a few basic questions. Starting with that short list in the last paragraph, here are a few samples:

- Precisely what is the record of (a) government and (b) the private sector in creating jobs? Why should the private sector realistically be expected to create jobs at all? Virtually every business I've seen at close range tries to destroy jobs, replacing full-time workers with part-time and replacing all workers with machines. What evidence is there that things can change merely because I've become prime minister?

- In this connection, what is a practical definition of efficiency in the public sector and the private? What meaning of efficiency covers an enterprise that uses or obtains public money to carry out its plans (as likely as not suggesting it will create jobs or do research, or both) and as a normal part of its activities goes on to pollute the environment, lay off workers, and even create ghost towns—all of which in one way or another become the taxpayers' responsibility? Why shouldn't any firm seeking federal help publicize as a necessary part of its documentation a list of all the assistance it receives from municipal, provincial, and federal sources, itemizing everything, from concessions on utilities, through land grants and other rights, to the expedients it uses to avoid paying income tax? Are firms that pay little or no federal tax nevertheless eligible for still more favours from taxpayers?

- Since the national public service is maintained entirely through laws passed by parliament, and since there are more female than male voters, what are the real reasons why females hold so large a percentage of the lower-paid jobs while males dominate the higher?

- What exactly is a deficit? Why should it be reduced?

If my former experience of getting answers to questions carries over to the prime ministerial level, those questions that I've just listed will naturally take months, if not years, to resolve. In the meantime, I'll need to do something to keep my party specifically, and the country generally, from falling apart while they are severally bedevilled by a prime minister who in private life earned much of his living by thinking. The pressing problems—unemployment, health and wel-

278

fare, grants to provinces, as well as all those others that are both perennial and always immediate—I'd have to delegate largely to my ministers, chiefly because I'd be hampered by knowing that each problem singly required lifelong study. There's no way I could master them all, and if I were prime minister I would not want to take shelter behind either euphemisms or claims to the sort of pseudo-omniscience the voters seem to expect, maybe because they've been trained to.

What I'd want to concentrate on would be the kind of long-range problems that many Canadians with children and grandchildren cannot help but think about in the 1980s. I don't mean nuclear war, whether undertaken deliberately or, as seems increasingly possible, accidentally. No Canadian prime minister has ever had anything of significance to do with the starting of major wars, and the only political point different about a nuclear holocaust, to Canada, is that for the first time it wouldn't matter which side we were on. What I have in mind, assuming Canada survives into the next century, turns on two basic trends: the fact that our population is aging, so there will be fewer workers to support us all; and the fact that the workers themselves face, on a growing scale, the disappearance of many kinds of work. So my concern would be how to cope with the massive amounts of leisure that are apparently going to be available to coming generations.

This problem will have to be solved primarily at the governmental level because the leisure now looked after by private enterprise, admirable as are many of the methods used, covers only that small fraction of the population who can afford it. What I'd like to look into is leisure that will be unavoidable for a very large fraction of the population on a permanent basis, and its handling will need many different kinds of policies. For one thing, our rapidly developing technology is accompanied by a rapidly developing and faceless bureaucracy—not in the government, where myth still stubbornly locates it, but in the private sector. It is far easier now to get a sensible letter from any level of government than it is to get satisfaction about unwanted advertising flyers in newspapers, irrelevant junk mail, or computerized financial or retailing services. These are just familiar examples, and they will undoubtedly be joined by many more in the coming decades. If I were prime minister, I'd like to do what I could to start training our leisured electors to cope with the private bureaucracies that threaten to engulf us. One alternative, let's face it, is rioting among a restless citizenry.

Bureaucracy, public or private, is impersonal (if not inhuman), and coping with it will be at least partly a negative operation. A large leisured population will need positive approaches to its contemporary life, and actual training for coping with leisure will be needed too. So if I were prime minister, I'd try to start (or at least lay the groundwork for starting) to build a whole new attitude towards the purposes of government. Government in the late twentieth century is not only preoccupied with mundane matters but is most successful when thus preoccupied. It is fairly good at keeping citizens from starving to death and at providing minimal health services. It succeeds in clothing and equipping small armed forces, and it builds sound sewage and highway systems. But it is far less impressive when dealing with things of the spirit, and if we are going to have a large leisured population it is things of the spirit that will have to be dealt with intelligently.

The idea of hugely expanded governmental programs to encourage all the arts and crafts and all the branches of athletics—all the accomplishments, in short, at which human beings can achieve individual excellence—is not popular as I write these words. But unless Canada is prepared to use oppressive means to curb the activities of leisured citizens who can readily become discontented, what other kinds of policies show promise? Already, newspapers and educational institutions try in their separate ways to help small numbers of the elderly to manage their retirement; but such solutions will not touch those retired in their twenties and thirties.

The policies I'm talking about all meet a useful criterion: they are labour-intensive, a piece of modern jargon which means that they occupy people. I do not have space here to offer many details, but if I were prime minister I'd try to make my ministers think as I do about planning for mass leisure. (If any disagreed, of course, I could always can them and get some sensible people.) I'd like to explore the potential of the education section of the Constitution Act. Since 1867 it has begun: "In and for each Province the Legislature may exclusively make Laws in relation to Education. . . ." I'd want to know about education that is not "in and for each Province" but is in and for Canada. I'd also like to think about the clause that says, "Until the Queen otherwise directs, the Seat of Government of Canada shall be Ottawa." I have nothing against Ottawa, and its original choice for the old Province of Canada in 1857 was sensible, partly because it was not Toronto or Montreal. But the new Canada has grown enormously since Confederation, and the capital is now not only well below the 49th parallel, while most of Canada is north of it, but it is in a part of the country that has become least like the rest of Canada, the parochial little island of southern Ontario. If the capital proved immovable, as capitals often do, I'd look at vast travel funds to allow Canadians to visit Canada—including Ottawa. Think of all the jobs that would be created!

If I were prime minister I'd clearly be a dreamer. But since I'd have no intention of retaining office past the next general election (a decision the electorate would probably settle for me anyway) I can tell you one thing: if I succeeded in persuading enough Canadians to follow up my ideas, we'd have fewer worries about our national integrity or about American cultural invasions. Among the world's industrialized nations, in short, we'd be unique. And if I'm wrong about all this, that's a prime minister's prerogative.

MEL WATKINS

If I were prime minister.... Wow! When I was a kid growing up in the village of McKellar, Ontario—which didn't merit more than a reeve—to have been mayor of the nearby town of Parry Sound was almost more than the mind could conceive. Even just mayor for a day seemed too much to hope for, while this present offer seems to be for as long as I want. (Surely longer than John Turner? Maybe even longer than Joe Clark? Speaking of which, are *they* in this book?)

Then I grew up and became both an economist and a socialist, and briefly flirted with what passes for the real world of politics. I remember someone asking me in those distant days if my ambition was to be Canada's first socialist minister of finance. I had enough sense of realpolitik, of the American imperial style—and of how the solid waste would hit the fan and gravitate northward at the prospect of a socialist Canada—to shudder at the thought, to demur, and to say that my secret desire, really, was to be the first socialist governor general. This was meant to be funny; little could I guess that Trudeau would stumble on that very idea, only to throw it away on Ed Schreyer in a doomed effort to win the West and the ethnic vote for Liberalism.

Now I am older and wiser, temporarily living in exile in Britain, undistracted by the flotsam and jetsam of the daily question period in the Canadian House of Commons, and depressed by the realization that the British economy has been going downhill for a hundred years, no matter which party is in power (much less which prime minister presides). Political junkie though I am, to be in a country not one's own is to be less mesmerized by familiarity with the names of all the players and to sense, finally and fully, how much of a mug's game parliamentary politics is—and how little you or I or anyone else could do if one of us were suddenly catapulted into 24 Sussex Drive.

Evidence abounds at many levels. Let me begin with the economic. It is commonly assumed that politics—meaning policy—affects the economy; but the obverse is much more the reality, with policy lagging behind the economy and politicians taking the credit for any random good that may have happened. Hence, if your economic advisers tell you that their reading of the chicken entrails, not yet made public, shows that inflation is moderating, you would immediately announce an anti-inflation program. This is commonplace and universally practised. A more sophisticated version is first to create a problem (this politicians are able to do!) and then solve it. When Ronald Reagan was elected president in 1980, there was 7.5 per cent unemployment in the United States. He forthwith introduced economic policies that pushed unemployment up to double digits. He then eased back; unemployment fell to 7.5 per cent again; he proclaimed an economic miracle and was re-elected with a larger vote than ever. (No wonder economics is called the dismal science.)

Or consider the following. By chance, I saw the *Toronto Star* of 17 May 1986. It contained a story by Rosemary Speirs, headlined "Peterson Switches Nuclear Power Sides," which reads:

> When he was leader of the Opposition, David Peterson voted on emotional grounds, against Ontario Hydro's plans to sell the nuclear byproduct tritium to the United States, against completion of the $11-billion Darlington nuclear station east of Toronto, and in favour of making Ontario a nuclear-free zone where no one could produce or sell components of nuclear arms.
>
> Today, as premier of Ontario, he says he'd prefer a nuclear-free province, but has inherited a power grid largely dependent on the atom and he has to be practical about it.

Ms. Speirs goes on to tell us how the conversion of Mr. Peterson has taken place notwithstanding the horror of Chernobyl (when you think about it, his timing is grotesque) and quotes him as saying about Ontario's reactors: "If I thought they were unsafe I'd close them all tomorrow." Ms. Speirs refrains from pointing out—but I will not— that the bravado is utterly unconvincing, the hypocrisy so deep that it could only be acquired by years of immersion in politics.

Imagine what you wish about what you or I could do as prime minister of Canada, being premier of Ontario (which is, after all, the largest and the greatest of the provinces) is demonstrably not worth the candle. In saying this, I mean no special offence to Mr. Peterson; nor am I, as a sometimes New Democrat, making a partisan point. The dulling of the senses in politicians—of which the first to go is common sense—is an occupational hazard. It will be recalled that the aforementioned Mr. Schreyer was elected premier of Manitoba on the promise to cease and desist from the flooding of aboriginal lands at South Indian Lake, which was being done for the production of hydroelectric power. (The well-known tendency of power to corrupt has, it would appear, a special meaning for Canadians.) Once elected, Mr. Schreyer settled for lowering the water cover from twenty-six feet to ten feet (or from eight metres to three metres, for those who can actually think that way); this was of slight solace to the aboriginal people, who couldn't touch bottom no matter how you measured it. As for today's Messrs. Rae and Broadbent, they are splendid chaps, I know. But I, a descendant of a Grand Master of the Orange Lodge, ask you: What are we to make of socialists who are regularly upstaged by Catholic bishops?

But what if, instead of going down the pecking order to Queen's Park, one went up it to Washington? Surely, to be president of the great U.S. of A. would matter. Now it so happens that just this point was once put to the distinguished American linguist and socialist libertarian critic of his country's foreign policy, Noam Chomsky of Massachusetts Institute of Technology. An election pending, he was asked: "Who should I vote for as president?" He said it didn't matter. But what, the questioner persisted, if Chomsky—or some like-minded person—was running? It still wouldn't matter, he said. One person, no matter how well intended, couldn't do anything.

Chomsky's point, of course, was that it would only matter if one were elected by an informed, aroused, and mobilized people. The implication was that one should stop day-dreaming about being president or such like and get busy informing, arousing, and mobilizing.

Nevertheless, if I were somehow to become prime minister anyway.... Well, I wouldn't want to be thought ungracious or unpatriotic, so I'd take the job, and this is what I would do:

– Move from London (England, that is), which ran the world in some previous century but certainly not in this one. Not to Ottawa though, which has never run anything, including Canada. To Washington, rather, where I would apply for *the* desk—the Canadian desk in the State Department—or, better still, for any desk in the basement of the White House; Ollie North's would do, and the ring of that surname would be inspirational.

– Name Brian Mulroney governor general. While he had no qualifications to become prime minister—and it showed—he is eminently qualified to be GG. He is bilingual. He dresses well. He has a smiling wife who walks one step behind him. He oozes unctuousness. He will not be missed in whatever it is he is now not doing.

– Agree to any free-trade deal with the United States that has the full consent of all provinces, territories, cities, towns, and villages—and of Tom d'Aquino and Shirley Carr. Meanwhile, leave Simon Reisman to negotiate with the Americans in a locked room. They deserve him; he deserves them; none of them will be missed.

– Appoint Larry Zolf to the Senate, and just as he heaves himself with difficulty to his feet to make his maiden speech, abolish the Senate.

Choose Gerry Caplan as Social Democrat of the Year and appoint him lifetime ambassador to Albania. Appoint a royal commission to study the futility (I do mean the f-word) of royal commissions; urge it to make a thorough study and, meanwhile, appoint no other royal commissions so that problems will actually have to be dealt with.

– Instruct the National Research Council to teach the Canadarm on the U.S. Space Shuttle to make obscene gestures.

– Do a Canadian-American version of a hostage swap: our Americans for their Canadians. We get John Kenneth Galbraith, they get Carl Beigie. We let them keep Zbigniew Brzezinski if they let us keep Jane Jacobs. They get James Barros gratis (and if you don't know who he is, be grateful).

– Appoint a minister of national defence from a well-inhabited area. Instruct him, or her (living in Thatcher's Britain has made me see the dark side of women's liberation), that any testing of cruise missiles and any low-level training flights by supersonic fighter aircraft from any NATO country must take place over his (or her) home in his (or her) constituency.

If I'm allowed to dream, let it be in technicolour—that I would be prime minister *after* the forces of goodness and light had been nourished and mobilized and had put me in place as their chosen instrument. Now this is interesting: the prospect exists of actually doing something.

You are warned that, for a short while, this is serious.

Two things matter most of all. They are peace and prosperity. Canada should do what it can to further both. Each goal aids and abets the other. A prosperous people is less easily seduced by false promises of economic benefits from arms spending; a peaceful condition frees up resources currently wasted on arms, making them available for wise spending on needed public goods and for capital formation that creates jobs and enhances productivity. The pursuit of each involves greater self-reliance for Canada.

So-called defence policy should truly become defensive. To do this, it must become non-nuclear, for it is nuclear weapons that above all fuel the arms race and put everyone at risk. Canada, to its credit, has long had the capacity to build its own nuclear weapons but has deliberately refrained from doing so. We have also discouraged our allies—meaning the United States—from deploying nuclear weapons on our soil. But this is not enough. We now need to make Canada a wholly nuclear-weapons-free zone.

There must no longer be the production of guidance systems for, and the testing of, nuclear-capable cruise missiles. As prime minister, I would prevent Canadian companies from bidding on Pentagon contracts that are related in any way, shape, or form to nuclear weapons systems (which includes Star Wars); jobs thereby lost would be offset by cutting back on purchases of weapons from the United States and by spending those public funds in other ways. The export of nuclear weapons fuel, such as tritium, would be forbidden. Ships carrying nuclear warheads would be banned from Canadian ports. If these measures proved to be inconsistent with membership in NORAD and NATO, too bad.

Canadian defence would be directed towards the patrolling of our land, sea, and air, the carrying out of search and rescue, and contributions to international peacekeeping. So far as possible, these tasks would be undertaken with Canadian-produced equipment.

As for the pursuit of prosperity, it must be threefold. Each measure is essential in its own right; together, the three make up a mutually reinforcing package. Firstly, there must be a guarantee of employment so as to rid the country of the long-term unemployment that is so personally debilitating and socially wasteful. The "right to work" must cease to be a code word for smashing unions and must instead become the guarantee of a job; this means work not pogey, and productive work not make-work. A measure novel to Canada would be used, namely wage subsidies to firms that increase the number of their employees.

Secondly, there must be a recommitment to equality and the elimination of poverty. The war on poverty of the 1960s has long since degenerated into a war on the growing ranks of the poor. No real improvement is possible without it being decreed that every government policy will be judged in terms of its effect on the distribution of income and on equality—not only of opportunity but of condition. Nor can such concerns stop short at our borders. It was a Canadian, Marshall McLuhan, who called our world a global village, and in it the poor greatly outnumber the affluent. Under my administration, Canada would commit itself to giving a larger share of its GNP in foreign aid than any other country; let us hope that this would become a race that we would have to keep escalating to win.

Thirdly, Canada is one of the world's largest importers of manufactured goods, both in total and in per capita terms. We constantly fret about getting better access to outside markets for our goods, and thus we risk going into a bilateral free-trade arrangement with the United States that would gravely erode our sovereignty. We should instead see our own market as one to which our own producers should be given first access and in which foreign companies should be given access in return for firm commitments to site production in Canada.

All of these steps towards peace and prosperity, needless to say, would have to be taken cautiously, because that is the Canadian way and because it is the only way the Americans would let us.

If I were prime minister.... Say, I'm really getting into this. I can't wait. Alternative summits are held, alternative Nobel Peace Prizes awarded, and the left is full of alternative economic strategies. Can I be alternative prime minister?

ELSIE E. WAYNE

Regrettably, this country is currently in a state of drift. What Canada so desperately needs is a vision of its potential greatness, as well as the political leadership and courage to seek the achievement of such a vision. The absence of a vision—or a national dream, if you like—creates doubts about our future, fails to instil confidence in our potential, and erodes our sense of opportunity and enterprise. In fact, the by-product of our current national aimlessness is cynicism and scepticism about our future. I believe Canadians are prepared to sacrifice and to submit to some short-term discomfort in order to participate in the renewal and reshaping of our future. But if they are to feel confident about the future, they must have faith in our national purpose.

I recently had an opportunity to speak with a group of new Canadians, who had left their home in the Philippines to start a new life in a strange land. While speaking with these proud citizens, I was struck by their fierce allegiance to their new country. They talked excitedly about living in Canada and about their dreams and hopes. Already, many had established successful careers and their lives in Saint John were thriving, with a rosy outlook.

I had seen this before in other new Canadians—a passion for their new home and a strong allegiance to the Canadian flag. Yet this appears to be sorely lacking in many native-born Canadians. I am convinced that the values one must have in order to be proud of Canada are not being instilled in our youngsters through our educational system.

Educational Policy
One of the first steps I would take as prime minister would be to attempt to develop a new Canadian policy on educating our young on the Charter of Rights and Freedoms and instilling in them an allegiance to their country. While I appreciate that education is a provincial responsibility, someone must take the appropriate steps to ensure all Canadians know and appreciate what they have in Canada. School children in Saskatchewan must learn that a vital part of their great country lies east of Montreal. Conversely, students in New Brunswick

should know that there is more to Alberta than the world's largest shopping mall.

What the Americans emanate in patriotism is an example for all native Canadians to adopt. We have failed to give our children, as our parents failed to give us, a deep sense of joy about being Canadian. New Canadians are required to learn about this wonderful land, but native Canadians take their rights and freedoms for granted. I would therefore advocate a uniform system to be established across Canada and to be taught in all schools about our heritage and "how great it is to be Canadian."

Military Service
Many young people in the Western world lack a sense of direction. I believe that all male high-school graduates should spend two years in the Canadian Armed Forces before continuing their secondary education. There is a great need to have this type of discipline, training, and respect taught to our young people. I think the result would be many more productive Canadians who would be more willing to apply themselves and who, in the long run, would become better citizens.

By increasing funding to the Canadian Armed Forces to allow this policy, we would also help alleviate high unemployment levels among our young people. They would leave the military with valuable training and with the maturity to accept responsibilities much earlier in life.

Review of Welfare System
As prime minister, I would advocate a complete review of the Canadian welfare system. I believe we should turn welfare into "workfare." Most Canadians who accept social assistance do not wish to be dependent on welfare. They have lost their hope and their dignity, and would much rather be part of the work force. The Government of Canada could restore their sense of worth by allowing them to work for their assistance payments. I say, let us pay them to make a valuable contribution to society. Federal regulations similar to those enacted under health-care financing would force the provinces to re-evaluate their view of social assistance as more than a "handout."

Term of Government
I believe Canadians are ready to limit the number of consecutive terms that any government's leader can stay in power. At the very least, we should follow the example of the United States and limit the number of consecutive terms for the prime minister to two.

History has shown that politicians begin to lose control of their own destinies after a period of service. Arrogance and disrespect for public monies and the public's opinion are commonplace after two terms in office. Too many favours become due for repayment. It is an unfortunate fact of political life that there are people who make their living off the backs of politicians. These political leeches eventually gain control of our elected officials, who then apparently lose the intestinal fortitude required to make fair and equitable decisions.

Dignity for the House of Commons

Canadians have been shocked in recent years to witness the decline of decorum in our House of Commons. Unfortunately, the introduction of live television to the House has turned many of our elected members into actors. They seem to have lost their sense of duty as managers of the billion-dollar budgets they are elected to oversee. One of the first steps I would take as prime minister would be to remove the television cameras from the House of Commons.

Canadians are looking for honesty and integrity from their leaders— not showmanship and partisan replies, which are often ridiculous and which disparage all politicians. Politics in Canada has become the politics of the party—at all costs! Federal politicians have long forgotten that they have been elected to serve their country and their constituents: they have not been elected to ensure that their party remains in power for as long as possible.

Our federal politicians must once more become accountable to the people. This restoration of integrity would be one of my top priorities as prime minister. I truly believe that the Canadian people's cynicism and mistrust of their leaders can be reversed. Good, honest, forthright government can do that.

Restoration of Department of Urban Affairs

Previous Canadian governments supported municipalities through the federal Department of Urban Affairs. This department has since been eliminated. This was a most unfortunate decision. The majority of Canadians are urban dwellers. Their homes and livelihood depend upon the success of their communities. Yet no government vehicle exists for municipalities to bring their concerns before the government.

The Federation of Canadian Municipalities (FCM) has done a yeoman job of bringing local concerns to the government, but greater recognition must be given to Canadian municipalities. Local politicians are those who are closest to the people. Mayors, councillors, aldermen, representatives—all local officials—are made aware on a daily basis of the needs of the municipalities and the citizens. They know what needs to be done in order to make the municipalities grow.

As prime minister, I would immediately make a close examination of the FCM proposal which recommends a $14 billion investment in the repair and upgrading of Canadian roads, streets, sidewalks, sewers, water systems, and bridges. There is no doubt that infrastructures in Canadian cities are deteriorating at an alarming rate. The FCM's proposal would create 45,000 to 60,000 person years of employment for each of the five years of the program. If the program was implemented, we would not only be improving the environment within our municipalities—creating cities more attractive for businesses to be established and for residents to make their homes—but we would also be creating employment for Canadians.

If the Urban Affairs office had not been removed, the Neighbourhood Improvement Program (NIP), the Urban Transportation Assistance Program (UTAP), and other community services programs would still be in effect. A revitalized Department of Urban Affairs would also be able to address the current inadequacies of the federal government in respect to intergovernmental planning and economic development for municipalities. As the Federation of Canadian Municipalities has noted, it is of the utmost importance that a review of the uses of property taxes and of alternative methods of financing municipal government be undertaken. No other developed country in the world is without a national agency which conducts affairs as stated above.

Intergovernmental Co-operation
As the mayor of Canada's oldest incorporated city, I realize there are economic difficulties and uncertainties about the future. These are in large part a function of basic structural changes in the demands for products, resources, and services, and in the means of production, extraction, and delivery. A major challenge facing all levels of government is to try to ensure that Canadians continue to enjoy a high standard of living, that we return to higher levels of employment, and that all have equal access to opportunity and range of services. This cannot be accomplished exclusively by one economic sector or by one level of government. Yet municipal governments have a significant role to play in this co-operative effort. I believe a Canada in which the municipal capabilities were more greatly emphasized would be one in which the well-being of all Canadians would be enhanced.

There also needs to be a closer working relationship between the provinces and territories of Canada. Currently, the lack of co-operation and cohesion between these governments is making it very difficult for Canadian municipalities to move ahead. One does not need to look elsewhere for direction but only to apply home-grown common sense to recognize that we are in the midst of an historical period in which we will prosper only if there is some degree of co-operation among the various participants. The prime minister must take the lead in uniting the various levels of government across Canada in a national, co-operative effort. Municipalities must not be left out of the decision-making process.

Revenue Sources
As prime minister, I would study the present system and determine if there was any source of revenue other than property tax to finance the needs of Canadian municipalities. For example, consideration could be given to the creation of a national, municipal development fund to enable municipalities to complete necessary capital work and infra-structure programs. I believe the three levels of government should work together to support municipal effort and to assist communities to deal with problems which are impeding their economic develop-ment. If this was accomplished, I believe we would find that we could put many people back to work.

Priorities should be given to developing municipal programs and projects involving joint efforts between the private and public sectors which serve to help with the economic diversification; to create new and expanded markets for Canadian goods and services; to increase plant modernization; and to foster research and development activi-ties. Meanwhile, federal policies and programs should help to rein-force the existing strengths of municipalities.

Support for Excellence
While the notion of pursuing and supporting excellence has become somewhat clichéd, particularly in the literature of business and man-agement, it is nevertheless critical for Canada that we do in fact pursue such a course. I say this because of Canada's relatively small popula-tion, its vast resources, and its vigorously competitive regions. Regret-tably, it is simply not possible, in this country, to provide a level of opportunity in every conceivable economic sector in every corner of the country. Rather, we must recognize that excellence and enterprise exist in varying strengths, in diverse sectors, and in different parts of the country. However, these individual strengths must be reinforced and supported if we are truly to build centres and indeed regions of excellence and enterprise throughout Canada. It will take political courage to provide the critical mass and resources to support and nurture these clusters of excellence. But it will be essential if we

intend to challenge the world's best, as we must do if Canada is to prosper.

Environmental Policies

It is time to take a far stronger position with respect to environmental affairs. In eastern Canada, acid rain is no longer a nuisance; it is a life-threatening environmental hazard. Canada must confront the United States and demand immediate action that will put a halt to the most serious environmental problem of this century. But if we are to have credibility in our dealings with the Americans, the municipal, provincial, and federal governments must demonstrate that Canadian standards are above reproach. If I were prime minister, acid rain—not free trade—would be the number-one area of negotiation between Canada and the United States.

The Need for Political Courage

It is some time since Canada has felt so despondent and so discouraged about the quality of its political leadership. Our news reports are filled daily with suggestions of impropriety and near scandal. Tragically, this is occurring at a time when Canada so desperately needs prudent leadership in both domestic and international policy. The absence of this leadership not only robs us of our national opportunity to reshape and rethink our policies and strategies for change; even worse, the pervasive sense of corruption serves to promote cynicism and scepticism about our political institutions. This makes it increasingly difficult to mobilize a nation which so desperately needs to be galvanized for action if we are to move aggressively into the twenty-first century. This malaise saps the country of its national spirit and patriotism; and without a strong and deeply rooted belief in the greatness and the future of our country, we become victims of divisiveness as we engage in regional grasping and squabbling, which serve only to distract us from what must be our national priorities of economic growth and reconciliation.

Citizens expect their leaders to give direction and to conduct themselves in a manner befitting the position. As prime minister, one must have the courage to do what is right, the strength of one's convictions and the dignity and integrity to carry out the job of looking after the interests of all Canadians. This is the manner in which I have conducted myself at the local level, and I would do no less at the federal level if I were prime minister.

For me to write my thoughts on "If I were prime minister," I must qualify my remarks by saying that they come from my view and experience as a mayor of a city and from the fact that I consider municipal government "the government of the people," whereas the provincial and federal governments are the governments of the parties. We are the closest government to the people and we understand more fully the needs of all Canadians. One only has to ask oneself, "What constitutes Canada?" It is the towns and villages and cities and unincorporated areas.

As mayor, I have had to take many unpopular stands. Eventually, citizens realize that these positions have been taken in their best interests.

Our leaders must show us once again how to reach our goals and objectives by our own devices. Canadians will enjoy satisfaction they never knew possible when they are the authors of their own accomplishments. It is the role of the prime minister to instil and encourage this new sense of pride and entrepreneurship among Canadians.

ROBERT WHITE

It's been my first day as prime minister—I've only had the job for nineteen hours. But I've already established two task forces, recalled Ambassador McDermott, assigned him to his new post of labour attaché to the United States, and replaced him in Ireland with Simon Reisman. And I've already had my first social talk with the president of the United States of America.

It began with a call from the American ambassador, congratulating me on my victory and assuring me that the president fully understood that my statements on peace, Nicaragua, and South Africa were just normal campaign rhetoric. I politely explained that I fully understood that the ambassador's call was just the normal post-election feeler but that I was quite serious in carrying out my party's platform of banning cruise missile tests in Canada, ending any participation in Star Wars, establishing full diplomatic relations with the people of Nicaragua, and calling for full sanctions on South Africa. A coughing fit on the other end of the line prevented me from hearing his reply. It ended only when I finally broke the connection.

Twenty minutes later, the president himself called. He warmly reminded me about the Shamrock Conference and I reminded him that that was the other guy. A little more businesslike, he promised that if we just continued to act like an American colony on foreign policy, we could have that free-trade deal we wanted. I, in turn, promised that if he accepted our sovereignty, we wouldn't force free trade on the United States.

I held the line while he checked this with his advisers. When he returned, he was less friendly. He had seen *Final Offer* twice, he said, but was not impressed—he'd had much more difficult roles when he was in movies. And he warned that if my members didn't go back to work, he'd decertify the union like he had done with the air traffic controllers.

This led to another interruption from his advisers. The president returned to ask me if I understood how economically dependent on the United States Canada was and suggested a formal meeting shortly to discuss the relationship between our two countries. I agreed to the meeting.

Before that conversation and since, I have been meeting with top civil servants to be briefed both on the mechanics of office and on policy issues. The common theme from the majority of them—there were some exceptions—was not with how we could actually get things done, but with impressing upon me all the reasons and excuses for why things couldn't be done. Their real concern was not that we might fail but that we might succeed. What characterized them as "bureaucrats" was not any lack of talent but their hostility to the mandate we had won, and fear of rocking the boat.

The difficulties are, of course, immense; they should be openly addressed and debated, and I certainly don't underestimate them. Our majority was small, and even some of our supporters will get nervous about staying the course when some of the warnings made during the campaign (for instance, that business will leave to where it can get a better deal) turn out to be true. But if we do have any respect for the meaning of democracy—and I consider our whole campaign, and in fact our existence as a party, to be about giving Canadian democracy a much deeper and broader meaning—then we must press ahead.

The two task forces I have established to deal with this issue will, I hope, prove to be different from past government task forces, which emerged more to limit public debate than to stimulate it. The first task force is on "Democracy and Sovereignty." Amongst other questions, it will ask:

- If democracy is about giving people some control over their lives, doesn't it have to guarantee certain basic rights in one of the most important spheres of our lives—the workplace? Why doesn't the Canadian constitution include the right to a job, the right to a safe workplace, and the right to form unions?

- If democracy includes the sanctity of the individual, doesn't this also imply that everything must in fact be done to develop the potential of *all* citizens? My own experience as a trade unionist has introduced me to hundreds of workers who, because of the trade union movement, had a chance to develop their organizing skills, to articulate workers' needs with confidence, to go beyond being a cog in a machine and play an active role in the workplace and in society at large. But the flip side of this is the millions of workers who are never given such opportunities and who do have skills to offer and potential to develop. What stands in the way of such development?

- Can a society be truly democratic if it is unequal? When corporations threaten to leave if concessions aren't made or if the "investment climate" isn't favourable enough, doesn't this power of the few to undermine the mandate of the many also undermine the meaning of parliament and democracy?

296

– Is our ability to determine the direction of our economy and society limited by our dependence on the international economy? What does this imply for national sovereignty? And without sovereignty, what does democracy mean?

This last question makes the link to the second task force: "Alternatives to Free Trade." It will address issues such as:

– Trade will continue and is important, but why must the level of our trade-dependence grow every year? Rather than trying to accelerate exports each year to offset the growing penetration of imports, can't we redirect a significant portion of our productivity activity towards replacing imports and meeting domestic needs?

– Are the marketplace and the multinationals the only mechanism possible for continuing trade? Can't we continue to trade with other countries but find other mechanisms—like government-to-government agreements—which are mutually beneficial and less likely to hold us up to blackmail?

– Does trade in its present form and direction enhance or undercut our ability to define what kind of Canada we want to build? Or, more precisely, whose goals does it limit and whose goals does it enhance?

These issues and these task forces are obviously related. They tend to challenge the ideology that still dominates our country. The fact that my party won the election shows that there are cracks in that ideology.

In the past, we commonly expected each year to be better than the present one, and we expected our children to have it better than we did. But today, in spite of greater productivity than humanity has ever seen, in spite of the promises of what the new technology can bring in terms of goods, leisure, and services, we are told to expect less of everything except insecurity. With this kind of vision, is it any surprise that people have begun to ask whether things can be done differently?

It's been a long day, a long week, a long year. I'm excited, a little nervous, and—right now—very tired. I remind myself of how great Ottawa is after the snow melts and slide into bed. For the first time in a long while, my mind joins my body in sleep.

LOIS M. WILSON

In the best tradition of Canadian prime ministers, I have consulted the spirits and my deceased mother before writing this short article. They advised me to follow the example set by living mortals, such as the wives of cabinet ministers. Here are the visions that emerged.

If I were prime minister I would strike a gold coin imprinted with the images of Adam and Eve (appropriately clothed, of course) for sale in the year 2000, in commemoration of the "whatever" anniversary of Creation. Proceeds from the sale of this coin to the public would be directed to renewing the face of the earth and stopping the destruction of Paradise. (I would direct the fund particularly to stop the logging on aboriginal lands, to clean up the Great Lakes, to stop acid rain, and to care for Canada's precious supply of clean water. I would put clean water at the very forefront of the possibility of achieving world peace in the next forty years.) I have not talked to my husband about this idea. I did, however, consult the World Council of Churches, and although it was thought to be a splendid idea, something in the World Council by-laws precluded involvement from that body.

I would build a federal penitentiary in my home riding, Spadina (Toronto). I first heard of this idea in the Royal Canadian Air Farce's radio program in December 1986. Although the program did not suggest that this building go to Spadina riding, it very helpfully suggested that the current prime minister, Mr. Mulroney, could use the project not only to create jobs but to serve as a halfway house for former cabinet ministers. I would do the same.

Meanwhile, I would try not to pat any of my male colleagues on the derrière. Certainly not in public. And if it happened when the television cameras were on me, before I fully realized its implications, I would ask forgiveness and put it all behind me. I deeply respect men and want them to have equal opportunities. This will be obvious by the number of men I would select for cabinet positions, albeit fewer than I wish because so few of them are really equipped to handle the job. As we all know, policy-making for the nation is really housekeeping writ large; and so few men have had the mandatory housekeeping experience, although more are now qualifying than ever before.

I would award a medal, "Wilson's Wonderful Winners," to the group of persons who contributed most to the development of affordable housing in this country, the medal to be awarded on site.

On a more serious level, if I were prime minister I would:

- stop cruise missile testing over Canadian territory, particularly since the United States broke the SALT II treaty;

- prohibit Canadian research institutions and commercial firms from participating in SDI research;

- bring NORAD under the North Atlantic Council and under responsible political control, or get out of NORAD;

- spend as much time and money and research, as is presently given to military production, on converting the economy to the development of a permanent peace economy;

- make it firm government policy to retain abolition of capital punishment;

- restore the cuts made to the budgets of the National Research Council, the Canada Council, the universities, and the CBC. I would not countenance budget cuts that cripple Canada's cultural sovereignty or the development of future leadership.

I would separate the refugee determination process from the immigration laws so that bona fide refugees could be admitted with dispatch, while those abusing the system could be found out early in the proceedings. I would support refugee policies for humanitarian assistance, kept quite distinct from our domestic and foreign policies. I would make the licensing of "immigration consultants" mandatory. I would have Canada take the lead at the United Nations in redefining the definition of a convention refugee to include "sex" as a legitimate ground for a well-founded fear of persecution, and to broaden the convention to accommodate present-day realities, such as mass movements of people due to the shortcomings of the present international order. If I were prime minister, I would actively direct Canada's foreign policy in search of solutions to the root causes of refugee migrations, which can be found in underlying economic and social injustices and related human rights violations.

I would devote more than a few lines to Canadian foreign policy in the Speech from the Throne. I would shape policy on the premise that Canada is, in the best sense, "a friend of the United States" when it maintains a little distance from the policies of our neighbour. While we Canadians share many values with the Americans, many of us do not share the way these values shape the foreign policy of the United States. Too often, U.S. policies appear to contradict the values we thought we shared. There are occasions when our assessment of a situation requires Canada to take an independent position, such as is the case with Central America. Canada has a natural affinity with such middle-power countries as the Netherlands, Australia, and New Zealand, and could work with these countries in establishing good relations with other blocs. To break through the stalemate of three opposing camps—East, West, and non-aligned—Canada could take the lead in creating an alignment of smaller states, friendly to the United States but not threatening either to the eastern bloc or to the non-aligned nations. I would give a strong lead to Canada playing a constructive and creative role as a friendly critic of the United States in this area.

As prime minister, I would initiate a reversal of the trend in Canadian aid policies over the last ten years, which I perceive as a significant retreat from the policy statement of 1975, *Strategy for International Development Cooperation, 1975-80*. That statement gave highest priority to assisting poor countries and poor peoples to meet their basic needs. Any consideration on government policy on North/South issues would, under my leadership, have three central ethical concerns:

- a commitment to solidarity with those who suffer;

- support for reforms for greater international equity;

- a commitment to assist Third World communities and states to develop economically and to become more self-reliant and more able to avoid dependency in their relationship with richer powers.

These three concerns would be the basis for policies on aid, trade, and to the international financial institutions. For example, it would mean CIDA immediately permitting tenders from Third World countries in relation to the development assistance projects administered by its bilateral programs. It would mean Canada progressively untying its bilateral aid so that the countries being assisted could use competitive international tenders for projects financed by Canadian aid. It would mean an end to Canadian government funds being used, directly or indirectly, in association with export credits to secure capital contracts for Canadian firms. It is shabby to present as "aid" funds spent in the promotion of Canadian exports.

There are countless other policies I would like to have set before you: free trade, adequate economic support for the disadvantaged and hungry, etc. But it would take more than an article to describe them. To know *all* of my mind, you will just have to elect me the next prime minister!

GEORGE WOODCOCK

There are two reasons why it is of course absurd of me to answer such a question as that posed in this volume: What would I do if I were prime minister? The obvious first answer is that as a lifelong philosophic anarchist I would never be prime minister, even if the fates were improbably to offer such a choice. Besides, though Canadian prime ministers in recent years have assumed powers to which in a democracy they are not entitled, their ability to change things fundamentally is hindered by all the interests on which their power depends. And in our world of looming twilight, the fundamental changes are the only ones worth making.

So it is an absurd question that I am asked. Yet as all good existentialists know, one deals with the absurd by engaging it. And so I engage this question, not by assuming that I would ever be prime minister but by considering the fundamental changes I would like to see in our society.

Most of these changes are related to power and its reduction. Karl Marx and his followers taught that the real motivations in society were economic and that once the control of production was taken out of the hands of individuals and transferred to the community, tyranny would end and men would be free. History, which they were always so fond of invoking, has turned against the Marxists and proved them wrong. Their error was that they did not understand the psychological basis of tyranny: that it is based on power and the addictive desire for power. Lord Acton had a better insight than any proclaimed by Marx when he declared, "Power tends to corrupt, and absolute power corrupts absolutely. Great men are always bad men."

Not recognizing this truth, the Marxists imagined that it was sufficient to transfer power rather than to destroy it. Marx and Engels talked of the dictatorship of the proletariat, under which Engels at least imagined that the state would wither away. Lenin amended the formula to talk of the rule of the party that represents the proletariat. What none of them took into account was that power corrupts whoever holds it, party cadre or capitalist politician, and that the only way to freedom is to get rid of political power altogether; the beginning of the process is to reduce it by dissipating it, as confederal societies have tried in the past to do.

So far as Canada is concerned—and, indeed, most other countries—we can consider power externally and internally. The foreign policies of most countries in the world today are based on the concept of the balance of power. Major countries with their military and economic strength and their open or disguised territorial ambitions seek to create positions of power in the world so that they can dominate ever-increasing portions of it. Middle powers seek, by suitable alliances, to limit the ambitions of the great powers—to balance them off against each other. All such calculations are based on the proposition that physical power in the shape of military force is the dominant factor in world relations.

That proposition can be challenged, and nowadays the obvious challenge is that physical power of this kind has become obsolete because it is self-defeating. In any conceivable major war in the future there will be no victors. In the first hour when the missiles fly, the earth will be condemned to destruction on a scale that will render armies and navies and other instruments of world political power immediately ineffective. So, clearly, it is better to make a fundamental shift of assumptions, to abandon any solution that depends on the illusion of a balance of destructive forces and to find some other way, a way by which the peoples of the world can be brought to living in harmony.

It has often been argued by the proponents of "realism" that any country which steps out of the pattern of competing alliances places itself in dire peril, because it does not enjoy the umbrella of protection offered by one of the great nuclear powers. The obvious answer is that quite a number of countries have in fact prospered and survived, in some cases for centuries, as perpetual neutrals. Switzerland and Sweden are the best-known examples, but there are others among the smaller states that make up the multiplicity of the United Nations. It is true that Canada doubtless could not defend itself in a conventional military manner without aid, though its terrain would probably make it as difficult to hold down as Afghanistan if its people decided not to accept an invader. But invasion is not the threat nowadays. The threat is that umbrella of mythical protection, which in fact means that in any future nuclear war Canada will be implicated immediately on the American side and will be in the front line when the missiles race for their targets or are blown out of the sky to scatter radioactive material over the land, under the impact of Reagan's Star Wars system, should that ever materialize.

Canada's best protection would lie in neutrality, and its neutrality could be of a different and far more positive kind than the passive neutrality of the European countries that keep out of military alliances merely to save themselves from the perils of war. Canada's neutrality could be an active one, aimed not at keeping out of international problems but at resolving them peacefully and rationally. It would proceed from a perception that Canada's interests are not in fact those of the large military and industrial powers who attempt to control the world's destiny. Canada has been and still is a colonial economy, dependent on the purchase of its primary products by the economic imperialists, and its interests lie with the countries of what we used to call the Third World, the disadvantaged and exploited countries that are struggling out of a historic client status. The important difference is that Canada's land mass and its wealth of natural products have made it more prosperous, at least for the time being, than the other countries that up to now have been forced into the situation of perpetual exploitation. And it is this extra prosperity, precarious though it may be, that would make it possible for Canada to assume a leading role in the world outside the two great imperial camps if it turned to positive neutrality.

Specifically, I would like to see Canada leaving NATO and NORAD, expelling American military units from its soil, turning the armed forces into a corps devoted to cleaning up and preserving the environment, and diverting the vast sums earmarked for replacing obsolete weaponry to two important peaceful purposes: rebuilding our shipping services and our merchant marine so that our products would sail to the world in Canadian ships; and devoting a much higher proportion of the community's wealth to foreign aid, aimed at achieving a situation where the just anger of poor people would no longer remain as a threat to the world's peace. The main difference from what the Canadian International Development Agency does at present should be the phasing out of government-to-government aid (which is wasteful, ridden with corruption, and likely to help mainly the elite of the recipient countries) and its replacement by direct non-governmental assistance between Canadian and foreign voluntary agencies and between Canadian and foreign communities—towns and villages—a process that would cement world relationships on the basic level of peoples and communities, not of political bodies and bureaucracies. To increase international understanding further, Canada should initiate a vast exchange program for students and other young people so that every Canadian will eventually have experienced life abroad.

Talking of political bodies and bureaucracies takes one from the matter of powers on a world stage to that of power on a national stage and the need for its dissolution. We are often told that Canada is a popular democracy. But a popular democracy is a democracy where the people are sovereign. In Canada, sovereignty still legally rests with the crown, that feudal fiction represented by a dutiful matron living in England. By delegation, it rests with a parliament, elected every five years, which the people are unable to call to order between elections; and in practice this means that the real sovereignty rests with the small circle of leading politicians and bureaucratic mandarins who dominate the cabinet and the higher ranks of the civil service, and who shape the policies which the caucus of the ruling party follows, ensuring their acceptance by its voting majority in the House of Commons. Nothing could be more remote from a true popular sovereignty than this government by whip.

My own model of the ideal society is a libertarian and participatory one of a loose confederation of co-operative working groups and of neighbourhood associations coming together to administer their mutual interests, with co-operation and consensus rather than coercion the dominating principle, and with most of the action going on at the lower levels of the pyramid, where people's real interests lie, and very little left to be dealt with on a national level.

I do not know of any society, except for parts of Spain during the Civil War and parts of the Ukraine in the early years of revolutionary Russia, where a real attempt to create a society of this kind has taken place; but some countries have not only acknowledged the people as sovereign but have given a fair degree of practical application to that concept. Switzerland, with a confederation much more radically democratic than that of Canada, is one of them.

To begin, Swiss confederation has three, not two, levels. While municipalities in Canada are the creations of the provinces, with no more power than provincial governments choose to give them, in Switzerland their rights as communes are constitutionally guaranteed, and they form the first level of law-making and administration. In many communes, and even in the smaller cantons (or provinces), the laws are actually voted by the assembled people, meeting—as in ancient Athens—once a year in a great open space. Such meetings are not possible for the larger cantons or for Switzerland as a whole with its six and a half million people, but on these levels the *landesgemeinde* (as the method of government by popular assembly is called) is replaced by an elaborate system of referendums and initiatives. Some laws, particularly those affecting the constitution, have to be submitted to the popular vote; there is no possibility of a deal like that between the prime minister and the provincial premiers, without any reference to the people, by which our constitution was repatriated. With regard to other laws, if fifty thousand people demand it, a law must be referred to the people for ratification by referendum; if it is voted down, this law does not appear on the statute books. If a hundred thousand people want a new law, then the Initiative, as it is called, must be put to all the voters; if they approve it, the measure becomes law, no matter what the national council may wish.

Such a system takes the power and the glory out of politics, and a flamboyant personality like Trudeau or Kennedy would have no chance in Switzerland, where the president holds office only for a year and even then is *primus inter pares* in a six-men-and-one-woman Federal Council that reaches all its decisions by consensus. Power is not abolished in Switzerland, but it is notably reduced and greatly diluted by being spread through so many different decision-making groups, from the directly voting people, through the communes and the cantons and the confederation, up to that almost anonymous Federal Council, which advises more than it decides and always in the long run defers to the will of the people. I would like to see Canada veer in that direction, with more decisions in our hands (the people's) and less in theirs (the politicians') and with a great increase in local self-government, so that the people involved make the decisions on matters that concern them directly. Indian self-government would be a good place to start a process which by example could become widespread, so that our fate will no longer be decided by party hacks and bureaucrats nursing their careers in the isolation of Ottawa, a city that for many of us is farther away in distance and in spirit than many great foreign cities.

What else? I have left no room for more than a few final sentences. Capital punishment? The point here is not pity for the murderer but pity for a society that brutalizes itself by taking the life for the life; we have surely grown up beyond Old Testament dreams of vengeance. The environment? All sensitive areas where activities like mining and logging and hunting might harm unique ecological systems or rare species should be turned into national parks, and one function for the demilitarized army might be to set them up. Factories polluting the environment should be subject not to fines but to expropriation without compensation. The CBC? We need public broadcasting, but bureaucracy has killed initiative and originality in the CBC, and it is time we dismantled it and replaced it by a network of regional broadcasting centres operated by co-operatives of producers, writers, and artists. The Canada Council? It has its faults, but political inter-ference would only do harm. Criticize it, replace the political appoint-ees on the council with creative people, and leave it to find its own solutions. Abortion? Nobody regards the rights of the dead as more important than those of the living, and where a choice has to be made the rights of the living must also take precedence over those of the unborn. If we believe in freedom, we cannot impose on women, against their wills, a servitude that can be prevented. If we don't believe in freedom, why not bring back the Inquisition?

PETER WORTHINGTON

If it is true that absolute power corrupts absolutely, it is even truer that absolute lack of power can be more corrupting—witness the NDP in opposition, who have a certain power of influence without the power of implementation or accountability. Thus they can vigorously propose any policy without concern for cost or practicality.

In a way, it is the fantasy of power without responsibility that seems a theme of this book. Without knowing what any of the individuals appearing in it are writing, the thought of some of them ever being prime minister is even more unnerving than the thought of the present PM being re-elected! As it is, only one of the authors participating in this upscale version of the public school exercise, "How I Spent My Summer Holidays," actually tried to become prime minister. (Jim Gillies contested the Tory leadership in 1976 until he switched to Joe Clark.)

As one whose trade of journalism is more often associated with tearing down prime ministers than building them up, I suppose it's fair occasionally to be called upon to put up or shut up. So what would I do if suddenly I were PM, either by magic wand or *coup d'état?*

Well, the first priority of any national leader is, or should be, leadership. It is a quality Canadians have had little exposure to in their prime ministers in my lifetime. If not our most serious failing, lack of leadership is perhaps our saddest as a people. John Diefenbaker came close when we gave him 208 Tory seats in 1958. But his vision blurred as his foibles took over, and we turned against him—as did his own party. In 1968 we *thought* Trudeau was the leader we wanted when he promised nothing except a Just Society and participatory democracy. But again we were disappointed. As for Mulroney, who we *hoped* was the leader the country yearned for, we have landed ourselves with a PM who sometimes seems better suited to selling snake oil and whose vision for Canada was fulfilled the day he became prime minister.

Okay, so what would I do if the good (or bad) fairy tapped me for the job? First, after phoning my mother about my promotion, I would set out my vision for Canada—which in rhetoric might be compatible with the goals and dreams outlined by my predecessors. To avoid the inevitable and justified cynicism of the people, I would try to do something dramatic to show I meant what I said—that I would be different in that I'd tell the truth, get off the fence, and not govern by bribery and opinion polls.

The virtue I would strive for in government and policies would be common sense. Plus the courage and will to follow or implement common-sense decisions. You don't have to be a genius to lead, but you have to believe in yourself, your ideals, your country. And you have to convince the people of your resolve and your goals.

Domestically, I would make it clear that I don't have all the answers but that I would hire or appoint people who I felt could achieve the goals I aspired to for Canada. I would tell Canadians that we cannot continue to run our country in a manner that would land citizens in jail or bankruptcy if they ran their personal lives or businesses that way. Hence, as a nation, we would have to start living within our means. That would mean reducing the deficit, and that means trimming government spending. Would that mean cutting social services and welfare, and ending universality? You're damn right it would! The means test would come back. We would implement a system of welfare that would never make a person appear a sucker for working for minimum wages instead of going on the dole.

I'd want to be able to supplement the incomes of those who choose to work at minimum wages rather than taking welfare, so that they aren't punished for the work ethic. I would put "insurance" back into unemployment insurance and stop the rip-offs. The Forget Report on unemployment insurance would be the basis of new legislation. And I'd end, immediately (if not sooner), the baby bonus, especially for those who earn over a certain minimum.

I'm afraid I would also have to revise the Canada Pension Plan and make it applicable only to those who need it—make it the Canada Pension-Insurance Plan—not because I want to or because it is fair but because a succession of provincial and federal governments have borrowed from pension funds and not repaid them, but merely guaranteed them. You try that stunt in the private sector, and it's jail if you're caught. Do it in government, and you get the Order of Canada or go to the Senate. Incidentally, I'd scrap the Senate forthwith and replace it with an elected body that would enable the regions, or provinces, to have equal power.

And speaking of equality, I'd start making Quebec equal to the other provinces—not more equal. The parts whose sum comprise Canada should be equal rather than weighted in favour of one over the others. I would not be blackmailed by Quebec—nor by the spectre of separation. (In certain circumstances, Quebec's separation might be a solution more than a problem for Canada.)

I'd instantly scrap programs that foster discrimination and racism. First to go would be quota systems, which are demeaning and unfair, and which create resentment among those who are unfairly legislated against. Next, programs like affirmative action would go, on the grounds that they represent reverse or unfair discrimination because they assume that the minority group targeted for help can't get ahead without favouritism. I'd replace them with equal opportunity programs for the disadvantaged so that they could compete as equals.

I would put a quick halt to the nonsense of equal pay for work of equal value and would insist that equal pay for equal work was adhered to, and equal opportunity. I guess I couldn't dump our written constitution, but if I became PM through a revolution I would do so and I'd reinstate the unwritten constitution that worked so well for so long and wasn't a make-work boondoggle for lawyers.

I would end our policy of two official languages, whereby the 15 per cent of Canadians who are presently bilingual are the only ones who can now reasonably aspire to be PM someday or to hold top posts in government. I would give extra pay to all who spoke more than one language, since this is an extra qualification which should be rewarded. And I'd put French into the schools by paying the provinces if they did it. If Quebec opted for French only, I'd not object, but no one who couldn't communicate in the language of North America, English, would be eligible for a federal job outside Quebec. Language would be free choice and removed from the constitution if possible.

The role of the Canadian government would be to assist immigrants to be better Canadians and to be at home here—not to make it easier for them to be Italians, Greeks, or whatever. Multiculturalism would be a reality rather than consisting of government policies and programs that encourage professional ethnics to pillage the taxpayer. Speaking of ethnics, I would open up immigration on the basis that the more people we have, the more wealth we will generate, the more jobs will be created, and the better off we all will be. More people mean more jobs, not fewer.

I would be selective in immigration. I would try to attract immigrants who reflect our values or who want to adapt. Europeans and Asians would get preference, because they work hard. I would encourage Slavic peoples, who make superb citizens. Selective immigration from Africa would be encouraged. I would be wary about immigrants whose cultural values are likely to produce problems and divisions. I would not want open immigration, since the country would lose control of its destiny. Racial origin wouldn't interest me as much as cultural attitudes.

Any union leader from Glasgow or northern England who sought to come to Canada, I would send back on the first Aeroflot plane— they've done enough damage to Canadian unions and our economy over the years.

I would revamp the Canadian military and get out of trying to be all things to all people. Neglect of the military by past governments has made it prohibitively expensive to catch up in needed equipment to fulfil traditional roles. I would make a virtue of necessity and change the role of the armed forces. I'd increase the numbers of the military by opening up recruitment. Boost the forces from the present 83,000 to, say, 150,000 and use the services as a means of training and educating our youth. I'd build a commando-style army, similar to the British SAS, capable of functioning and fighting in small or large units. Individuality would be stressed, making every soldier elite in his way so that if Canada were ever invaded it would be impossible to occupy.

I would get rid of tanks (sob!) and would stress an anti-tank role as being more economical, practical, modern. Ours would be a missile army. I'd end participation in most (but not all) U.N. peacekeeping forces, which are not right for soldiers. I'd develop a coastal navy and have an air force that can do the job we need for Canada. I'd stay in NATO and NORAD. When our allies needed help in worthy causes, I'd rent or lend our troops—on a voluntary basis—for training or symbolic co-operation.

I would expand the militia or reserves from their present pathetic 20,000 to 200,000 and would use them for training or teaching young people—the militia rather than welfare. Those who did well could go to university or trade school for free, rather as the system worked for veterans after World War II and Korea. Pay for reserve training would be tax free.

I'd do all possible to get a free-trade deal with the United States, in the belief that anything Canadians put their minds to they can do as well as, or better than, anyone else.

I'd take government out of culture. Culture is something that can't be stopped—only controlled or diverted. If people prefer to look at American or European TV and movies, so be it; let our culture industry adapt to the people's interests. I would end or curtail the Canada Council. The Mel Hurtigs of our country would have to make it on the open market, not with public funds and grants. Being innovative and dynamic, they'd succeed there too.

I would encourage Canadian culture not through regulations or restrictive laws, which prevent easy access to our market, nor with Canadian content laws, but by quality. Take movies. *Breaker Morant*, *Gallipoli* and *The Getting of Wisdom* are great Australian films not because of how they were financed, filmed, or who acted in them, but because of their scripts. In Canada *Meatballs* is no more Canadian than Oliver Twist, despite it being named one of the best Canadian movies of the year.

I'd have the CBC take lessons from Public Broadcasting in the United States and have it concentrate on excellence, no matter its source, on the grounds that quality encourages quality. In order to improve CBC quality and efficiency, I would drastically cut its budget—and would give the scalpel to directors and cameramen, rather than to accountants and managers whose main concern is to save the bureaucracy.

If I were prime minister I would work to establish a flat-rate income tax and close tax loopholes, and I'd get rid of all those tax bureaucrats by shipping them to the United Nations or Tanzania—and would then reduce our commitment to the U.N. I'd also have no capital gains tax for Canadian investments, on the grounds that those who produce wealth also produce jobs. If Canada became a country where reasonable profits could be made safely and honestly, industry and enterprise would flourish and tax revenues would increase as unemployment declined.

I would cut foreign aid so that instead of aiding ninety countries with $2.5 billion annually, as we now do, we would aid, say, twenty countries which practise values we respect or which show signs of improvement. I would give *no* aid to repressive regimes like Ethiopia and Tanzania. Instead, I would concentrate on helping the Caribbean, where there is democracy and hope. Canada would operate on the principle that aid to dictatorships entrenches the despot and makes it difficult for democracy and the people in question.

I would take Canada out of the Commonwealth, unless that body smartened up. As it is, I'd urge that the United Nations be moved from New York to, say, Uganda or Ulan Bator for a few years, since so many U.N. members seem to dislike America and the West. Perhaps it's Moscow's turn to host the U.N.?

I would also read the riot act to the Commonwealth unless it showed signs of living up to certain human rights codes. Who wants to be a member of a club that has no standards or ethics? Over half the forty-nine Commonwealth countries practise repression that civilized people abhor. We should be more choosy about those nations we associate with. Put the Commonwealth on notice to change—or lose one patsy.

As for Canadian politics, I would encourage Canadians to vote for individuals who will best serve their country, their constituents, their conscience—in no particular order. Lastly they should serve their party. The way Canada is run now, politicians must pledge loyalty to the party above all else. In this, Canada is unique among the democracies. Our party structure tolerates little deviation. Our political parties demand blind subservience that is matched only by the Nazi and Communist parties.

In order to get sincere individuals who seek to serve rather than to feed at the public trough, I'd cut the pay of MPs, end their indexed pensions, and stop the lunatic practice of severance pay when they are defeated at the polls. Also, for every percentage point of inflation over a certain acceptable point, I'd make a rule that senior civil servants and politicians forfeit an equivalent percentage of their pay.

I would revise our policy with regard to native peoples and would move to end the reserve system. I would phase out paying Indians to stay in ghettos, which is what reserves are. I would start helping Indians to blend into Canadian society and end their isolation in apartheidlike "homelands." All could live where they wished and do as they wished—but not get handouts for doing it. Within a generation, Indians would become functioning first-class citizens.

I would end the "founding races" nonsense and make *all* Canadians equal, regardless of French, English, Indian, or Inuit heritage. I would let women into the armed forces in any capacity they can handle, be it fighter pilots or paratroopers, just so long as they meet the requirements.

I would start reducing the federal government's powers, get it out of the private sector, and would put profit back into being a law-abiding Canadian. I would not bring back capital punishment per se, but I would end mandatory abolition and allow judges discretionary power to order execution for murders of perversion—especially murders involving children, torture, sex, terrorism, or contract killings.

As prime minister I wouldn't have all the answers, but I would get people around me who were smarter and more able than me. As PM, I would be setting the tone, providing leadership for the sort of a Canada I want. Mine would be a Canada of freedom, individuality, independence, confidence, progress, and fulfilment, with all citizens being first class. Canadians would never have to worry that their government wouldn't come swiftly and resolutely to their defence if they were unfairly held or badly treated abroad.

How many would like to live in my Canada?

Well, find me a dozen MPs who are willing to break with their present parties and form a new one, and I bet we would be on the way to winning popular support.

Meanwhile, it's not going to happen, so Mel Hurtig and the CBC are safe....

THE CONTRIBUTORS

Doris Anderson is a former editor of *Chatelaine* magazine and former president of the Canadian Advisory Council on the Status of Women and of the National Action Committee on the Status of Women. She is currently a columnist for *The Toronto Star*.

Dr. Thomas S. Axworthy is an associate of the Center for International Affairs, Harvard University, and vice-president of The CRB Foundation in Montreal. He was formerly principal secretary to Prime Minister Trudeau.

The Hon. Leone Bagnall is leader of the Progressive Conservative Party of Prince Edward Island. Between 1982 and 1986 she was P.E.I.'s minister of education and minister responsible for the Advisory Council on the Status of Women.

George Bain writes the Media Watch column for *Maclean's* and contributes to various other publications. He has been a newspaper columnist on national affairs since 1952 and is a former director of the School of Journalism at the University of King's College, Halifax.

The Hon. David Barrett is a former premier of British Columbia and former leader of B.C.'s New Democratic Party. Since 1983 he has pursued a career as a radio and television commentator, as well as writing articles and lecturing across the country.

Carl E. Beigie is director and chief economist of Dominion Securities Inc., a professor of management studies at the University of Toronto, and an associate professor at McGill. He is a former president of the C. D. Howe Institute and was the institute's founding executive director.

Ruben Bellan is professor of economics at St. John's College, the University of Manitoba, and author of *Principles of Economics and the Canadian Economy, The Evolving City, Winnipeg First Century,* and *The Unnecessary Evil.* He contributes articles to *The Financial Post* and numerous other publications.

The Hon. Nancy J. Betkowski is minister of education of the Government of Alberta and the Conservative MLA for Edmonton Glenora.

Before her election to the Alberta legislature in 1986, she was executive assistant to the provincial treasurer.

Shirley Carr is president of the Canadian Labour Congress and a former executive vice-president and secretary-treasurer of the CLC. The daughter of a coal miner from Sydney, N.S., she has been active in the labour movement for more than twenty-five years.

Dian Cohen is a principal of Cohen Couture Associates, an economic communications consulting group. She is financial editor of CTV news and appears twice daily on "Canada AM." She writes a syndicated newspaper column on personal money management and economic policy, is co-author of *The Next Canadian Economy* and author of *Money: Financial Strategies for the 1990s*.

Marjorie Cohen, a feminist economist, is a professor at the Ontario Institute for Studies in Education and the author of a recently published book on women and free trade.

Sheila Copps, Liberal MP for Hamilton East, is opposition spokesperson for health and welfare and for fitness and amateur sport. She is a former member of the Ontario legislature and in 1982 was a candidate for the Ontario Liberal leadership, placing a strong second.

David Crane writes for *The Toronto Star* on political and economic affairs and is the author of *A Dictionary of Canadian Economics* and *Controlling Interest.* He is a former director of corporate affairs for the Canada Development Investment Corporation and a former member of the Ontario Economic Council.

John Crispo is a professor of political economy in the Faculty of Management Studies at the University of Toronto. A frequent media commentator and public speaker, he is the author of several books, including *The Canadian Industrial Relations System* and *A Mandate for Canada.*

Senator Keith Davey has been political organizer of the Liberal Party of Canada for more than a quarter of a century and masterminded many of the Liberal election campaigns. In 1986 he published his political memoir, *The Rainmaker—A Passion for Politics.*

Georges Erasmus has since 1985 been national chief of the Assembly of First Nations, the national representative body of status-Indians. He was previously northern vice-chief of the Assembly (1983–85) and president of the Dene Nation (1976–83).

Peter Ernerk, president of the Keewatin Inuit Association, was born in an igloo and lived a traditional life until sent away to school at the age of eleven. As a member of the Legislative Assembly of the N.W.T. 1975–79, he held three ministries: Social Development, Economic Development and Tourism, and Renewable Resources.

Jacques Francoeur is the president of UniMédia Inc., the holding company that publishes more than thirty newspapers, including Quebec City's *Le Soleil*, Ottawa's *Le Droit*, and Chicoutimi's *Le Quotidien* and *Progrès-Dimanche*.

Dr. E. Margaret Fulton, currently an education consultant in Vancouver, is a former president of Mount Saint Vincent University in Halifax, N.S. She has earned three degrees and holds seven honorary degrees, in addition to the Human Relations Award from the Canadian Council of Christians and Jews.

James Gillies, professor of policy at York University, is a former Conservative MP and in 1979–80 was senior policy adviser to Prime Minister Clark. The material in his essay is more fully developed in his recently published book: *Facing Reality: Consultation, Consensus and Making Economic Policy for the 21st Century.*

Dr. John F. Godfrey, former president of the University of King's College, Halifax (1977–87), is editor of *The Financial Post*. With Peter Dalglish and Dr. Arthur Andrew, he co-founded Ethiopia Airlift in 1984 and, in 1985, Adopt-a-Village Degahbur. He is a modern European historian by training.

J. L. Granatstein is a professor at York University, where he teaches Canadian history. He writes on Canadian politics and on foreign and defence policy, and his most recent books include *The Great Brain Robbery* and *Canada 1957–67: Years of Uncertainty and Innovation.*

Ray Guy, Newfoundland journalist and broadcaster, is currently a columnist with the St. John's *Sunday Express*. He is the author of several books, including *You May Know Them as Sea Urchins, Ma'am,* which won the Leacock Medal for Humour.

The Hon. Céline Hervieux-Payette is vice-president, Corporate Development, of The SNC Group in Montreal. A former Liberal MP for Montreal-Mercier, she was minister of state for fitness and amateur sport 1983–84, and from January to June 1984 was Canada's first minister of state for youth.

The Hon. Dr. Hugh M. Horner, currently a consultant on rural development, agriculture, and transportation, was the Conservative MP for Jasper-Edson from 1958 until 1967, when he was elected to the Legislative Assembly of Alberta. From 1971 to 1979 he was deputy premier of Alberta.

Stephen Hume, general manager of *The Edmonton Journal*, served as its editor from 1981 to 1987. He was originally posted to the paper's Arctic bureau and travelled widely, visiting all but two of Canada's settlements north of the 60th parallel. He is also a poet, author of two published books of poems.

John Hutcheson is the editor of *The Canadian Forum*. He is also an associate professor of social science at York University and writes on Canadian political economy and cultural policy.

George Ignatieff, president of Science for Peace and a former chancellor of the University of Toronto, served for thirty-three years in the Canadian Foreign Service, where his appointments included Canadian representative to NATO, to the United Nations, and to the Conference on Disarmament.

Janis Johnson, who has been involved in Conservative politics for the past twenty years, was national director of the Progressive Conservative Party of Canada 1983–84, the first woman to hold the position. She lived in Newfoundland for many years and now lives in Winnipeg, where she manages her own public affairs consulting firm.

Steven Langdon, New Democratic Party MP for Essex-Windsor, was formerly associate director of the International Development Research Centre. Previously he taught economics at Carleton University and worked with trade unionists at the Canadian Labour Congress's Labour College.

Daniel Latouche is currently a professor with the Institut national de la recherche scientifique in Montreal. He is a political scientist and political commentator, and worked briefly in the Quebec premier's office during the premiership of René Lévesque.

Dr. Richard G. Lipsey is senior economic adviser at the C. D. Howe Institute and a professor of economics at Queen's University. He has held a chair in economics at the London School of Economics and was dean of the Faculty of Social Science at the new University of Essex, England.

Dr. John S. McCallum is a professor at the University of Manitoba, where he teaches and does research in capital markets, financial institutions, corporation finance, and investments. He is a columnist with *The Financial Post* and has been a financial consultant to a number of corporations and governments.

Thelma McCormack, a professor of sociology at York University and former president of the Canadian Sociology and Anthropology Association, is a feminist who was the first incumbent of the E. Margaret

Fulton chair in women's studies, Halifax. She edits a series on *Studies in Communication*.

The Hon. Donald S. Macdonald, former Liberal MP and cabinet minister, was a member of the government from 1968 to 1977, and in the early 1980s was chairman of the Royal Commission on the Economic Union and Development Prospects for Canada. He is currently a lawyer in Toronto.

Alexa McDonough is a social worker and leader of the New Democratic party in Nova Scotia. She has been a member of the Nova Scotia legislature since 1981, and for the first three years was the only woman and the only New Democrat in the House of Assembly.

The Hon. Dr. Patrick L. McGeer, a former member of the provincial cabinet in British Columbia, was the MLA for Vancouver–Point Grey for twenty-four years and was leader of the B.C. Liberal Party 1968–72. He is currently professor of neurological sciences at the University of British Columbia.

George Manuel, who was president of the National Indian Brotherhood 1970–76, has travelled worldwide in support of indigenous peoples. In 1972 he was an adviser with the Canadian delegation to the U.N. Conference on the Environment, and in 1975 he became founding president of the World Council of Indigenous Peoples.

Robin Mathews, writer and cultural critic, known for his work on Canadianization, has taught in the United States, England, and France as well as in Canada, where he is professor of English at Carleton University and currently visiting professor in Canadian studies at Simon Fraser University.

John Meisel is the Sir Edward Peacock professor of political science at Queen's University and a former chairman of the Canadian Radio-television and Telecommunications Commission. He has written extensively on Canadian parties, the politics of ethnic relations, and cultural policy.

William R. Morrison, professor of history at Brandon University, is author of *Showing the Flag: The Mounted Police and Canadian Sovereignty in the North, 1894–1925* and other works on northern Canada.

Peter C. Newman, former editor of *Maclean's*, is author of a dozen books, the latest being *Caesars of the Wilderness*, the second volume of *Company of Adventurers*, a highly unofficial three-part history of the Hudson's Bay Company.

Patrick O'Callaghan is publisher of the *Calgary Herald* and former publisher of *The Edmonton Journal*. A native of the Republic of Ireland, he came to Canada twenty-nine years ago and has since been involved with a number of newspapers and news agencies, and is vice-president of Southam.

Gilles Paquet is professor of economics and dean of the Faculty of Administration at the University of Ottawa. A broadcaster with Radio Canada, he is also the author of numerous works on the economic history of Canada, regional development, private and public management, and the regulation of socioeconomic systems.

Arthur Phillips, founder of Phillips, Hager and North, Ltd., one of the leading investment counselling firms in Canada, served as mayor of Vancouver 1972–76 and as Liberal MP for Vancouver Centre 1979–80. He was British Columbia's commissioner of critical industries 1985–87.

Walter G. Pitman is director of the Ontario Institute for Studies in Education and a former dean of arts and science at Trent University, former president of Ryerson Polytechnical Institute, and former executive director of the Ontario Arts Council. An Ontario MPP 1967–71, he was deputy leader of the Ontario NDP.

W. Gunther Plaut, rabbi, senior scholar at Holy Blossom Temple, Toronto, is the author of historical and theological works, as well as fiction, and is also a journalist, human rights activist, and public servant. His autobiography, *Unfinished Business*, appeared in 1981; his novel, *The Letter*, in 1986.

Major-General Richard Rohmer, former commander of the Air Reserve Group of Air Command and former chief of reserves of the Canadian Armed Forces, is chancellor of the University of Windsor, a lawyer, a business executive, a syndicated columnist, and a best-selling author.

Thomas K. Shoyama is currently a visiting professor at the University of Victoria. He was economic adviser to the Saskatchewan government 1950–64, was federal deputy minister of energy, mines and resources 1974–75, and deputy minister of finance 1975–79.

The Hon. Nick Sibbeston is government leader of the Government of the Northwest Territories. A former lawyer in Yellowknife, he was first elected to the N.W.T. Council in 1970.

Dr. Stuart L. Smith, chairman of the Science Council of Canada 1982–87 and a former leader of the Ontario Liberal Party, is visiting professor of health sciences, McMaster University, and adjunct professor of psychiatry, University of Ottawa.

Stuart A. Thiesson has been executive secretary of the National Farmers Union since its founding in 1969. He was previously secretary-treasurer of the Saskatchewan Farmers Union and secretary-treasurer of the Interprovincial Farm Union Council.

William Thorsell is a member of the editorial board of *The Globe and Mail*, books columnist for *Report on Business Magazine*, and was formerly associate editor of *The Edmonton Journal*.

Norman Ward, a professor emeritus at the University of Saskatchewan, is a professional writer, broadcaster, and scholar who has supplemented his academic books with humorous essays and stories. His *Mice in the Beer* won the Leacock Medal for Humour.

Mel Watkins, professor of economics and political science at University College, University of Toronto, is currently on leave in London, England, where he is a visitor at the Institute of Commonwealth Studies, University of London. He has published extensively on matters Canadian and is a regular columnist for *This Magazine*.

Mayor Elsie E. Wayne of Saint John, N.B., is the first woman mayor of the first incorporated city in Canada. Originally elected to Saint John Common Council in 1977, she served two three-year terms before successfully running for mayor in 1983.

Robert White, national president of the Canadian Auto Workers Union since its founding in 1985, was previously UAW director for Canada and international vice-president of the UAW. He is also general vice-president of the Canadian Labour Congress and vice-president of the federal New Democratic Party.

The Very Rev. Dr. Lois M. Wilson, former moderator of the United Church of Canada, is co-director of the Ecumenical Forum of Canada and is one of seven presidents on the praesidium of the World Council of Churches.

George Woodcock is one of Canada's most prolific men of letters, with more than sixty books to his credit. Two of his books, *Anarchism* and *The Crystal Spirit*, a study of his friend George Orwell, are classics in their field. In 1959 he founded *Canadian Literature*, which he edited until 1977.

Peter Worthington has had more than thirty years in journalism and was co-founder of the Toronto *Sun* and its editor-in-chief 1971–83. He has won four National Newspaper Awards. He now writes a column for *The Financial Post*, is editor of *Influence* magazine, and broadcasts for Toronto's CHFI.

Editor: Carlotta Lemieux
Design: First Edition Book Creations / Doug Frank
Typesetting: Attic Typesetting Inc.
Printing: John Deyell